A BOTTLE
IN THE SHADE

A Journey
in the
Western Peloponnese

A BOTTLE
IN THE SHADE

A Journey in the Western Peloponnese

Peter Levi

SINCLAIR-STEVENSON

First published in Great Britain in 1996
by Sinclair-Stevenson
an imprint of Reed International Books Ltd
Michelin House, 81 Fulham Road, London SW3 6RB
and Auckland, Melbourne, Singapore and Toronto

A CIP catalogue record for this book
is available at the British Library
ISBN 1 85619 588 0

Phototypeset by Intype London Ltd
Printed and bound in Great Britain
by Clays Ltd, St Ives plc

N.G.

A poem lived: a bottle in the shade,
the music played, the old artist is dead
I am afraid: and I can hear him wade
through shallow water, where the stream is wide.

Contents

Introduction

Things do not turn out as you expect, however you may concentrate on planning them, and books as you write them have a will of their own, an unconscious or underground stream that is not revealed until they are over. I intended this to be the simplest of books, like a sea-otter or polar bear leaping from a crystalline cliff of ice into familiar green water, but memory disturbs purpose, and the senses being no longer young are more determined by memory than one thought they would be. What I had in mind was a clear, definite journey to Greek lands, a small and necessarily elderly adventure undertaken with one of my oldest and dearest friends in the world, who is a Greek poet. I thought I would speak just a little about the captivating problems of archaeology which have obsessed me ever since I began to discover them in 1963, and where I lacked freshness, I hoped that a touch of nostalgia would not be out of place. One of the things I most wanted to see was the fall of the River Styx, a legendary and inaccessible waterfall near the ancient town of Nonakris, which has never been found. I had read about it and dreamed about it for more than thirty years.

I thought I would be writing in an afterglow of gratitude about what I had most loved, but Greece would not submit to that role. I remembered an old man coming into a London club, humming a tranquil but spirited rendering of a hymn tune. He was a retired publisher I had known for many years, a man taken in Oxford to represent London and business, but taken in London to represent the severe unworldliness of an Oxford college life. I asked whether he was humming 'The day thou gavest Lord is ended'. 'I can't get the tune out of my head,' he said, 'but the only words I put to it are "O Syros, Seriphos and Tinos" . . . I've just had such a good holiday there.' He died not long afterwards, and I wanted to write my book in the same spirit as his tune. I assumed of course that to write with the excitement I had first felt about Greek things, and first expressed with an accumulated passion in the Sixties when they were transforming my life, would now be beyond me. I was leaving my wife at home in Gloucestershire, so I could write my book for her, as one might write a letter.

In fact I had already written the first few pages of this introduction, when we went by chance on an afternoon visit to Worcester, to photograph some tombs in the Cathedral and look round the Dyson Perrins Porcelain Museum, a collection housed in part of the old Worcester china factory, in a long, bending Victorian street that winds its seductive way down from the Cathedral to the river. The collection there was exciting in many ways, but what electrified me, and brought back a swift memory of my first steps on the Athenian akropolis, was a plate of about 1813, decorated with a circular painting I had never seen before, of an artist at work inside the ruined Parthenon, near the east end, facing north so that he must be drawing the Erechtheion. Below the Parthenon on the north stood a simple cottage or shed that I have never seen before, but behind the artist was the Turkish mosque with its red bubble roof like the smaller domes of San Marco at Venice. It took me some minutes to realise what it was, but recognising it, as suspicion turned to certainty, was like turning a new page in Stuart and Revett's *Antiquities of Athens* of the 1760s, the volumes of which I used to haunt in the Ashmolean Library forty years ago. There was the same element of puzzle, and the same invitation to observe accurately; the same avenues of conjecture opened before me now as used to open all those years ago, when I was innocent of archaeology, and thought Pausanias little more than a guide-book to ancient landscape (I had never been to Greece) and to ancient religion.

I was shaken by this experience, and that fact among other things made me remember the past more accurately. For one thing, it explained those hours on end in the Seventies when I was content to hang over the railings of the eyrie in Metz where I had nested, staring at the perfect Parthenon. It was not that study did not attract me, it was just that the thing itself was so beautiful I was content to worship it. For more years than I can remember, I have felt a lot of sympathy with the early inhabitants of the British Isles in their apparently simple-minded worship of stones, but the Parthenon is for me at least the central discovery or revelation of the renaissance; it is august as nothing else is on earth. It is a very great privilege, as well as a never-failing pleasure, to be able to study it, to observe its behaviour in different lights and to gloat over the survival of what is left of it. How typical it is all the same of the nature of our 'rediscovery' of the Parthenon, that it was swiftly blown up by a German gunner working for the Venetians, and then when the mosque shown on the Worcester plate had been built and in use for about a hundred years, the numinous marble columns around it were stripped of their decor-ations and sculptures by the servants of Lord Elgin. Then when the akropolis had been fought over and the Turkish garrison marched out, the mosque was desecrated by a passing Englishman who got his horse to shit in it.

It seems not unlikely that the artist on the Worcester plate is Lusieri, a Neapolitan who was agent to Lord Elgin. It is a fragile surmise, but the colour-tone of the stones does suggest a Neapoli-tan origin, so that at first glance I wondered which of the known Italian ruins this could be: the mosque, and when you consider them the two fragments of the east pediment, are what confirm it as a scene in Athens in about 1800. The plate itself, with whatever companion pieces it must once have had, was made by a copyist in about 1813. The mosque is small enough to be designed to fit inside the rectangle of the columns.

The mosque that was blown up by gunfire at the end of the seventeenth century had simply been an adaptation of the Christian church of the Parthenon, which had been an adaptation of the ancient temple. The Christians had it longer than the Turks, of course, and some of their graffiti or *dipinti* can still be made out on the outside wall at the west end: there is even a small painting of the Virgin. The Royal Society has a manuscript, which descended to them through Robert Hook, of the travel journal of a seventeenth-century Englishman called Francis Vernon, a kinsman of the Admiral, who is the only scholar since the renaissance to describe the Parthenon in any detail as it was before the Venetian guns opened fire. The journal is fascinating and adventurous: Vernon was murdered in the end in Persia. The journal is full of information about flowers, which lurk under their Italian and Linnaean Latin names, of inscriptions and of information about fortresses. Of the Parthenon he tells us that the pillars inside its four walls were two storeys high and Doric when he saw them in the 1670s; but some twenty pages of the journal are about Constantinople. A version was printed in 1676 in the *Philosophical Transactions of the Royal Society*, by Henry Oldenburg, the diplomatic representative of Bremen at the court of Cromwell, a close friend of John Milton and an early member of the Royal Society, who had Vernon made a fellow in 1672. They both died in 1677, Vernon at Isfahan in a quarrel over a penknife: in his youth he was one of the few members of Oxford University to be sold as a slave by Barbary pirates, but he was home in time to take his MA in 1660. It is a pity no one any longer consults his travel journal.

This year there is stranger news about the Parthenon. From a careful examination of every block of marble, a Greek archaeologist called Korres has made the astonishing deduction that four

Victories stood or flew on the corners of its roof: or at least on three of the corners, where the heavy blocks of marble show the mark of iron clamps that will have held the statues in place. I am old enough to be alarmed by this alteration in the shape of an old friend. The new model is not without analogies and the evidence of the clamps is hard to resist, but it is not certain when the Victories like migrant birds may have appeared or disappeared, and still less certain why there were three of them and not four. They are just another of the many puzzles about that wonderful temple: the longer one stares at it, the more surprising it becomes: the proportions of its columns, the details of the mythology on its pediments, the meaning of its marble procession of 'horses and horses of the sea, white horses', and on the east end the mysterious eager horses of the sun, hungry for daylight, and the weary horses of the moon vanishing, or the sun descending. Korres has published the first full study of the physical marble of the Parthenon and of Pendeli, the mountain and the quarries that generated it, but he has produced such photographs of the marble hanging like vast ocean clouds in those quarried cliffs, that one is disposed to change religions and transfer one's worship from the ruined Parthenon to the quarry and the snow-white, unhandled rock itself.

However that may be, I found myself flung backwards in time; I could see as many pathways of research as ever in the past, winding and intermingling ahead of me. In a scholarly lifetime devoted to the travels of Pausanias I had hardly begun to scratch the surface of the subject. When I first went to Greece it was still not difficult to follow the old mule tracks and footpaths of ancient communication, and the migration routes of sheep and goats, though those had begun to alter under the influence of the newer, bulldozed routes of village buses and the depopulation of the countryside had already begun. Now not only do I feel a lack of time and physical energy, but the countryside is altering again, as I was to discover. The great flocks are a thing of the past, but

the European community favours small-scale sheep-farming in
Greece, so the fields where the old flocks wandered freely are
fenced off and subdivided with wire, and the flocks of several
hundred sheep that one used to see have disappeared like a mountain mist. Admittedly, by May they had gone up into the high
mountains, but even there I did not see them, I only heard once
or twice the faint jangling of the sheep-bells, far away across a
valley or on the other side of a hill. We have passed the time when
it was easy to explore the tracks they used. My first decision
therefore was to avoid Athens with its purple pea-soup fog and its
smells, and to take my time in a part of the Peloponnese I already
knew in outline, though I must admit that in the event I found
the detail terribly hard to remember. You do not remember a
hillside or a village where you explored thirty years ago.

Exploration loses its excitement and the world shrinks, until
the only coast that attracts old people is the most unattainable of
all, past time. The buried ages of the world and their surviving
monuments do not altogether lose interest, particularly when they
are mingled with terrific landscapes as the Greek monuments so
often are, but in going back to take another look at places one has
seen before, there is no doubt that it is one's own past, as well as
the Greek past and present, that one is exploring.

The Peloponnese is like a leaf dropped from a plane tree and
floating on turbulent water. In the height of summer, as I first saw
it thirty years ago, it was like a dead, brown leaf, but when I went
back this year the leaf was that magical and vivid light green of
plane trees rustling among divided rivers; the season (which was
spring) made as strong an impression as the place. One can never
go back of course, because nothing is the same, but if, like me,
you are lucky enough to have lost most of your memory, you will
have the advantage of freshness, and most of all in spring. The
trouble is that with the increase of age you will also have the
disadvantage of diseases, and so will your friends if any survive, so
that you can no longer do the heroic journeys of former times:

the pair of you will stagger along together like the four ill-assorted legs of a pantomime donkey. In my own case I have been used to polio since I was sixteen, and more recently to diabetic feet and the queer effects of various strokes, but my friend the poet Giorgis Pavlopoulos, whom I set out to visit and with whom I planned some thrilling expeditions, not only had polio as a small child, but had recently evened matters up by falling down some stone steps in Athens. The excavations of Gakellarakis on Kythera had stirred me: the bronze figurines of worshippers, the votive hands and feet and legs, the women of Peloponnesian coloured stone: but Kythera was probably out of our reach and beyond our range.

We had to confine ourselves to the western Peloponnese and the most easily attainable islands. This suited me, because the magnet of all my happiest expeditions in the past was always Arcadia, and the no man's land called Triphylia to the south and west of it. I was for some reason determined to steer clear of Athens and its overwhelming pollution; indeed my ambition was to arrive at the local port of Katakolo, but I was told no passenger ship called there before the end of May and the schedules of Greek shipping lines are seldom available in advance. My journey was paid for by the Society of Authors, which offers elderly writers the chance 'to renew their acquaintance' with their foreign colleagues. Most Greek writers live in Athens, but Giorgis, who is among my oldest Greek friends, lives in Pyrgos, a large town, indeed a city, where the waters of the River Alpheios have combined together and left their mountains to make for the sea. Olympia lies some eleven or twelve miles further inland, and at Pyrgos the road turns north towards Kyllene and Patras. Kyllene is little more than a castle and a harbour; the harbour entertains the island ferries and their lorries, but the castle is a romantic shell that was the last Greek stronghold of the last Palaiologos, who held out there against the Turks until the late fifteenth century.

Kyllene used to be the most romantic of ruins. The Spartans used the harbour in the war against Athens in the fifth century BC, and the Villehardouins had this castle fortified in the middle ages: Chlemoutsi was its name. Twenty years ago it was overgrown with brambles and the remains of desultory excavations were lying about in its courtyard, because of course the castle was built on the partly buried, partly reused ruins of a classical town. Now, with the increase of tourism the state archaeological service have cleaned it up and labelled it clearly; it is easier to understand but less fun to explore. Even the view has altered; from the old road that took you south from Patras to Pyrgos, the keep of Chlemoutsi kept you company for an hour, but the big new road lies further from the sea and you scarcely catch a glimpse of it. Even if you take the local bus, which dodges here and there between nineteenth-century villages, you see less of it than you used to see. The best view now is from offshore, where the mound appears as a splendid green bump from as far away as Zakynthos if the weather is right. Kyllene is a small, almost an insignificant problem in Greek history, though its story is typical of the region; I was interested in it years ago because it helped to fill the puzzling gap between ancient and modern Greece. The French contributed some dramatic ruins to Greece: Kyllene, Karytaina and the extra-ordinary Cistercian monastery in an ancient temple at Lake Stymphalos, where Herakles massacred some murderous birds. They also contributed some robust vines: one of the best late-autumn grapes is called Santomeriko, because its vine was introduced by the Lord of Saint Omer, a ruffian Baron from near Calais where his town is called St Omère; he held a Barony in Greece as the Villehardouins did. The other thing that the French left is the name used for donkeys, which are still commonly called Baron: though the word Baron may be older in Greek than we think because it existed in Latin, and come to that, in Etruscan.

How have I strayed into this wilderness of queer information? It is because the many years I have spent studying the country have not resulted in concentration, and particularly because when I came to the Peloponnese it was usually on holiday: I gathered whatever offered like blackberries in a hedge, but without a great deal of system. Take for example the head of Saint Andrew. This alien object was the prize possession of Thomas Palaiologos, who had it with him at Chlemoutsi. It appears to have come out of a holy well described by Pausanias at Patras, where Sir William Gell drew the few remaining stones of its classical shrine. My friend Ian Watson was inspired to trace its strange and highly scandalous history, how Thomas used it to buy himself recognition from the Pope, who had a far grander reliquary made to contain it, but luckily kept the old head-reliquary (like a hollow bronze sculpture of a head) and found a use for it in the course of time, when it became politically expedient to return the holy head-bone to the Greeks. The Vatican preferred to retain their pretty and apparently more valuable reliquary, which after all was fifteenth century. It was not long before a mad monk smashed the head-reliquary which had reached Patras, because he was convinced the Vatican had not really put the skull inside. Luckily the head was tough enough to resist this treatment and even the bronze head-reliquary could be repaired. But meanwhile my friend Ian had set off on an odyssey of North Greek and Serbian sacristy cupboards, in search of more and better head-reliquaries, and I do not think that is the kind of quest that can ever end. Yet I must admit that in all the labyrinth of research that preoccupied me for so many years, almost nothing ever seemed to end, and least of all in the western Peloponnese. The medieval, the Venetian and the Byzantine seemed so to overlay the classical that one was constantly thinking again, starting again, wiping away the cobwebs from one's eyes as if oneself were the skull of Saint Andrew.

There is no excuse really; mine has been from a scientific or a severely scholarly point of view a wasted lifetime, although it has not been idle. I first hit on Pyrgos because I made friends there with Giorgis Pavlopoulos. Luckily it was near Olympia, and at Olympia I once worked for an entire winter with the snowy crests of the Arcadian mountains rearing up beyond me. In summer they are not so visible, though my eyesight is not good and I can no longer tell. One of the things I was anxious to notice in Greece this year was the stars in the sky. Years ago, I remember an archaeologist who had worked in Greece before 1939 telling us that before the war the sky in Athens blazed at night with thousands of stars, and now (1966) you had to go to Australia to see what Greek light used to be. I had scarcely believed that and I thought the trouble was old age; now I had suffered that myself, and it was years since I had seen a sky full of stars: but I was not sure whether that was due to the Severn mists and clouds, which are prodigious in the estuary, or to decay of eyesight. Fortunately in the event I found it had mostly been the clouds.

Now I must clear the cobwebs from my eyes yet again, to confine myself to what happened. Before I set out for Greece, having chosen the flowering season, I had kept a Greek notebook for some months to get myself in the mood, stirring dull roots with spring rain. Looking at it now I find all the scholarly remarks and receding vistas of research quite futile, but the bits and pieces of Greek news surprising and interesting. I had wanted to come through Serbia and Macedonia, but that was impossible, and all I could do was make my way to Italy, where I had the idea of finding a boat at Ancona or Brindisi. I travelled by rail under the Channel, herded like an animal through the nasty terminals and regretting the antique ironsided Channel ferries of the past. I carried almost no foreign money, but English notes, so that I lost less by needless exchanges. The food on the train to Paris was terrible and the drink worse, but after the Gare du Nord it improved.

I had not heard about my friend's misadventure in Athens before I arrived, so that some of our expeditions had to be abandoned at once. I had wanted to go to Kythera and Antikythera, a small island half-way to Crete where the weather is as bad now as it was in the *Odyssey*, particularly if you sail from Gythion as I had in mind; it was the stub end of a wish thirty-two years old, conceived because the French guidebook I used then reported seals in the sea-caves and blue grottoes of Antikythera. But the weather this year was uncertain and the crossing dangerous, particularly for a man who walked with difficulty. We had wanted to visit friends at Kardamyli, where the Spartan mountain Taygetos crawls southward to die in stormy water, because we remembered arriving there together through a clashing wood in a high wind with lightning at dusk, on an evening twenty years ago, when the arrival was the most romantic event we remembered. We did not feel it was possible, unfortunately, to negotiate the stone walls and other hazards that might lie in the way, so in the end I went alone.

We had one other plan that came to nothing; I wanted either to begin or to end my Greek journey with a visit to Reggio, where two bronze statues live that were fished up from the sea off southern Italy. They are life-sized Greek bronzes of naked men in full maturity or middle age, holding spears: they are heroes out of mythology from Olympia or Delphi that were being taken to Rome when they were shipwrecked. There is a quality about them that reverses all existing ideas about Greek sculpture and the ideal body. In date and style they seem close to that terrifying Poseidon with a trident or Zeus in the museum at Athens; and they are like Argonauts or the fearful forefathers of the Greeks, and they embody the truth about heroes in ancient religion, who died by violence and had to be placated or they would do violent actions from beyond the grave. Stories about them most flourished and their miracles were most recorded from about 520 to 460 BC, about the time these awe-inspiring figures were cast in bronze. Neither of us had ever seen them. From Brindisi we might have travelled by road or small boat around the instep and the sole of Italy, past Tarentum where Virgil describes a garden, past Metapontum where a temple is still standing, past the great medieval mosaic pavement at Otranto and many old towns, many crumbling baroque churches, to the straits of Reggio: but we left it too late, Giorgis had an appointment in May to read his poetry and to lecture on some mid-Atlantic island and I had one to lecture to the Virgil Society in London, and we had to abandon the wild scheme. It was wild because it is impossible to plan such things in advance. The only way I could obtain a ticket in advance for the night sleeper from Paris to Bologna was by ignoring the gloomy prognostications of all the idiot travel agents, of whom Cook's were the worst, and telephoning an office in Glasgow. Calabria might as well have been the dark side of the moon.

Now I must go back a little, in order to describe my arrival in Greece. It was no ordinary arrival. But before I do so may I very sincerely thank P. J. Kavanagh, Paddy and Joan, Mary Burn, Giorgis and Mitsa, Theodora, Iannis Siderokastritis, and Christos Kalamatianos for making this book possible. There were many others too, but the list is too long. Most of all I am grateful to my wife, Deirdre.

1 : *The Foot Less Fleet*

I HAD stayed in England until the last Saturday in March for a friend's memorial service, and said goodbye to my wife on Oxford station with the last kiss in the world. I was panic-stricken, and although I travelled as far as London with James Fenton I talked to him non-stop about the poet Milton out of nerves, and what I talked about to my cousin Zoe, in whose house I spent the night, I do not dare to imagine. Andrew Hewson, who is my literary agent, picked me up at Paddington and took me to Zoe's, and handed me over a reassuring £2,000 in English money; Zoe took me to Waterloo and my troubles should have been over. I traversed the station in a bright yellow electric van that seemed to have strayed from a golf course. From the moment I left it the hellish torments devised by the railway company, the lifts and moving staircases and formidable crowds began to close in. I crossed to France pressed against a girl with dyed-red hair and a Sony Walkman which leaked the dreariest music. We passed leafless vines and empty hopyards, and suburb transformed effortlessly to seaside and suddenly to darkness, then to the misty plains of Picardy where for ten or twenty minutes we attained 300 kilometres an hour: it felt like no more than 30.

At Paris the crowd were shepherded like football fans, down dark and winding ramps into a tunnel full of fuming taxis. My driver was Malagash, and flashed me a brilliant smile because I knew

Madagascar was very beautiful and contained *lémuriens*. At the Gare de Lyon I came near to collapsing with exhaustion, because there are no more porters in France than in England, and I was dragging heavy luggage. I was not sure where my train left, but I went as far as you could go ruling out alternatives, and where I slumped down to rest turned out to be exactly the right place. My sleeper was in the rear coach, which was the nearest, under the charge of an Abyssinian who looked like a Masai. He was gentle, sweet-natured and efficient, and I decided that the take-over of jobs like taxi driver and sleeping-car attendant by black people was a change for the better. The train itself was admirable and the service excellent; it was all worth every penny that it cost. The Masai advised against the dining car, which was far away, and brought me *foie gras frais*, a luxury I last tasted in Moscow where there was nothing else to eat, navarin of lamb which was delicious, and a rather good claret which he had carefully put on ice; it was surprisingly enjoyable and I slept well on it.

That train is really intended for Venice, but I got off at Bologna. It was seven in the morning, a bad hour to find oneself in the hands of Italian railways. It is, as Baudelaire says, the hour when they cough and die in the hospitals, when the dawn shivering in her pink-and-green shift comes slowly forward down the deserted Seine. The train to Brindisi is no fun, of that I was sure because I had often travelled on it, and I had not fully decided where to go next. But there are trains to Ancona which are comparatively frequent and I was inspired with confidence by having secured the help of the only porter I ever discovered in all Europe, so by half-past eight I had a corner seat in the Ancona train, which takes two or three hours. In Paris I had translated for an American who claimed to love London and said of Venice, where he was going, 'Oh, is it pretty?' Someone had told him his seat was at the top of the train, which he thought might mean on the roof. He called me Doc, which cheered me up a bit. By now he must have been crossing the bridge in that eerie silence of the lagoon, to step out of the station into a painting by Guardi. I admit that I envied him a little, but I had once been by car to Ancona and my memory of that was thrilling.

The journey was suburban at first, though even so with a difference. There is something that excites and satisfies about the small churches with the grandiose towers, the judas-coloured blossom of the peach trees in the orchards, the dusty fields and the small hills that screen the bigger mountains. I had been reading Attilio Bertolucci, the old poet who is the father of the two film-makers, and my head was already full of North Italian landscape, the way it melts in the mind as the words of the poems melt in the mouth. Admittedly Bertolucci is a poet of autumn, when the spaniel ages on the warm brick floor and the straw hat disappears into the shadows; his springs tend to be sharp and mountainous. In this fashion I dozed my way past Rimini, where luckily the train revealed little of the renaissance wonders of the Tempio Malatestiano, or I would have been tempted to get out and spend the night, as indeed I would have done at Bologna if I had not been so dazed and so anxious as to how on earth I would get to Greece, which I still did not know. Past miles and miles of sandy beach and many little harbours we dawdled our way to Ancona.

The town lies along the shore under some green hills; the ancient city is at the far end of it. First you pass an old quarantine building in Venetian brick picked out with white stone. It was being repaired that year but it is a very fine place with a moat and a bridge. It lies just outside a monstrous gate or triumphal archway, a baroque extravaganza of white stone like the stiffest of whipped cream adorning the most elaborate of trifles. I was told by my taxi driver it was Roman, but it is too amusing to be imperial: I think it might be Papal, because Ancona was once the boundary of the Papal states. They must have extended alarmingly far, since Ancona is more or less due east of Florence, but to judge by the condition all these territories east of the Apennines were in when Edward Lear explored them a hundred and fifty years ago, when they were

Neapolitan, they had not been very actively governed for many centuries. The gate is called the Porta Pia and the quarantine building, which is low in the water, is called the Mola Vanvitellana. Above them rises a little hill with a Citadel on it, and a Residence, enmeshed in roads named after Verdi and Titian and Raphael and Crivelli and Michelangelo and the Martyrs of the Resistance, and a little park with a Monument to the Partisans, so it is easy enough to date the expansion of the city. The hill with the Citadel on it is much inferior to the green hill to the south, where the ancient church of Saint Cyriac towers above an entire Vatican of old buildings, and over the harbour and the sea.

Ancona is a pleasant place to pass a few days and full of excitements for anyone hooked by the ancient world. We rolled along the seafront to a respectable ancient bronze of the emperor Augustus and then cut away uphill past an amazing baroque church with a tower that can only be called rococo, through a discreet commercial area as tranquil as the old city at Geneva, to a large old-fashioned hotel called the Roma e Pace, which was exactly what I was looking for. I no longer regretted Bologna or Rimini, and having left my Bertolucci in England, I swiftly acquired a fatter one that lacked the brilliant facing translations by Charles Tomlinson I had got used to, but made up for that by the number of poems in it I had never seen. At the top of the hill above the hotel the big commercial roads, of which they were two parallel ones, ended in an enormous square, and then a little further on yet another as big. I found to my surprise a thirteen-spouted Papal fountain, not precisely in working order I admit, and downhill again various gates and arches, imperial as well as Papal, around a busy harbour where boats left every night for Patras. Old men in the upper squares nodded to one another like retired trade unionists, a cat scampered into one of those clumps of palm tree that all grow from the same root, there were children's trains. The size of the great palazzi occupied by the banks alarmed me rather, but a university building, very smart and 1830-ish with thin tall pilasters, suggested that the palatial standard was set by the aristocratic private houses, some of which still survive in the old city, on their last legs and crumbling to death. The city was all of a piece: in the restaurant attached to the hotel a beggar circulated among the tables, no one troubled him and everyone gave. Women as well as men had mobile telephones and used them as they ate.

I had slept all afternoon, and having telephoned home from the bedroom, which required cunning and persistence, I slept again more deeply than ever. My diary in Ancona becomes hazy. 'Few restaurants, hotel spaghetti marinaio and some roast meat flogged to death with rosemary; wine in jugs, excellent ice-cream as the coffee bars promise. The further you get the brighter the green, the better the wine, the lazier the sun; even the sea is green. Blossom like Gloucestershire pear blossom in small confident orchards growing nothing else.' In England there was an icy arctic wind, with snow expected next day. I slept the deeper for that thought, only to be woken at four in the morning by storms of cold wind and heavy rain at Ancona. I blamed a mountain called S. Vicino, but in fact the hill with the cliffs called Conero attracts any wind there is in the Adriatic because it sticks out into deep water: hence, I suppose, the deep-water port. This was a north-east wind from Croatia, but the Ancona people say of all bad weather that it comes from the sea.

In the morning I took a taxi to the Archaeological Museum, high up in the old city towards S. Cypriano, and I had not got beyond a sort of vestibule or entry hall lined with Roman stones mostly of indifferent merit before I was very surprised indeed. There was a stone relief carved on a big block that had once been part of a monument, representing twelve figures lying in a semicircle on those benches where the ancient world reclined at dinner. The round table was very simply furnished with one large cup and some smaller objects. The whole design was not more than two feet square or so, and no inscription was anywhere near it. Was it Christian, or the dinner of a guild, or a dinner to celebrate the dead? It is a moving sculpture, but no one knows. The figures are crowded together like close friends: I felt that in them, Jew or Christian or pagan, I had friends whom I respected.

The museum is housed in the biggest of the surviving aristocratic houses that once lined the hill above the harbour; a few of its upper rooms still have their splendid painted ceilings. The collection is rich from the eighth century BC onwards, from the time of Homer, but the Greek connection begins to be strong in the seventh and the sixth. Since this is the national museum for the whole of what are called the Marches, it is more important than the one at Brindisi, and one must keep an eye on the whereabouts of the find-spots, which may be far from Ancona. Still, it is evident that Ancona with its deep-water refuge from the sea had become a centre of Greek influence before history began to be written. The local swords and pots and crested helmets have a dignity of their own, and the small Greek bronzes are wonderful: the most memorable a tall helmeted warrior holding two horses by the mane or the ears, one on each side, while two hawks fly above them and a pair of lions sit above them at head height of the man. There are also a pair of healthy-sized snakes which the hawks or eagles are carrying off, though neither serpent has given up the struggle. This was the decoration of a bronze pot now lost from Belmonte Piceno. There is a coin-like disc from Pitino of a charioteer with two horses seen from the front, which is a little earlier, even more beautiful and ingenious: it is a symphony of curves.

The entire collection is astonishing, and not widely known. It reveals the interweavings of tribes, at which Virgil in the *Aeneid* could only guess, and of course the enormous importance of sources of iron and bronze in the ancient world. The fifth-century vases are fine but with few if any great masterpieces: the truth is that the archaic bronzes spoil one's appetite for the smoother nudities exported from Athens. Someone in Monte Fortino had a golden wreath like Philip of Macedon's, and it is only a piece of Hellenistic luxury, it does not impress. What does impress is the formidable stone tablets deeply inscribed with letters but not readable as any known language. The alphabet was newly discovered I suppose, from the Greeks, but its use was magical or decorative at first, like the kufic Arabic decorations on Asian minarets. To make things worse these stones are extremely hard to date. They too are part of the historical hinge that elsewhere we call the classical age, and they depend as much as the temples of the south and the Apollo of Veii on wave after wave of the Greeks breaking in surf on the Italian coast.

It was time to consider Cyriaco of Ancona, the first western traveller ever to explore Greece, a merchant and a diplomat who is last heard of reading Livy aloud to the Sultan in his tent, just before Constantinople fell. Cyriaco was baptised at the Cathedral on the hilltop, and he learnt to draw and to record by noting down the monuments of his home town. It was still a trading city, still pointing towards Greece in the fifteenth century. Today it is the port for Croatian Rjeka and Dubrovnik, but the trade with Greece is far livelier. Cyriaco's journals were boiled up into letters so that several versions of one description may survive. Mommsen refers to his documentary remains as Sibylline leaves, laurel leaves swept by the wind, but gradually, with tact and patience and a kind of scholarly brilliance, he has come in our lifetimes to offer an invaluable witness to a lost age of ruined antiquities. I first visited Ancona to venerate Cyriaco, named after the Saint, and the Roman antiquities that had inspired him. As I write this, a new volume of his journals and letters has just appeared.

Last time S. Cyriaco, Cyriaco's patronal church, was shut for repairs after an earthquake; this time I adventured on foot up innumerable steps, in gusts of wind that I was told later had been Force nine and ten: the sea was like a fleece, and I passed a number of broken umbrellas. But the church itself was even more thrilling than it had been twenty years ago. The pillars of the porch at the west end rest on the backs of lions, as further south they might rest on elephants. Inside is a world of tall shadows and silvery grey stone, spoilt, if at all, only by the Bishop's grand silver candles; here the eighteenth century and here and there the nineteenth intrude ungracefully into the twelfth. I was lucky to find a certain peace of soul in the Cathedral because it was late in the morning and the place was shutting at midday. There was an innocence and a tranquillity about it outside and in. The rain was still dripping from the bushes, but the freezing wind was luckily beginning to die. I plunged with relief into the dark, narrow street where the museum was, which had no pavement and some swift traffic that luckily had good brakes. It was a journey of many surprises, roads swooping through renaissance arches, toppling baroque palaces, vast flights of stairs going nowhere: but the greatest surprise was the little church of S. Maria della Piazza. It was a building of modesty and integrity with elaborate decorative arcading on the east end, and the same little carvings as there are on the outer wall of the Cathedral, in the same silvery white stone.

At six that evening the sun came out in a sky of blue crystal over the harbour. I found a ship for the next evening that got to Patras in two nights and a day, arriving at seven in the morning. I had heard it was a journey of twenty hours, but that service had not been introduced. I did not mind because I was enjoying Ancona. I did not even regret Rimini any more, though I saw from a poster I had missed an Alberti exhibition. I tried to make up for that by a visit to the Ancona art gallery, which was a mistake except for some bits of medieval sculpture downstairs in the courtyard, a Crivelli Virgin with a marrow and a peach painted in a miniaturising way somehow more attractive in England than in Italy, and finally the discovery of a local painter called Lilli (1570–1630), who in one picture is almost exactly like El Greco, who I had supposed was inimitable. This Lilli is a large canvas of saints: the colours, the faces, the movement all recall El Greco so precisely that you could easily mistake it for his work. It is also the only picture of its kind, so far as I could see, that Lilli ever painted, and has great merit. On the whole the art of painting at Ancona did not flourish, it hangs dead between idiotic baroque saints on the walls of expensive churches, and in the art gallery attains only to the phoney dignity of the bourgeois portraits of those who paid for the paintings in the churches.

I was happy enough just observing Ancona. I stumbled somehow on a huge piazza of about 1760 where a double flight of stone steps frames the statue of an enthroned Pope. The conception is baroque, but the Pope's head is fatally realistic, nodding wearily and lined with unhappiness. Behind him soars a Dominican church (the Jesuits are shut for repairs) rebuilt to suit the statue: here in the provinces the Pope could order the entire piazza from top to bottom from one architect. For the same reason it has curiously little relationship to any other street or building: a wonderfully shadowy medieval gate of the city is hidden away behind the top left-hand corner. In general the outer façades of noble houses in Ancona are distinguished with a certain lightness, within the same space as other buildings, by their *piano nobile* decorated with perhaps a balcony half-way up. Later the Ruskinian grandiose takes over, and the third-storey *piano nobile* becomes absurdly exaggerated. The classical moment is understated, like the small gorgon's head that Augustus wears over his corselet, scarcely bigger than a medallion. The oldest house was occupied by the Faculty of Commerce and Economics near the museum: its face had a mass of unlikely and reused ornamental sculptures built into it more or less higgledy-piggledy. There are such houses in eighteenth-century drawings of Athens, but this one was probably the first of its kind Cyriaco knew.

I never discovered who the band in uniform were who stayed a night in my hotel, but they cannot have had good weather for their performance: only a sun like a crystallised apricot in a sky of ice. In the shade of the older, darker streets the cold may get into your bones: and yet their life is kinder than the bustle around the enormous transports that filled the harbour. It had a railway line still in use that wandered along the street out of sight. But I preferred the medieval gate called S. Pietro up behind the Pope's sad statue, where cats wandered in and out of a library built inside the arch, and the heads of two unlikely stone lions peered out of the solid stonework. In the newer city towards the station beyond the Place Cavour I found a tiny Greek consulate above the office of Olympic Airways. Huge container lorries with Cretan surnames rumbled by, driven by boys as agile and as nonchalant as Cretans. It is a curious thought that George Seferis might have been a consul here instead of in Albania, before the war. He would have been more comfortable. Lost in this thought, I had lunch at the Moretta, a luxurious Italian restaurant near the stony Pope.

My diary reads, 'Remarkable prawn cocktail where everything (dill, etc.) smelt and was delicious except the prawns, from the freezer. Good local wine and water Levissima naturale. Grilled sole and olives all'Ascolano, which turns out to be where they stuff olives in meat and not vice versa. The sole in crumbs and a bit of raw carrot and celery to stay your immediate pangs.' It is here, I think, that my sought-for but mysterious transformation begins (the descent and the ascension in Greece). Over my lemon sorbet I worried about the Stazione Maritima and the luggage tugging I had to face there, while I listened to the boss on the telephone about money, and preferred my lot to his. Had I then realised that the harbour had no porters I might have preferred his. I snoozed away the afternoon in a huge room with a twenty-foot mirror fringed with a bank of dark-red geraniums the colour of Calabrian tomatoes. It was apparently reserved for this civilised use, and for smoking; I was admittedly woken three or four times, but only by mobile phones. Otherwise the sleepy provincial propriety of the nineteenth-century Papal states still prevailed.

Outside it was raining quietly to itself. I wondered whether an Italian cook could explain the uses of the enormous variety of cooking pots in the archaeological museum; it was an idle speculation. The place where I got my ticket yesterday was slow to fill up, dirtier than an airport and smelling of cheap cigarettes, but somehow more cheerful. I got among a crowd of Canadian soldiers in sky-blue hats, off to Split after 'leave' in a rest camp, for the final sixty days of their tour of duty in Bosnia. It seemed a preposterous waste of life. 'One of the guys from the battalion had meningitis and they wouldn't let him back in the country. So we stayed there in dock till three in the morning. And they left the bar open, but they shut down the casino.' A casino which all these boats boast means an array of fruit machines and other automatic gambling devices. Children play them without even talking to each other. My chief friends in the crowd of soldiers were a tiny, very polite Filippino and his enormous, beaming, inarticulate black minder.

With many struggles and heavings of luggage I got on board *Daedalus* of the Minoan Line, a large and bad floating hotel with an enormous garage for container trucks. In fact I had never seen so many truck drivers in one place, and that part of the journey was fascinating. I even met one from Gloucestershire who told me of bizarre adventures in Russia. They were independent to the point of being solitaries, but their lives were based on economic calculations that seemed to me extraordinary. Most of them, I suppose, will end up prosperous heads of small or not so small businesses. The queerest thing about the departure was that there were no seagulls whatever at Ancona, and none offshore, only a glittering greenish-black sea miles below us, flecked with white foam. No dolphins kept us company either, and at lunch-time next day when we came into the shipping lanes between Brindisi and Greece you could see only long caravans of dung-beetles like ours moving this way and that across the mildly heaving sea. At four in the morning I had been woken by being thrown about in bed, but the storm appeared to be nearly over. Italy was grey though you could see no mountains; it just tailed away to a final lighthouse and was gone, but the clouds in the sky were like those you see in the west as you drive towards Wales, heroic and abstract. At six or seven in the evening, water and whisky bubbled like volcanoes in the glasses.

Suddenly about seven in the evening the sea quietened, and we ran between Paxos with its twin and then northern Kerkyra and the

Albanian coast. This was exciting to me because Albania was so long forbidden, ever since the mines blew up a British ship in the Albanian Channel in about 1946. The Albanians refused to accept responsibility, in fact they were thought to have done it on purpose, and on this excuse the British confiscated a huge sum of gold which King Zog had left in the Bank of England. He must have had a lot of money, because he had a plan to buy the *Times* newspaper, and run it in the Albanian interest. I remember King Zog as elderly in a hotel in Bath when I was a schoolboy; he seemed an attractively unlikely figure. His financial adviser survived the war, and twenty years later he was an Anglophile Communist Albanian minister of finance: he used to parade beside the sea as a dandy of the Twenties, in spats and a straw hat with a gold-topped cane, and was a friend of a friend of mine who used to visit Albania to buy books for an Oxford library. To me the thrill of the place was that archaeologically it was close to being virgin territory; the only English expert was Nick Hammond, who was lucky enough to be sent there during the 1939 war. Now, as the dusk closed in and the islands swam away into the mist, you could have thrown an apple into Albania. I did once seriously attempt to learn Albanian from an old exiled bar-keeper in Athens, but he just roared with laughter at me.

The sight of the place altered my perspective, and so did the rings of bright blue water round the beaches of Kerkyra, and the elephantine light grey of the Albanian hills, which is one of Edward Lear's colours; indeed he uses it for the chromolithograph of Paxos. I heard an anxious voice saying in Greek, 'They talk of getting to Patras by seven in the morning, but I have to be in the village before that.' We passed small islands or headlands of Albania, hills steeply sloping into the sea with just a few olive trees, that might be the ideal place to test the influence of the Corinthian colonists on Kerkyra on this opposite coast: was it as unoccupied then as it seemed to be now? In Kephallonia the Myceneans coexisted with a native culture of great simplicity, and one wonders about the archaic and classical period. The answer must be, I suppose, that by then

24

everyone spoke Greek, on the Albanian coast as well as in all the islands. The differences had become merely class differences.

That evening I ate prawns 'fried with cheese', which turned out to be the old Spetsiotic dish you could get thirty years ago at the Kokkini Barka in Piraeus, a lethally delicious mixture of hot feta cheese, prawns and resinated wine bubbling in a deep earthenware pot. The waiter was a Kephallonian and wondered whether perhaps the idea was Cretan. There was more wine in it or stronger cheese than in Piraeus. It may not have been quite the same thing but it was a haunting ghost and to be taken seriously. After that I remembered my wife's advice and tried the veal, but fell into the trap that in Greece all beef is sold as 'veal', just as in England all mutton is called 'lamb'. The wine was rough and rather strong, from Archanes in Crete, and I was tempted to stay up all night and see Levkas and Kephallonia and the rest flitting by like black clouds. We might pass inland of Ithaki. Even at Igoumenitsa, which has about a thousand times more lights than it ever used to have, I felt the overwhelming excitement I have always felt at every Greek arrival. Half a mile away to the right the Brindisi ferries were unloading.

At dawn there was a hailstorm with thunder and lightning. I woke early in my dog kennel and dragged myself to the place near the head of the stairs where passports had to be checked. In order to do this the police handed out bits of blank paper and collected them up again, still blank. Unluckily, in the press of people I had to negotiate a downward moving staircase, something I can hardly do on dry land, and I tripped up. It might have been serious but it was not, and I staggered out into the hailstorm with only a broken watch-strap. I fell at once into the arms not of Giorgis but of his friend Dinos Eliopoulos, now retired from a career of thirty-one years as a psychiatrist in America, and photographing the wild flowers of the Peloponnese. Giorgis had sent him to meet me, not because of the earliness of the hour, since we were an hour and a half late and it was now nearly nine, but because all the Greek farmers were on strike, and had made all the roads impassable.

Dinos took my luggage and we were off to his flat in Pelicano, which was once an old marshy area of Patras near a brewery, where a wounded pelican settled itself in a taverna and left its name to the district. Dinos proudly showed me his own contribution, a Michigan Chinese elm, which is going to be a wonderful tree if only the municipality would stop pruning it. In the shaken condition to which I was reduced, I felt considerable sympathy with that fine young tree and its lopped branches.

Patras was not as I remembered it. It was once a town I had slowly come to like, grubby and old-fashioned with a ridiculous public garden and arcades of shops climbing straight uphill to a nondescript castle. One of those streets contained the best home-made chocolate shop in all Greece, better than Flocca's in Athens and more inventive in its variety and ingenuity. There was also a reasonable restaurant lower down. As the city grew, it had developed a pleasing and very dull museum much despised by Greeks, full of Roman rubbish. Augustus had depopulated a large part of the west of Greece after winning the battle of Actium, in order to found two powerful and favoured colonies, one here to replace Corinth, and one near Actium itself with a function like that of Igoumenitsa, as a port where the roads led eastwards. Patras had theatrical arrangements that startled Pausanias, and the same sort of portrait sculpture as Augustan Naples or nineteenth-century Ancona. I mention Naples only because the town council there have their heads in bronze mounted on blocks of stone like herms, but their courting tackle is also bronze, for fear of vandalism no doubt, and portrayed with the most whole-hearted realism. They are like portraits of elderly businessmen in a pissoir, but with no hands. I have never seen such a gallery elsewhere.

Now Patras had become a huge city. This was the sort of change I half expected, so I was armoured against it, but I was too dazed on that first morning to notice the extent of the new city. Pelicano was on the sea in the Athens direction; it must have been near a fourth-class hotel where I once spent the night, where there used to be a notice propped up in the lavatory, 'Do not stand on the pedestal in boots, danger of death.' That had crumbled to dust long ago, but I remembered the beautiful brickwork of the abandoned brewery chimney, which I had always assumed was an old brickworks. The flat where Dinos now took me to meet his wife and wait for a train was one of many hundreds, a garden suburb of flats, near the sea and not too tall. The sea is still narrowing at Patras, a mile or two out from Rion and Antirion and the straits, so that you can see the islands. On that day they were cloaked in evil weather, the sea was a dramatic black with white horses lit up by lightning flashes, and occasionally obscured by hailstorms.

As for the farmers' strike, that was a simple try-on that flared up as nearly as it could into a crisis, but it lasted only about a week. Wherever the roads were barricaded there would be a way round known to the local Greeks and it was possible to negotiate your way through the barriers in many cases. It was partly a matter of tele-vision, which gleefully spread panic, and of rumour, which multi-plied it. The strike was a demand for a new subsidy for farmers so that they could pay their taxes. They were already getting large subsidies from Europe and they had decided the government should do its bit to subsidise them some more. They behaved as if they were re-enacting some heroic scene of resistance from the past, but it had never happened, it was a myth. In the past, Greek farmers did not command enough tractors to block the main roads, and anyway Greece did not have much in the way of main roads: this strike was a creation of the new wealth and the new Europe. At any rate, that was how I came to read it, and in another ten days it was completely forgotten, as if it had all just been a bit of fun. Mr Papandreou, the Prime Minister, treated it scornfully and with a political dexterity that left the farmers open-mouthed. At that time he had just bought himself a new house of a devastating ugliness with three swimming baths for six hundred and something thousand pounds. But mean-while, Giorgis and Dinos had arranged for me to travel by train, which is what I would naturally have done on my own: the train is slow and quiet and I am used to it. It used to be so slow that you could pick lemons out of the train window, or have a long conversation with an old crone with no teeth and a goat she was taking somewhere. Athens to Pyrgos could take nine hours thirty years ago, and when I first took that train I got on at midnight at Aigion, just up the line, an important market town for currants where boats came in from Delphi, and I got to Pyrgos after the dawn had broken, about five in the morning. Now the train was a mere thirty-five minutes late at Patras and less than an hour late at Pyrgos.

At Pyrgos you could change to the heavenly little train to Olympia where you used to pass a field full of fireflies after dark; the winter I worked at Olympia I took that train once a week to see Giorgis. In summer there was the most rarefied train of all, with just one carriage to take children to the beach at Katakolo: it was originally a goods train to take currants for export to the harbour, and it was called *Kolo-syrtis*, the Drag-arse. In Pyrgos it once had its own special station, as grand as the main station at Lausanne or Geneva, of which nothing is left now but a four-storey neoclassic building. But if none of these things attracted you, and you just stayed in the train beyond Pyrgos, you came in the end after an odyssey of lakes and mountains to the south, to Kalamata, on the edge of the Mani, which in those days was bandit country. From Kalamata it is possible to take a train, and for all I know the same one, up to Tripolis, and so I suppose to Athens, but that I have never done. I am pleased to say, though, that this altogether delightful rail network which serves no purpose except pleasure was the result of English advice on how to improve the Greek economy at the time of the Crimean war. If goods circulated it was thought everyone would become richer, although alas there were never any goods to circulate.

So Dinos showed me into a seat in a first-class compartment, and the weather suddenly cleared up, though from the platform we had an excellent view of the lightning flickering over the mountains to

the north and the enormous ferry still tethered to the quay like a
sea-monster. As we hooted our way out of Patras, I felt for
a moment that nothing had altered: this was going to be the Greece
I knew. The first few hundred yards from the station really are much
the same. You notice the intense green and the jungle density of
people's back gardens, the lemon trees loaded with yellow fruit and
sometimes with light bulbs as well, and the few orange orchards still
burdened with their fruit. That was because no one can be got now
to harvest them, Giorgis said, and in the case of the single trees of
lemons, which are so picturesque, people simply leave them on the
tree to pick them at need whenever they want a fresh lemon. There
were lemons in people's backyards in Pyrgos, but at times as few as
two or three, or the last lemon. The light bulbs remain a mystery,
unless up a lemon tree is the most convenient place to hang them.
One bulb I saw in a tree was painted lemon yellow: was it a bird
scarer for use against owls, or was it that simple aesthetic wish that
accounts for so many mysteries in Greece?

So we ruminated our way along, stopping at stations and halts
with and without names. At times there was a small hut or a smaller
bus-shelter, but the train chose where to stop very precisely, often
ignoring these inconveniences. It would halt where it was easy to
step across a bank into a lane, or where tradition demanded and
some old lady waited. Sometimes the old ladies just waved to us
and on we went, or they had a little conversation with a friend
through the window. I began quite soon to notice the numerous
tiny flocks of sheep and lambs which have sprung up all over Greece
in the shade of the Common Market, but very few that collected as
many as fifty animals. Some quirk of regulations favours the small
owner and the enclosed space, just as it favours the disappearance of
the casual labour that once picked the oranges and lemons. Now
that we were out in the real country, the green was as green as it can
ever have been, the goats as familiar and inquisitive, the occasional
tree as old and gnarled as ever. At one tiny halt a dignitary of the
church attended by a village elder in a dark suit and armed with a

black, silver-topped cane skipped up and blessed us all and found himself a seat. A man came blushing and told him in his ear that he was from the same village as his holiness's mother; this went down well. We passed Skourochori and Lasteika and there in the distance rose Pyrgos like a mirage.

The Bishop was the Metropolitan of Pyrgos, and as he left the station he noticed Giorgis. 'What are you doing here?' he asked him. 'Is this another literary event?' 'No,' said Giorgis, 'I'm only meeting a foreign friend off your train.' 'A foreigner? Oh yes, I think I spotted him, but I can't tell because he didn't speak.' I was not expecting to be met at Pyrgos station, but there he was, hair gleaming with water and a smile on him like a ripe apple. It was worth the journey just for that moment. All the same I observed immediately that something had altered in his status. He had not had a lot to do with any Bishop since the one who gave him free use of the Cathedral printing press during the German occupation, the one who deserted Pyrgos to join the armed resistance in the mountains. Now Giorgis was a somebody in Pyrgos: he had always known a lot of people because of growing up there and working for the bus company, but this was something more than the democracy of small country towns. He had become famous as a poet. This process had been going on for years, but first in Athens and now and far more intensely in Pyrgos the tidal movement of fame had engulfed him. He was the President of the Library of Pyrgos, and everyone acknowledged him as a distinguished literary man.

This made a difference to the whole time I was in Greece. The physical circumstances of his life were the same, but now he was deferred to, he had disciples as well as friends, he was a highly respected writer in a society that was provincial enough to be perfectly sincere in its respect and even in the ceremony of its deference. Some of this new-found grandeur even rubbed off on me. About a year or six months before, a girl who was a Greek journalist had phoned me once or twice from London and asked me the usual daft sort of questions. Because I was in a good mood, the sun was out, or because I knew I would not have to see her, I gave her full and rather clear answers, without bothering about diplomacy, and she recorded the whole conversation, which was printed in her Greek paper, I think the *Free Press*, including whatever I chose to say not just about the Elgin marbles but about John Major, Mr Papandreou, Mrs Thatcher, the House of Commons and any other scum of the earth. This interview was utterly irresponsible, but apparently in Greece it was a sensation. So the Greek local television and radio stations showed an unnatural appetite for the pair of us. Through this minefield Giorgis was to guide me.

At a more serious level it is a great relief that he is now so famous. I have known for thirty years and more that he was an enchanting poet, even what I would call a great poet: happy the country that has such a poet lurking in the provinces. In the slow progress of his poetry he has moved step by step, like a man treading on ice, to a position where he is a master of his language and a master of clarity. George Seferis had already recognised the size of his talent and the moral dimension of his uncorrupt life in provincial Pyrgos, and came in the end to love him as a son. Unhappily, that great man died in the early seventies at the moment when Giorgis's first book was published, and the critical essay he had intended to devote to him remained unwritten, or at least unfinished. But I had known just what a good poet he was from the days when Seferis sent me to see him in 1963. At that time he and Takis Sinopoulos, the doctor and poet who was our friend and the sweetest and funniest of men, seemed to be as entangled with Giorgis Pavlopoulos as if they were two bodies with one head. Now they have grown apart and are easy to distinguish, but then they used to write bits of one another's poems. When Takis published his first book of poems, which I think was *Knowing Max*, Max being a dog, he spent his entire profits from the book on buying Giorgis Pavlopoulos a glass of beer.

Things change, and there is no consolation for it. Takis is dead now and seriously famous. He was an asthmatic with very bad general health who drank and smoked as if there was no tomorrow;

he died comparatively young; he was a few years older than Giorgis, who is about seven years older than me, about seventy. Takis suffered anguish all his life from his experiences as an army doctor in the Civil War, when he treated the wounded and dying of both sides. That comes out in his great poem '*Nekrodeipnos*', 'Dead Men's Dinner', about the ghosts who haunted him for ever. He was warned about his life-style naturally, but he said he intended to live to the fullest degree possible to him, for whatever time he might have left. Now he has three roads named after him, one in Athens, one in Pyrgos and one in Epitalion where he was born. He was astoundingly loyal to his patients and to Giorgis. They knew each other as boys and he would always want to be at Pyrgos for Easter, even though it meant travelling all night on the Saturday and doing the same again on the Sunday night, so as not to miss his surgery at Perissos. Takis embodied provincial feelings in a quite different way from Giorgis; he had a frantic hunger to be recognised and to know what was what in French poetry, German poetry and every other kind, and he attacked the centre of the literary game in Athens with passionate bad temper and genuine fury. If on some night he chose to offer you a private reading of his poems, it might go on all night. If it were tonight, I wish it would.

This was intended for a celebration and yet the reader will see that I was haunted by ghosts; even when I met people I had known in the past they did often seem very old and frail and shaky, as if I found myself in a new stanza of a very old poem whose lines were laid down long ago. What impression I may have made on them I shudder to think. The first I met was Theodoros who was the tavern keeper of the Lyra, the little bay near Katakolo where Giorgis had taken me on the evening we first met. He is dying of heart disease and the usual dramatic problems have arisen over the division of the property. Understandably he did not want to give up whole-heartedly with no right ever to enter his own kitchen again. The Lyra as I first knew it was undiscovered, with a huge vine, Santomeriko I think, trailing through olive trees above a path which was a sandy scramble down to the sea. It stood in the shadow of an ancient akropolis. In the distance about a mile offshore it looked at a small green island called Tigani, the Chip, crowded with the poor graves of early Christian fishermen, and beyond that it looked towards the hazy ghost of Zakynthos. It was the most beautiful place I had ever been in, or so I thought. Twenty-five years ago I must have taken Bruce Chatwin there and told him to bury me there if I should die in Afghanistan. He appears to have taken this seriously as a last wish and the practical difficulties alarmed him, but I only meant to rest there as lightly as ashes and free of all social bonds and religious links. Perhaps it was also to avoid those dank monuments where dons are buried in Oxford and where tourists penetrate among the brambles.

Pyrgos itself had altered in the 1970s when they cleared up and paved the untidy old hilltop, half-way between a garden and a rubbish tip at the edges, where Giorgis had played as a child with Mikis Theodorakis, where the last traces of the tower or fortified farm had been that gave Pyrgos its name. The ruin was that of a seventeenth-century house, but I think I discovered that it stood on the site of a thirteenth-century French or Byzantine tower: at least I have a note somewhere that says so. The stones that might have told us more were removed wholesale to build the parish church of St Spyridon, outside Pyrgos towards the sea. Giorgis had grown up in central Pyrgos; the family house was now a car-park near the new library, but his father's shop and café was two or three doors from the square, and the Theodorakis house was at the opposite corner. They went different ways as schoolboys, when Mikis was lucky enough to learn music from a singer in Tripolis, who sang the traditional chants in church all morning and the old songs in taverns all evening. He was a deep drinker and a deeply traditional man, who knew a vast repertory of music that was not all written down. The echoes in the music that Mikis composed when his day came are very powerful. Roots of this kind go back to a Greek life dead and gone these many years: it is only amazing that it lived so long.

Of course the roots wandered in many directions: Pyrgos before the war was a place where ladies held tea-parties, and there were dancing schools to learn the foxtrot and the tango. Giorgis and Mikis as little boys planned to write an opera together: it would be a pastoral opera with a flock of real sheep.

Old Pyrgos was a civilised, neoclassic city or small town, and it was comparatively wealthy because it was and is the wettest part of Greece, water was abundant, and the landscape comparatively luxuriant, so that the Athenian orator Lysias thought nothing more beautiful could exist on earth. He does not mean the plain, admittedly, but the small hills towards Olympia and the distant blue crests. Unfortunately, at the end of the Second World War, Pyrgos burned for twelve days and very little remains that was not then ruined, or ruined ten years ago by earthquake. In the Sixties and Seventies you got a vague impression of noble architecture going to ruin, of the astonishing survival in the provinces of enviable building. The old market rose like a cricket pavilion or a nobleman's stables designed in 1750, out of squalid streets; it seemed a discovery, yet it was and is the most meritorious bit of architecture in the world of its date, which must, I suppose, be somewhere in the 1870s. Pyrgos burnt because when the Germans withdrew and the resistance came down from the mountains, armed police were left in charge. They agreed to surrender next morning but in the dawn when the resistance arrived in the streets they were shot at: it seems likely that some of the police feared the future, a few probably escaped, but when it was over you could see the burnt bodies in the smoking ruins of the town hall. Giorgis's first cousin was an officer in the resistance; he was shot dead by a sniper from the Cathedral bell-tower. Old Pyrgos must have been something like a country town in Ireland, with horse-races in the streets once a year. The innocence of that world could still be sniffed in the atmosphere of the 1960s, but Pyrgos as it once was never really revived. For one thing, the currant trade had gone. Then came the traffic, then the big roads and then the holiday houses.

Giorgis's present house, which he won in a lottery organised by
the government to provide working-class houses, lay in a small
patch of forty of fifty similar houses called the Alpheios Workmen's
Houses, one of three or four such estates in Pyrgos. The estate was
as far as you could go towards the river within the town boundaries,
and it used to be isolated and raw-looking, but now Pyrgos has
crept out to embrace it, and the hens escape from their houses and
lay eggs in the olive groves, and the lemon trees and the flowering
trees have buried it, and you ask the taxi driver to turn right where
the parked car is, the red one, because that never moves. Most of the
houses are not in roads but in some four or five little courts, where
each house has a small forecourt or front garden, all defiantly
different, but at the backs they give on to lanes, and that is where
you hear the women's voices in a conversation apparently perpetual
between back doors, that is where the cats lurk and miaow and
where small presents of food and bits of advice about cooking,
salted with ironies about husbands, go flying this way and that. I
think Giorgis's wife Mitsa has been happy here.

The news began at once; it is best to quote my diary. 'The grass
like very bright green surf. Sun Sageika to Ampelokampo (and
Skourochori and Lasteika where Giorgis saw the huge water-snake
as a boy playing truant). Mitsa gayer and greyer than she used to be,
"and she don't eat much either".' We lunched on rice with a red
sauce and fresh rissoles and a marvellous wine from 'the fisherman's'
special reserve: him whose daughter fell for Charis at first sight, and
after a few weeks' determined wooing on his part, now they are
engaged and will marry at Christmas. Charis is Giorgis's son, a
mathematics teacher at Athens University, now about thirty. In the
summer of 1963 in a house in Cemetery Road, near the Marble
Spring, which flowed then if only through a tap, from an inscribed
marble slab, Mitsa and Giorgis were newly married and she was
pregnant with Charis. Now the house is gone, the tap is gone, even
the rose in the garden that was so good with salad is gone, since the

35

earthquake, but the street remains and my old friend Takis Loumiotis still lives in it, looking a little younger as his hair whitens.

That evening the new in-laws came to dinner and I liked them greatly. The fisherman turned out to be a highly successful fish merchant called Kalamatianos with two fresh-fish shops in Pyrgos and two sons like young giraffes. It was the first of April, with cold blasts disturbing a good sky. On this day I learnt for the first time that Giorgis had fallen in Athens, and that his leg still hurt. Only a few weeks before, he had written to me about our expeditions saying he could still ride a horse with one leg hooked up, which might be useful, and I remembered that he used to gallop a horse of his uncle's for many miles across country, through distant villages where they knew him as the mad boy. There would now have to be a change of tactics, which he had foreseen, and I found myself in his hands. At this time I was still dazed with sleep or the lack of it, and my stomach was still churning from the sea. Giorgis found that the cold affected his leg badly. Indoors, though, I felt perfectly at home, the house reminded me of Pasternak's father's drawings of his children. The bookshelves had overflowed, Giorgis's own paintings of female nudes, with a heroic nude by Takis the doctor, were stuck all over the walls, with one based on a poem by Giorgis, painted by an old resistance man called Captain Xanthos (Pinieros), a sweet and childlike man who had taken to painting in his old age, in a naive style of his own. Giorgis's had a lot of dead heads with two Glories of an angelic shape hovering above them. In Charis's old room, which was my bedroom, was a signed Henry Miller lithograph.

Outside, the olive field that separated the estate from one of the tributaries of the Alpheios was covered in great foaming patches of something I took for meadow cranesbill, far stronger and taller and healthier than its English cousin. These flowers swarmed like great clouds of migrating purplish-pinkish insects under the boughs of the old trees, and the hens hid in them. But no one now can command the labour to harvest the olives, except to share the oil on a fifty-fifty basis if anyone can be found to do the work. The new father-in-law had eight kids from three nanny goats, with which he was besotted; his face melted when he described the way they lay. I went for a walk along the perfectly flat mud road towards Salmone, past great carpets of flowers, lambs and goats and water-courses or canalised rivers, tiny farms to the right as I walked inland, and grand new houses to the left. But on this side of the water there was no doubt that gypsies still prevailed; it must be where those sweet insistent gypsy children came from in the square at Pyrgos, as warm as monkeys and highly intelligent: you see them sweeping through the square in droves, like young swallows. I found them irresistible, and so did Giorgis. He wrote a poem about one the other day, which perhaps I should give here, if only because I vividly remember a gang of gypsy children hunting for the new season's snakes at a bridge over a river where a tarmac road crossed the dirt-track over the fields. There were numerous sand martins and a dozen kinds of wild flowers, but no snakes. I remember a small farmyard with hens, sheep, goats and dogs, all controlled by an ancient and much wounded tom-cat who growled. The poem is called 'The Gypsy'; Giorgis read it to me that day.

> I said to a Gypsy girl
> I want to be a gypsy
> and have you.
>
> Can you eat bitter herbs with no salt
> for an evening meal she said to me,
> and then lie down?
>
> I can, I said to her.
>
> Can you lie down she said
> without weeping with cold
> on the frozen mud?

I can, I said to her.

And on that mud she said to me
can you set fire to my body
and burn it up to ash?

And that too if I can, I said to her.

Can you throw my ashes
into your wine she said to me
and get yourself so drunk you forget me?

No, I cannot do that, I said to her.

You will not make a gypsy she told me.

There is no doubt that this poem is passionately erotic and at a
deep level embittered: it is as much an epigram, though one like
a stone long polished in the hands, as many of the small haiku he
sent me. 'Little boat Shut in a bottle Where are you making for?'
There is another that mentions the sea and ships: he is like the
child in a poem by George Seferis, drawing by lamplight sea-shells
and sea-boats. No doubt that is ordinary, or once it was, for Greek
children. 'I heard oars And saw no boat In the sea-fog.' There is
something sad, something lost or frustrated in all these brief
poems. They are summed up in 'A peacock's tail On a donkey's
behind. That's this world.' They are not easy to translate, but they
express something in Giorgis that I like very much. Mitsa likes the
gypsy poem and laughs a lot about it. When it was read aloud on
some grand occasion, I got a heavy nudge in the ribs from her.
Still, this is not a book about his poetry, which I have translated in
the past, only it goes to explain what I so admire about him, and
his poetry was a constant presence in that month. When I showed
him mine I had the considerable burden of translating it
impromptu, line by line, though when he is left alone, he

produces translations of my poems that are better than the originals.

When I left the estate for that walk of an hour or two, a long procession was passing by of tractors and farm machines new and old, and some police cars and a breakdown van. I thought it must be reinforcements for the crossroads at Kalo Nero (Clean Water) to the south, but it turned out that the strike, which had looked so formidable on last night's television, when men with moustaches like the eaves of haystacks were setting light to tyres in the road for the cameras, was over. Politically, this strike was a curious bastard, being a product of both the parties in opposition to Papandreou's 'socialist' government: that is, a combine of the Communists with the Conservatives, manipulating the richer farmers. That was visible in the sheepish and rather well-dressed young tractor drivers, waving in the hope of sympathy. A toothless old crone of a traditional kind did give them a cheer. 'Poor boys,' she said, 'what can they do?' But most people were annoyed, half amused, and rather frightened by how swiftly the shops emptied. I saw a sweet little old man as brown as a nut far up my mud track trying to get a little cart with an engine to show some sign of life. His wife was helping him though she did not seem to know much about the machine. He came racing to meet me and was very pleased I was English. Lastly, as I came back to the main road where the estate is, I explored an abandoned-looking house of great if melancholy beauty. Its shape was classical, it had an iron balcony and some broken windows. Giorgis told me that inside its rooms had painted ceilings in the old Italian and Greek fashion, but a child had been killed by a fall from the balcony and the place was more or less abandoned: it belonged to a theologian, that is, to a man who undertook religious instruction in schools. He would sell it one day and make a fortune. I hope that all these things fit somehow together to make a picture of the provincial countryside in 1995.

In the early evening we went together on a little whizz in

someone's motor car to see the place where the Alpheios falls at last into the sea, and to see the driver's beach hut or house for the summer, which was in that marais or waste land behind the endless sea-beach. To get to the river you had first to head south and cross it, then take tracks or lanes across country towards the sea. The Alpheios is a mighty river and in the past it flooded mightily. Its mud was famous in ancient times: the nymph, Salmone, after whom the modern village is named, avoided rape by Poseidon by plastering her face with the river-mud, while Artemis the protector of nymphs craftily persuaded everyone else to do the same. There was an annual festival when this scene was re-enacted according to Pausanias, but now the mud has covered the temple or sanctuary and nothing remains of it but the moonlight on the wet heather. The beach-houses are much raided by poverty-striken Albanian refugees, who have settled in Eleia in huge numbers. They are only the latest of many generations of refugees: in the 1920s, Mitsa's father employed Asia Minor refugees to look after his cattle and George Seferis was just such a refugee, from Smyrna. In those days the Athenian opera house was crammed with refugees, a family to a box, now it is the beach-houses of the Pyrgiotes that they dismantle.

There is a wonderful desolation of marsh and puddles and heath, with a little stand of pines on a mound in the distance that marks the estuary. You can see Katakolo and headlands or islands far beyond it in the evening light, and, far away in the other direction, Kyparissia to the south. Kyparissia was an Arcadian port for a time; it was the only port Arcadia ever had, but they were unable to keep it and I dare say their heart was never in it. It scarcely connects with anywhere at all. That whole country from the Alpheios to the borders of Messenia is cobwebbed with mythology, but the ancient sites are queer ones: they were unambitious and fought no one but one another, in tiny quarrels over flocks and water rights perhaps. There were kingdoms there of which we know nothing and dialects of which our knowledge is insubstantial. These places are the opposite of Athens, and even more so of Sparta, and I have always tried to imagine the history of the fifth century through their eyes, but without success I fear. I wanted on this occasion to try to sort out more of the puzzle of the ground south of Alpheios called Triphylia, the three tribes, but I cannot say that I made a lot of sense of it. Yet it seems to me that it would have been in the fifth century the ideal place to live and the one most suited to my temperament. Giorgis lives on the edge of this territory and regards it with amazement.

That evening was the first of what the Bishop had called literary events that I attended. In the past, I gathered, there had been one exactly similar, when people had made speeches about Giorgis and he had read some poems aloud. There were sometimes events something like these in Athens many years ago, but only, I believe, among the post-war writers, and I had never felt they were much fun. I suppose what has happened now is part of the growth of literary festivals and the higher profile of poets in all Europe. I am all for them, but I have never been able to understand who attends them. A concert like the Three Choirs Festival draws on a clear constituency and so does a jazz festival, but poetry is published in books and the performance of it by its author is in my judgement either a luxury or a fearful illusion. This has become an old-fashioned point of view. The first thing you need is a building, and Pyrgos has the restored Apollo Theatre, the same one where Giorgis took refuge as a boy and crouched in the dark with a couple of friends when the Germans had suddenly imposed a curfew and were searching the streets, after the resistance had assassinated a general at Lasteika. It was where he and the boys in his group put on *Volpone* and *Six Characters in Search of an Author*, both in Greek of course. They published a magazine with a physically amateur appearance called the *Odyssey*.

But now, O Bottom, how thou art transformed! The Apollo in its new paint was a smarter, prettier, more appetising small theatre than I have ever seen in the English or French provinces. Even

inside, it was beautiful, though admittedly the inside of the Theatre Royal at Bath is better still. The Apollo at Pyrgos is more
comparable to the theatre at Richmond in north Yorkshire. On
that evening it stood blushing slightly in a side-street, pink and
white and Mozartian. All that time ago, the boys hiding there did
not dare shine torches, but they had one candle and played the
game over it that they were dining at Maxim's in Paris (how had
they heard of that?), for which they invented long and bizarre
menus of rhinoceros and so on. Now it was a crowded evening,
with all Pyrgos and even people from Athens all crammed into
the Apollo, to honour a writer of short stories called Papadimitrakopoulos who looks and dresses like Spike Milligan, and really
is an excellent writer. He is a retired army doctor with a high
rank, whose stories might, if his temperament were different,
have been combined into a brilliant memoir. They are extremely
truthful, particularly in the most bizarre details: he is a Tolstoyan
really.

His appearance was gleeful and half goonlike with the beard
and shoulder-bag, and he reminded me of John Wain's friends,
among whom he would have melted indistinguishably. He also
likes women, and adores Mitsa, who responded. At dinner Giorgis
and I were drawing hens, and he put the napkin in his pocket like
a handkerchief. I felt like a child at the circus whom the clown has
noticed. One of the speakers was a scholar with a refined manner
from Lamia. At fifteen he had run away to Eurytania to join the
resistance in 1944; that resistance was Communist inspired and he
might have had a bad time in the Civil War, but luckily
he celebrated victory over Hitler by running back home again.
The other speaker was a Professor of Philology (that is, of
literature) from the Albanian border, and looked like a fellow of St
Catherine's College, Oxford. The first one looked badly worn
out and shaken after talking. The Mayor then gave Papadimitrakopoulos a medal and was given an antique photograph of Pyrgos in
return. Cameras flashed the whole evening and the entire audi-

ence queued up to shake hands with the writer before they left. Slowly they disintegrated, and Giorgis said, 'This *is* Pyrgos, pure provincial life, as Stendhal says, in the provinces everything goes slowly.' The story the author read us was a fitting one, not only because it was very good but because it was about Katakolo. It was called 'Warm Sea Baths', and Mitsa assured me that the iron spike on which the hero gets impaled while diving is still to be seen there. On that night I was ready to believe her. The Mayor had taken a huge party of us all out to dinner at a restaurant with incredibly loud electric organ music: there were people dancing formally in couples who came from a class reunion of the Pyrgos grammar school; they were about forty years old, but to look at they might have been Godalming golf club, dancing to Sandy Macpherson's cinema organ amplified.

Now that the strike was over, our plan was to go on the next night to Kalamata, where another, similar literary event was due to feature Giorgis, so I rang Joan Leigh Fermor and arranged to stay the night at Kalamata, while Giorgis came home to Pyrgos, and then to go on the next morning to the village of Kardamyli, some miles outside which the Leigh Fermors lived. They are old now, and I had doubts about imposing myself on them, but there is more life in either of them than there is in me and I was swiftly persuaded. Going to Kardamyli used to be an adventure like hiking through the Hindu Kush, but ten years or more ago the government built a tarmac road right through the Mani to the very bottom, so once again everything had altered. The road used to be a mud track that broke every winter and got repaired, and the only tarmac was a length of about two hundred yards inside the tiny village of Kardamyli, which was once installed by a progressive mayor. The chance of Giorgis's engagement at Kalamata on the edge of the Mani was an opportunity too good to miss.

We rushed first to the next town towards Patras, which is called Amalias, because it has a proper bookshop which Pyrgos cannot boast. Giorgis needed a large supply of a book of his because (as

43

in England) the organisers of his appearance expected to sell them, but the author had to bring them under his arm. We went by car with Christos, the fish king, who had some equivalent of a BMW, and we slid swiftly to a halt in the right road: Pyrgos people have certain prejudices about their neighbours, particularly against the pretensions of Amalias. The bookshop, Dimitropoulos, was an extremely good one all the same. I bought a copy of the collected or selected songs of Nikos Gatsos, which I had never seen or heard of until Giorgis showed me a copy: it was published just after his death about a year ago, though I believe he had seen the proofs. Giorgis had wanted to give me a copy, but I needed to buy it and to carry it around. At a deep level of which I have not spoken, the reason I was in Greece was to visit his grave, which was in the centre of Arcadia, a long and circuitous pilgrimage from the western coast.

But how could I have grasped how distances had lessened? In that car they told me Kalamata would be only an hour or two away, and at once the flying landscape on the road took on the same eternal and dreamlike quality it has in the memory, the lonely stands of water-rooted trees, the sudden rivers and the endlessly dissolving and reassembling plain. Dark trees around old houses stood in bright-green fields, the nearer mountains snow-covered from the last few days had taken on a gilded tint, a kind of transformation scene towards the spring I had never seen before. At lunch Giorgis told me how the pop video advertisement was going to alter poetry: not for him because he was an old poet, but for everyone younger. It would take over memory, there was an inevitability about it. Mitsa told me about the deer in Western Virginia, where they had been to visit Charis, but Giorgis told me how he and Dinos had emerged pop-eyed from a session in the space-flight simulator which was open to the public at the Florida Disneyworld. It was a curious image that they raised, these two elderly, serious Greek gentlemen in Florida. They both agreed the worst part of their simulated flight was the bearing down on the earth and coming to rest. There is a surreal streak in both their imaginations which goes a long way back, as it does for many Greeks. Seferis had it in his way: Giorgis felt that Greek poetry would never be the same again after Seferis, as it never was after Solomos, and as English poetry never was after Eliot. He recalled a question about how to translate the *Odyssey* into modern Greek, to which Seferis had answered at once, free verse. I put in a caveat about the version by the Cretan Psychoundakis, which Giorgis admitted by wild exception was a masterpiece. And yet Greek poetry is full of wild exceptions.

On that day he told me things I had never fully grasped about his life. We had been watching television during lunch, which had given a background tone to our conversation. Then the machine turned to the elephants of Tilos, which is one of the thousand or so Greek islands. The archaeologists have found a forty-five-thousand-year-old graveyard there of very small elephants. They remain a mystery, no one know how they got there. In the same way, said my friend, there is a new adult generation that knows nothing about famine or the resistance, or even about George Seferis. Giorgis met him for the first time only in 1962, when he retired from the foreign service, which was late in the day. He had dropped out of being a law student in Athens, although the allowances the government gave to 'wartime students' like him lasted practically for ever, and they were pushed through the obstacle course as home students. He dropped out of the prospect of a lawyer's life and diploma, which now he said he rather regretted. I had never heard him say this before and I wondered whether it might not be a new thought: after retirement many of the struggles of one's life seem unnecessary in retrospect, and the mistakes take on a coherence as if they were bound to happen. What I was most fascinated to learn was that his wide acquaintance with artists as well as writers, of the Greek generation now so much respected, was based on the years

1940–2, which they all spent in Athens. It was by borrowing his paint box that Takis Sinopoulos suddenly began to paint.

At five we took flight to the south, taking the new turn left at Kalo Nero, a few miles before Kyparissia. I call it new since it was new to me, but the others knew it well, and it must have been twenty years old. Near where a dusty old mud track which we crossed over still ambled off towards Siderokastro and the Neda gorge below Phigaleia, which I had crossed in 1963, this admirable modern road cut across country, following and then ignoring the railway, to meet the old Megalopolis–Kalamata road a little south of the northern border of Messenia. Taken together with the new grandeurs of all these mains roads it must have cut hours and hours off the journey. Now perhaps a generation is already adult that does not know the beautiful Roman aqueduct one used to pass beyond Pylos and Sphacteria: perhaps the sandy beach that Homer knew and the island with its fifth-century BC history and its naval history will become unfamiliar monuments and sink back into obscurity and mythology. We did pass two fine railway viaducts and swished down a wonderful, dead-straight, tree-lined avenue for miles to Hagia Florina and south to Kalamata, to the Galaxia café, where we met a reception committee of old-fashioned and conservative gentlemen dominated by lawyers.

The evening was punctuated by attempts on my part to explore for a decent hotel; these were firmly frustrated for fear I might get lost. We held our meeting in an extraordinary marble building, a modern and extremely expensive-looking architect's dream. Inside, hall beyond polygonal hall, we came to a huge lecture theatre, a bemarbled emptiness with an audience that included a Bishop, two priests and a nun, all come to hear about Giorgis and to listen to two actors reading his works, and maybe to himself. But the programme was too ambitious, towards the end a rehears-ing orchestra in another room played havoc, Giorgis was begged to be extremely brief and the audience for whatever followed practically burst open the doors to get in. Still, honour was done and perfect courtesy was observed. The lecturer was very high-toned, like a late-nineteenth-century English lecturer, perhaps the philosopher Bradley on the poet Tennyson: there was a good deal about light versus darkness, and I remember little more; I had shut my eyes to avoid catching the poet's eye, whereupon Mitsa woke me, in case I fell asleep.

Dinner was much livelier, in a very good fish restaurant on the sea-front that looked like an old railway hut and had a superannuated shunting track passing the front door. I found it remarkable that fashion had moved on and mercifully now there were no bouzoukis. The people were the same rather educated society we knew in Pyrgos, and they talked sensibly and liberally about case law: about the story of a suicide and about whether the most murders in Greece used to happen in Pyrgos and in Agrinion. They said not; they thought it was a question of active local journalists whose pieces were always dated from these towns, though their information might really come from half Greece. There was a Maniote who told me he lived 'near Fermor Leigh', a man in a Savile Row sort of blue suit who admired the prose style of George Thomson in Greek: I did not like to tell him that his hero, a Professor at Birmingham I knew well, was a Communist, and dead into the bargain. He was I must say the mildest mannered man; he introduced mother goddesses and matrilinear successions into the study of Aeschylus and had a stomach ulcer. When I told Giorgis about the vehement denial of Pyrgos vendettas, he gave me a sly grin, and when I told him we had the same sort of thing as a speciality in western Gloucestershire, he admitted the same about Pyrgos.

On this evening I made great friends with Christos Kalamatianos, who I perceived was a very good man to be near in any large party, as he looked after his neighbours. But a flash of lights and he was gone, and they were probably in bed before I was. I settled for a hotel I would have called old-fashioned in the Sixties. There was a meagreness, a sourness, a scarcely held togetherness about it. The room was dirty, nothing worked, but the bed was clean and the bathroom got eight out of ten. How I pined for the Rex where I used to stay in Kalamata, which was a hotel of about 1930 miraculously preserved for fifty years, which an earthquake had wiped away. I began to see the extent of earthquake damage the next morning, the wan and wasted walls and the intrusive new buildings. One newly repainted town house stood out like a sore thumb for its beauty, for the gaiety of light-blue walls and white stucco, and one of those fine Nauplion iron balconies like a flower in its buttonhole. I tried to have breakfast in a ruined café resting on vast wooden crutches like an old man, but inside it was full of an Aristophanic swarm of very old men, buzzing with conversation and brandy and coffee, as if to prove there was life in its veins, and I did not dare to intrude. I found myself back at the Galaxia, opposite that queer modernist mausoleum where the arts took place in this strange corner of the provinces. After breakfast they summoned a taxi for me, and I set off.

2 : The Morning Dew

BY that morning I had plenty to think about. It was for one thing a great relief that Greek, which I had scarcely used for twenty years, had come back to roost quite effortlessly. There was a time when I had to undergo a psychological crisis ending in nightmares before I began to dream in Greek and to think in it and write poems in it. There was no need for that any more, and as for poetry one becomes wily as one gets older, and is careful not to use energy of that kind unless it will come to something. My ambition now was to enter more closely into Giorgis and his world, which had altered. His poems were better than ever, but the life they drew on had changed with his retirement and his new status. I did not know quite what to think of his new literary companions. They were not poets, but mostly consultant academics and inspectors of schools. They were a kind of people I did not know well in England and had never met in Greece. They were charming and bright in the sense of highly intelligent, and I suppose they were critics like Brian Cox.

Not having been trained in English literature I have always feared and frequently distrusted critics; I remember once telling Christopher Ricks most foolishly that I thought the only critics of poetry should be other poets. But here was Giorgis breaking tranquilly through into a world of writers and lecturers and words, such as I had never imagined. Milionis for example, one of the most charming of men, whom I had met the other day, has just written the

49

most brilliant tiny book about Papadiamantis, the great Greek short story writer and novelist of the Nineties, whose novel *The Murderess* I once translated under pressure from a feminist married to a Marxist; it is about a peasant woman who goes about murdering babies because poor girls had such a ghastly time. It is a memorable and Hardyesque story and I learnt from it, but when I went on to explore the western sources of Papadiamantis, I found only Victorian magazines and the idiot Bulwer Lytton, so I gave up. Milionis discusses a fascinating story full of ironies and contrasts called 'The Seal's Lamentation', about the dead body of a girl being washed up and lamented by the seal while her mother is busy lamenting other deaths. The story ends, 'The seal sat by her and lamented, and wept over her, until it was time for her dinner.' Milionis discovered a bit of folklore in which the Greeks speak of seals' tears where we speak of crocodiles' tears. What is worse, General Makryiannis, a peasant general of the 1820s, who is certainly the strongest and to my mind still the best Greek prose writer, speaks of a seal who lamented over a drowned man (that is, keened over him), wept salt tears over him, and then ate him. This is an insight that justifies the profession of criticism.

I had become obstinately opposed to most literary discussions in Greece as in England, because I preferred the starker and at times crazier style in which poets discuss one another's work, which derives maybe from Ezra Pound. There is an openness about it. But also I should admit that I hated reading very long books. I remember George Katsimbalis exploding one day about foreigners and saying not one of them ever read a novel through in Greek. Personally I seldom did so and seldom do so even in English. I said then that I did read them, but it was not as often as I pretended and I did not like to say how bad I felt they were, how unalive their language. I had to read enough long books for professional reasons at that time to blunt my curiosity. But with the writings of these critics, who were some ten or fifteen years younger than I was, a great deal about Greek literature in the nineteenth century and the early twentieth was somehow dropping into place, however much I had resisted it. Poets like Karyotakis and like Giorgis himself and like Photos Paschalinos, a boy who was hanged by the Germans at Patras when he was just coming into flower as a poet, no longer seemed lonely lights as they had done, but now they had a context and a whole literary world which made their attainment seem greater, not more ordinary. What I could not quite make out at that time was whether all this was just the influence of my friend or whether it was progress on a broader front. I have no doubt a great deal of it was his influence. He had been after all an expert for thirty or forty years on writers who are still only names to me.

It was a great pity he was not coming to Kardamyli, where he was actually expected, but I had not realised that the new road made it possible. It is hard to describe the journey because it has so utterly altered things. We trundled easily along, as if we were in the highlands of Scotland, with plenty of soarings and loops and spirals up or down over the impossible crags. The houses had spread far along the shore into the Mani, like a continuous suburb of Kalamata. There among them was the lugubrious-looking luxury hotel where I ought probably to have stayed the night. At Stavropigio someone was attempting to build an artificial village, and where there would have been nothing there was now a dubious-looking antique shop. What looked like cranesbill had swept across the roadsides in a surf of purple, not of pink, with the last of the red anemones, the first few poppies, bright yellow furze and the thousand shades of dark and pale green, and the Mani's extraordinary repertory of rocks. In spite of the road, it was still a place of refuge with the sea hanging like a backcloth at crazy angles behind it, curiously untattered. In the foreground lay deep ravines under our feet where the cliffs were forested, and the taxi man stopped at the sight of one to tell me in an awe-stricken voice about a village bus that had gone over the edge of the cliff opposite and hung there teetering for an hour and more until the people could get out of it.

It took us hardly an hour or so to get to Kardamyli, though I have known it take two or three. As a result the village has become a resort, there are new houses everywhere, the tiny village hotel is unrecognisable, the village high street with its one sad café and its ruins is now done up like somewhere in Provence. There are houses all over the mountainsides, many of them German, all of them of an astounding ugliness and impertinence. And yet it is not ruined, its bones are the same, it just looks like some place in Provence. You might even argue that Paddy and Joan have gained more than they have lost. They are both now within a few years of eighty, in remarkably good health by normal standards, but the road which has obliterated the landscape and the loneliness of the place has, I suppose, brought some degree of convenience and the luxury of a track to their door. More important still, within the boundaries of their estate and their view, it is the same, unchanged, perfect.

You used to know where it was, because of the track into which the road degenerated as you bumped towards Tainaron and the cattle of the Sun, the gates of Hades, Poseidon's sanctuary and the Cape of Quails, you came to a pull-in where two cars could pass or one could park. That was where you left the road and explored the olive groves by footpath, crossing certain hazardous dry-stone walls which it may be that memory exaggerates, and descending towards the sea past a lonely and completely mysterious chapel on some rocks, until suddenly you came to the house. Unfortunately my taxi proceeded masterfully into a close of German houses, dumped me and withdrew. After some difficulty I came back to the road, where a kennel full of vigorous dogs were giving voice. They appeared to be a cross between a large hound and something more brutal, more effective no doubt, from further east. What it was they hunted I dread to think. The owner, whom I half recognised, had been Paddy's foreman of the works when he first built his house and brought water to the hill. He said if I just went the other way round his houses I would easily see what I was looking for.

Seeing is one thing and getting there is another. I descended by waterfalls of steps dying out into trickles as the houses died out into house plots, and the path, which was now close to where the taxi originally left me, wandered off into the wrong direction, becoming a kind of overgrown trench. From this scarcely negotiable hazard you could indeed see a roof, hovering or rather shimmering through an olive grove, but you could not be certain whose it was or how to get to it. Still, I followed the path in the trench and came across the ashes of a bonfire, which suggested human habitation, and then the mysterious chapel, tightly shut and hemmed in among rocks and the shadows of rocks. The path wandered more boldly on until you came to a delicious smell of wood-smoke and wisteria intermingling beyond a high stone wall. This wall was newly built on the apocalyptic evening when I brought Giorgis, and not know-ing what it was or where the entrance might lie I do believe we climbed it. Wisdom comes with years, and I followed it round to the front door, which gives directly on to the great highway of Mavromichalis, or a fragment of it, the stone mule track that served the Mani from about 1800, before there were any roads at all.

Until the war or a little later, the tiny coastal villages used to be served by cargo ships which traded from port to port. In the war when the British retreated, this was where the remnants of the army had got to when the bombers found them. The Greek war office had supplied a hopeful map in which the road from Kalamata south was marked as a substantial route, but there was no room to turn around on it, and headquarters were still near Kalamata while the front of the retreating force had got to Kardamyli before they realised that the 'road' died out there altogether. Some men took to the mountains, a few got away by sea. In western Europe we have forgotten the war, or forgiven it, but that generation of Greeks have not, and it must strike them as an irony that their rockiest, more implacable refuges are now colonised by summertime Ger-mans like migrant birds. As someone said to me on Zakynthos, 'When we complain of the English occupation here in the nine-teenth century, do you know how many there were? Seventy. Now it's more like 70,000.'

You enter into a new world, as if you had dived down into a grotto under the sea and come upon the court of Amphitrite. It is quiet, set among gardens that are now mature, an oldish stone house which from above has the lightness of a Chinese pavilion, but it curls around an inner courtyard decorated with pebble mosaic, into which stone stairs flow down from the stone arcade of the house. One wing that lies towards the sea is a big room with a huge Turkish bay window over the courtyard below and French windows into the gardens. Plants and vines climb and coil, a stray classical pillar marks a path into the olive trees and kittens, for whom this house is a sort of paradise, lurk and observe. It is really the nicest house I was ever in, and completely expressive of its owners. In early days the chickens used to roost in the olive trees and one would hear Joan's plaintive individual voice coaxing them down at dusk. 'Chick chick chick, come along down. Come along down then. Oh *if* you won't come down I'll break your ★★★★ necks.' Now she has them in a shed under sterner discipline: there are foxes on the hillside.

One of the exciting things about the house is its paintings, a Ghika landscape painted on stone, some seventeenth-century Japanese hawks, some Craxtons, one by Takis Sinopoulos; the antiquities are a terracotta gravestone that appears to say Hail Nemesis, but probably only said Hail Nemesius, and a small marble mother goddess whom I once remember cleaning. The books are equally expressive and personal: I found one that afternoon which was a Life of Aubrey Herbert, in which Raymond Asquith speaks about a combination of 'the passion of Shakespeare, the precision of Pope'. I really know of no house anywhere I so like being in, and I have scarcely any older close friends left alive. The other day Philip Sherrard died, with whom I was staying in Euboea as a student on my first outing. He had let the Leigh Fermors a cottage there for the summer, and Maurice Bowra was staying as their guest. I remember that he appeared booming and sparkling, only at lunchtime, having spent the whole morning happily rereading Euripides;

we all met in the evening at the tiny tavern, which in those days had only one table.

I had known Philip for longer, heard him lecturing about modern Greek poetry in the Fifties when I was an undergraduate, and then got advice about Greece from him through Nancy and Betty Sandars, when like some improbable butterfly he came to tea at Little Tew. He was not physically like a butterfly, though he had a certain pale and flitting appearance. He had known Nancy from the British School of Archaeology, and his Oxford lectures were probably the result of one of Maurice's many attempts to fit him into an Oxford career. But he could never face it, he was a poet and in his way a loner, and a not untypical intellectual of the 1940s, who flitted mothlike and improbable through charcoal soot-streaked Oxford. His mother had been one of a family who were close to Rupert Brooke and famous for going barefooted in about 1910; Laurence Olivier was his first cousin. As a boy I believe he ran away from home and lived as a tramp for a time, but when I knew him he was the sweetest, shyest man. He had not only married a Greek but a Mavromichalis, and he took a very firm Greek line in theology. He was a redoubtable, somewhat Dostoevskian theologian, which used to terrify me and may have annoyed Maurice, but Philip was impossible not to forgive. When I last went to his stronghold in Euboea, his huge garden turret or gun emplacement like a castle over the Rhine was still in use, which Paddy built him in 1963, because he had expressed a wish for a stone seat to admire the view. The urge for architecture of that wonderful construction flowered in the end in the house at Kardamyli.

It was Philip who introduced me to Greece and to the others, whom he produced somehow like a conjuror. It was at Limni in Euboea, where he had colonised a slaggy hillside above the sea – an old bauxite or magnesium mine – that he showed me the remarkably pure lines of the mountains at sunset and pointed out their relationship with Greek sculpture. He was also a remarkably sensitive and admirably devastating critic of poetry and of the life that underlies it, of the soul for want of a better word. He had come to Greece by chance, towards the end of the war, and met Paddy by wandering into the library of the British School of Archaeology which had not yet reopened, and finding another officer there who recruited him to lecture on a voluntary crash course for British troops on ancient Greek archaeology and civilisation, set up by some general (can it have been Scoby?) to give the soldiers something to do; Paddy had already been recruited. Later in life Philip wanted to become a monk, but marriage of course does not make such a wish any easier to fulfil. As it was he remained in the fullest sense a humanist, a description he would strongly have resented: except that what else is there to be?

There is a grace and a strength in Philip's poetry that tell me it will live. George Seferis whom he translated has been an influence, and was so at a time when in English the alternative would have been T. S. Eliot, who dried up many poets at the roots. George Seferis before he died wondered to me once what had happened to Philip's poetry. 'Tell me, is he still a poet?' George did not live long enough, but twenty years later Philip published his brilliant last book, less than twelve months before he too was gone. It was Philip who first introduced me to George Seferis, with a letter which was enough: it is hard to express or to imagine now to what an extent that very great poet was the sun in the sky to all of us who loved Greece from the late Thirties to the early Seventies. He was well translated into French first by Robert Levesque and later into English by Durrell and Valaoritis, so that from 1945 or so a reader without Greek could make out the outlines of his magnitude. In him the light dances more generously, the frost of modernism, almost more necessary in Greek than in English, was more kindly and more fertile. There have been few critics to attend on the double sunrise of Seferis and of Boris Pasternak, but of those who knew and admired both their work, the two who come to my mind are Maurice Bowra and Philip Sherrard. What they had in common was their passion for the greatest modern poetry.

George Seferis had known Paddy and Joan from the time they became inseparable, long before they married; he knew them in Cairo in the war, and perhaps earlier still. He wrote to Joan in English on Christmas Eve 1954 from Beirut about England as he first knew it, in Balham. 'Sometimes we get up talking to a faraway friend. Today I got up talking to you. The conclusion of this nice association is that you are perhaps my best friend in England. . . . mist and Christmas pudding, ennui in a suburban common . . . I think I ceased to be poetic since I started publishing poems. My two great impressions there were the fog (I had never seen a real fog) and the beggars . . . I remember the song they were playing, "Say it with a ukulili". Sometimes I think I am so shocked by England because I am so different, because I get there some sort of repose from being the same. I am glad you like "The Mules". If God extends his benevolence upon me, I shall try to write now a poem about the Cats of S. Nicolas, and when I have dealt with that fauna I shall return to men. Be happy Joan. Love, George.' The three mules were published in a Cypriot periodical in 1955, so Joan must have had an advance copy, but the cats were begun in 1952, abandoned in 1956 and begun again in October 1968 and finished in the following February. The letter to Joan was among nine edited by A. Dimitrakopoulos for Akti, Levkosia, 1994. (Most of them of course are in Greek.)

There is one more old connection I must discuss, though I had not known of it. On the mountain above Paddy and Joan at a small monastery in the middle of nowhere rest the ashes of Bruce Chatwin. When he was dying of Aids and all his deepest fantasies came back to haunt his conversation, he told me of a plan he had to hire a *kaiki* and take the monks with him from a monastery I think he said on Athos, and conduct them all to Patmos to arrive there for Easter. His eyes were like beacons and he clutched at a cross or a medal the monks had given him. When he died his wife Elizabeth took his ashes back to the Kardamyli monastery as he had asked, so that they lie in holy ground. There were other slightly crazy stories as well, one about a snow leopard made of a single precious stone, discovered in the depths of Asia, which was being brought for him, and another about being incredibly wealthy at the moment because he had just run down Bond Street trading art objects from shop to shop until he had made above a hundred thousand pounds in an hour by the skill of his eye. Bruce was a man deeply ploughed by his obsessions and one for whom truth and fiction mysteriously intermingled. I remember when he was doing the fieldwork that led to the Black Hill novel and film, that he came to see us at Stonesfield full of his discovery of the two twins, and told us the whole story with eyes glittering. It was a true story at that time, not a fiction, but it was already deeply touched by his imagination. Paddy and I agreed that of all his books, that was the one we liked best, and we both agreed that although *Song Lines* was fine as a story, the lore about aboriginals was mostly fantasy.

Bruce had lived a year in a cottage at Kardamyli when he was writing *Song Lines*, and then his last winter on earth. His father had come down for a time to be with him, and so had Dr Juel-Jensen, who so brilliantly cured his illness when he was dying of a disease only known in a remote part of China which Juel-Jensen diagnosed. In fact Bruce already had Aids, which he got in central Africa, but he lived another two years or so. One of his half-crazy obsessions at that time was to go back to Africa and inoculate everybody against Aids. These fantasies were never harmful, often slightly messianic only at the end. On a more normal level they did of course make him an unreliable teller of tales: I got a severe telling off from his widow Elizabeth for some appalling lies I told in his obituary, all of which came straight from Bruce's own stories that he told me. I see from bits of his diaries which were edited, not without malice, that he told someone he was writing a book about our Afghan adventures, and decided not to do so only when mine appeared as *The Light Garden of the Angel King*. That is not true either: he was then in the process of transforming himself from an anthropologist into a writer, and so far as any advice was called for, it was I who advised him to make the change. We both influenced each other at that time I think. The life of writers is an attempt to alter oneself, if it is anything: it is a journey that leads to metamorphosis. The clue to Bruce's ideal of writing I am certain is the prose of Mandelstam. He had written a long anthropological book about nomads with a huge tangle of footnotes, but later he foolishly took the advice of a girl to throw it away and start again. Of course that did not rid him of the obsession, and he wrote it as fiction at last in *Song Lines*, printing his old notebooks as an appendix. He met that girl through me, and Paddy and Joan through the girl, but I think at that time it was Joan who liked him best and spotted his remarkable quality. I am glad he found peace at Kardamyli, if he found it anywhere, and not surprised.

When I woke in the afternoon from the sleep that always compels me at Kardamyli I could smell mowing wafted down the hill from where the hotel is. From near the house I could see the new road with its coaches and lorries buzzing to heaven knows where, and the large unfinished construction like a smashed aeroplane on the hilltop towards Exochori where Bruce's ashes rest, which is to be a German hotel should it ever be finished. It is the only novel or ugly object in sight, and it does not matter much. It is like a pre-1914 flying machine or a bizarre smashed beetle on its cliff. My eyes were sinking into sleep like pebbles into the sea, and they did so all evening. The sea was a Connaught green, and a dense, sweet twittering of birds signalled better weather as the sun at last sank; it slipped down as easily as it sank thirty years ago, in a pink colour like pink gin, and the new moon swam on her back. When I first came to Kardamyli I came with a hurt knee and had to take to bed in the tiny village hotel; I had given myself housemaid's knee by clambering about a wet, preposterous akropolis in the rain in pursuit of science. Paddy and Joan lived in a tent, the house was in the last stages of building. It seemed the fulfilment of a dream, in which I had shared since I read *Mani* on its first appearance, and was taken over by it, in January 1959, as I never have been by an account of a place since. Now that fulfilment seemed to me superabundant. Not since the eighteenth century has any English writer so created a reality from an idea, a house and a garden and surroundings that add to nature with such modesty and such conclusive harmony. The only true analogy is Pope's Twickenham, not poor Shenstone's estate, which is now a golf course.

My diary descends to the details of meals. Lunch had been kolokythia tiganita with taramas and aubergine (home-made) and then gigantes (large beans) à la Philemon and Baucis, perfect. Dinner was the most delicious pork chop with onions and Byzantine-coloured mashed potatoes with garlic, like the green-yellow face of a martyr off to heaven. Conversation was about Bruce. The next morning I got up very late after not a bad night and a delicious bath. Then toast and coffee and a seat in the sun where one of the kittens made friends. Paddy is hard at work in the mornings, and I see that I noted, 'This is a place of healing, and where one could write, but I can't between English and Greek.' Paddy told me again the story of Weckherlin, which I had quite forgotten. His manuscripts have just been saved by Lord Downshire's agreeing to sell them directly to the British Library. Weckherlin was Latin Secretary to Charles I before Cromwell took over the state and Milton the job, but he also succeeded Milton when that poet went blind. He wrote a thrilling, baroque sonnet on the death by assassination of the Herzog von Buckingham which Paddy translated thirty years ago and gave me a copy, which I have somewhere, but where? Weckherlin was born in 1584 and married a Miss Elizabeth Raworth, which is how his papers were preserved in the Downshire family. He published *Odes and Songs* (1619) and *Spiritual and Secular Poems* (1641) in German, and died as Milton's assistant or substitute in 1653. He was a good and most interesting poet.

My diary flits from this unexpected bit of scholarship, most of it gleaned from the *Oxford Companion to German Literature* (1976), to remarks about the landscape. 'Mani has the hugest, queerest bugs: e.g. giant black in wisteria, faint bee-hums. This house and landscape have an amazing exuberance and yet frugality, like Cyril's habit of peaches for lunch, when in season. Paddy wondered if his wisteria was almost too much, but this was said with a giggle, he did not really think so.' I seem to have been sitting indoors, reading about Herbert, to whom Raymond Asquith remarked, 'You have a rapid and contorted mind, like the poet Pindar.' I noted also a nineteenth-century Albanian or Greek servant called Kiazim, who despised evening dress because it included no provision for a revolver. Someone remarked (it could have been me) that the little hanging woods on small hills in English landscaping are not put there for their picturesqueness, but in order to get high shots at pheasants. Paddy suddenly said:

> 'Great Chatham with his sabre drawn
> Was waiting for Sir Richard Strahan,
> Sir Richard, longing to be at 'em,
> Was waiting for the Earl of Chatham.'

We had lunch at a restaurant in the village run by Lella, who for years was Joan's servant and housekeeper. It was a meeting of old friends that generated pure delight; she was wreathed in children and grandchildren. One of the boys wore a shirt advertising a dog club. I asked if he knew about sheepdog trials. He not only did, but he had been to Aberdeenshire to see dog and hawk trials as well. We ate very good fish, *barbouni* which is 'mullet' but is never the same in two seas or two bays, and something for which the English is 'rowlock'. Paddy needed a hat and Lella brought us three straw ones, all three feet across. Later there was a conversation between Paddy and Joan that has certainly been going on since 1963, exquisitely courteous, almost Chinese, about who would drive the car. I do not believe they remember any longer who does or does not want to drive it, but they defer to each other in a waltz of words. 'Do you know' (as if they only just became acquainted) 'I never like to drive it after lunch?' The sun was light silver in the olive trees and gleaming on the vast cypresses from the west as it had done earlier from the east. Where it struck fullest on bushes and walls it was almost white. Those cypresses around the house have grown to a gigantic size.

Diary: 'In the afternoon I slept again, motionless apparently because my spectacles were in my trousers pocket and came to no harm at all. Later I wandered down to look at the light on the sea, with a wild ginger kitten that flirted gently in and out of the rosemary hedges and topiary. There were kittens everywhere it turned out, all with lemurian tails. One climbed up a spiring cypress to the top, to whizz down the empty middle as if it were a slide. Then he settled on my knee with much rubbing. Vines were just in leaf, blackbirds calling all over the grove, and late last night I heard one like a nightingale, but the Mani is not wet enough for those. The vast squares and barricades of seats and herbs on the upper terrace were new to me, so that the pleasure of wonder gave me almost as much as the pleasure of familiarity can give in a garden: in fact I had a mixture of the two, as one has exploring a garden in a dream. As I sat down I spotted a kitten chewing an olive leaf about four feet above my head against the clear blue sky. The sun slipped down very coolly, as swiftly as time itself. Those great quiet terraces at dusk that seem all but buried in clipped rosemary, and the Japanese stone-garden round the fountain, are like one of Basho's places of pilgrimage. Only now does it strike me that it was through Bruce I first discovered Basho in 1969, who has remained to me an ideal poet, as Mandelstam was the ideal and only travel writer for Bruce.'

The diary goes on; it is unsatisfactory but I can do no better now: 'The green waxed paper leaves of the young fig tree fresh from winter and the distant column of white smoke from olive pruning, let alone the evening fires of olive spitting and smouldering, all say Enough. The sun on your shoulder or your back and shadows draping your eyes. It is almost such an extremely good (Horatian?) poem it seems a pity to write it down: foolishly and ineffectively competitive. Reading Bertolucci's version of

Adlestrop, it occurs to me that with us (in Gloucestershire) the West begins, we live under (want to ride to) the ridge where the west commences. This place seems as far away as India or as Prospero's island, from *tutti gli uccelli delle terre di Oxford e di Gloster*. The continual repetitions and slapping, slopping, slapslop sea on pebbles, and the sighs under cliffs unite us . . . Walked to Kardamyli to feel the flowers through my footsoles. Purple and white cistus, yellow "May" and furze. White small rough delicate kind of horse-parsley. It was hot and I was not disappointed to be overtaken by Joan in the car, as I descended on Kardamyli past the house with a new swimming bath and other wonders. The last unbought and unexploited ground is the island.'

Paddy had a last uncollected remark or two of Maurice Bowra's, '*Pelvis et umbra sumus*', and 'Look, a dear little crab' (said I cannot reveal to whom). He also had a query about the origins of a story about monastic chant. Thurstan, a Norman-trained monk who was Abbot of Glastonbury, stamped out the deviant English chants by stationing archers in the clerestory to shoot (given the Abbot's nod) any elaborator or descanting monk in choir. It is a curious and alarming story, which if it were not true I cannot imagine who would have invented it. I do recollect a martyr story of some holy monk shot in the throat by a Viking while singing a long and elaborate Easter Alleluia, but that is different. The time came when I must leave, and so I did, but sadly: one hates leaving friends and nowadays any time may be the last time. Alas, I could not have stayed as I had been told I was off to Zakynthos, and Paddy was about to set off for Crete with another widow with the ashes of her husband, Paddy's wartime brother-in-arms and friend, Xan Fielding. I took an early afternoon train from Kalamata. It was a hot, windy journey, slowly past the long-remembered landmarks, Thouria, Meligala and Dorion, then by an upper plain as the mountains close in, and by viaducts to Kalo Nero. Had I but known it, I could have got off there while the train shunted and puffed and hooted down to Kyparissia and back again. Then came the slow, pleasing journey through the woods between Kaiapha and the beach, and the long last pull across the Alpheios bridge, which has two stations, one on each side of the river, both called Alpheios, and by the last, tiniest, craziest, most lost of cottages to Pyrgos, where Giorgis was waiting. Somewhere near Dorion I had seen an eagle.

Philip Sherrard once wrote in an Oxford lecture about Yeats that 'The symbols and images of a great art can only really function on condition that the artist himself has experienced something of the realities of which they are the expression'. I have always doubted the cogency of this view, and it would be fair to say that Philip was to some degree a mystic *manqué*, and that this was the tragedy of his life, or, for all I know, of all life. A hundred years earlier he could easily have become a sage in India, a kind of saint, as some of the more sensitive British officers did, though none of them that I know became a poet. I think Philip's hesitations about his own poetry were a re-enactment of those he felt about his mysticism. But in those realms there is no 'success', and failure is a relative word that also scarcely applies. 'The nineteenth-century magus taught that all great art emerges from and controls supernatural mysteries.' One can see how Philip felt this was not his own calling. He did not seek to discover either 'powers over nature' or the 'laws of the imagination'. The lecture in which he speaks of these matters was a good one, and he follows Yeats on to more acceptable ground. The lecture was in 1975: since then he has written the best long essay ever published about Edward Lear and last summer he gave a most brilliant and vigorous lecture, the best I ever heard him give. We have all of us gone different ways. Paddy is and was the most cheerful of men, as well as one of the deepest; he is a writer who knows enough about mysticism (which he treats sympathetically) to set it at a distance among the wide variety of human experiences that fascinate him. Bruce probably never knew Philip, but he was a writer consumed in and by the mere act of writing: his writing was a passion, he was one intense flame, though the more soberly he wrote, the better. I feel sometimes that my poetry has usually been mothlike, a hover, and is therefore weak, but the last thing we can any of us choose or alter is our principles as writers I suppose.

Why did it mean so much to spend a few days there? It was a place I wrote poetry when I was younger, and sitting on the same stone seat over the courtyard where the mother of the gods gleams mildly in her niche, I began some twenty-five years ago to translate the Psalms of David. I found the first far the hardest, because it meant picking on a style. This visit was more than just calling on old friends. It was the refreshment of a dream deeply buried, which had never been refreshed and needed it: and as one loses one's memory with old age such a process becomes easier. Affection increases and experience distils, but most of the rest of life becomes loss. As I have said, my eyesight is fading and when there was a brilliant sky full of stars I did not dare go outside with the others to enjoy it, for fear I could no longer see it. The next night I did dare, on my own, and I did see that virtually everlasting firework display. When Paddy and Joan went off up a mountain one afternoon to see the spring flowers I did not go for fear of delaying them, but I should have gone because the top of the mountain is a flat meadow of fantastic wild flowers. With Giorgis I felt I could go to such places on more equal terms and we did go to see the spring flowering on a mountain-top quite soon afterwards. It was of a marvellous beauty, flowers of individual delicacy but wild profusion had taken over the surface of the earth.

Observing Paddy at work has always been to me an astounding spectacle. He works in a small garden house of his own, dominated as I recall by a gigantic Turkish stepped fireplace, but the striking thing about this process is the amount and variety of material he consumes and distils down to make a few sentences, or just to see how to come at a chapter. He has been a writer in search of material, well served on the whole by the distraction of that side of his nature which is a man of action, but only because that furnishes a necessary ingredient to the astonishing variety of knowledge, reading and scholarship which he inhales. The whole of his jingling set of alembics and phials and alchemical instruments are animated also by such a sense of humour, such a love of life, that while Joan is like a Taoist sage full of years laughing at the shadow of a tree on a mountain-top, Paddy is more like an old Turkish poet beaming at the most delicate of tulips. When I first knew them, they seemed the incarnation and reincarnation of the spirit of an earlier world, a generation I had never known, but the difference now is that their atmosphere has settled round them; they are better than members of Bloomsbury, and wiser and kinder than the generation of Raymond Asquith and his friends: they are intransigently liberal, admirably fastidious. The only bad effect of age for them is occasional forgetfulness. The other day, a stranger arrived at the top of the steps as they sat eating eggs for lunch in the courtyard. Paddy asked if he could help him? It was the Australian Ambassador, whom they had invited to lunch that day and completely forgotten and failed to recognise, after an invitation agreed in Athens and two or three phone calls to confirm it.

The streak of sadness that has run through this account has arisen from the necessity to recall Bruce Chatwin, which I had not known would come about at Kardamyli, and from the brutally sudden death of Philip Sherrard, who like Paddy and Joan had attained in the end the lightness and the twinkling humour of the sages. Maybe all sages are similar, or more similar than other people, like those ring-tailed lemurian kittens to which years make no difference, but which one always seems to meet in that shadowy western garden. If anything could, they would reconcile me to reincarnation.

3 : Transfigurations

THE lady from the Lyra had given Mitsa a present of amazing appearance. It was an opaque plastic pot with a handle to it like a bucket, containing two large cactus plants side by side, that dull green colour that they have and a terrifying repertory of needles, one shaped like an obelisk and the other more like a pineapple, each of them in vivid red flower. Mitsa liked them, she was defiantly proud of them, though when I laughed she joined in, and when I tried to draw them, they were removed from the centre of the room to a sideboard. It was hot, earthquaky weather, the taxi drivers at the station were surly brutes, and we talked over the past again. The most recent earthquake was three shakes within a quarter of an hour, the last of them fatal to fifteen hundred houses. Giorgis's mother was carried down into the street by Mitsa's brother who still lived opposite, as Giorgis and Mitsa had done until they married. We talked about the perception of the world, and how it alters. He remembered a story of George Seferis walking in some mountains above the sea before the war, and being discovered by Maro sitting on a rock and howling, really howling, with grief. When she asked what was the matter, all he could say was: 'How can one stand' or 'I am unable to stand such beauty.'

That night we drank a remarkable new claret from the Mercouri estate. The owners are remote cousins of old Spiros of the far left, and his daughter the film actress, but their branch went away to

Australia in the nineteenth century, came back rich and planted vineyards behind the hill that separates Katakolo from Hagio Andrea.
The house, which for Greece ranks as an old one, is on the bottle
label. The wine is the kind that used to be such a discovery years ago,
when it was marketed locally from the barrel, or when one got it
through some special connection of one's aunt's cook's cousin, but
now here it is in bottles as smart as any in Europe. Soon we shall be
seeing it in our supermarkets. I slept extremely well after it and
woke to the light blazing on the other buildings of the court. They
reminded me of Kardamyli for some reason and the dense stars I was
too lazy or really too cowardly to go and see, which now I regretted.

It is seldom remarked that Shakespeare, who is often quoted for
his belief in the heavenly music of the spheres, which is supposed to
mean the natural noise made by the onion-skins of this universe as
they revolve one inside the other and carry the stars with them,
does not believe anything so queer. Look on the floor of heaven:
''Tis thickly sewn with patines of bright gold, There's not the
smallest orb that thou beholdest But in his motion like an angel
sings, Still choiring to the young-eyed cherubims.' I have begun to
wonder whether this does not reflect the teaching of the Digges
family, who were his friends, and who left moving notes about the
stars. 'This orbe of stares fixed infinitely with perpetuall shininge
glorious lightes innumerable.' Father and son, two members of that
family invented the astronomic telescope fifty years before Galileo,
in 1570, but it appears to have been kept as a state secret. Thomas
Russell, who was a friend five years younger than Shakespeare,
married the widow of the astronomer Thomas Digges, and young
Leonard Digges lived long enough to write affectionate poems
about the poet. It looks as if Thomas Russell paid for the wall
monument to Shakespeare in Stratford church, and young Leonard
Digges wrote the English verses on it.

Stars are the same, but birds are fewer in Greece even than they
were twenty years ago, when I met a clucking, shivering quail that
had flown in on its own to the hill above Katakolo. They are still

shot, and many of them poisoned, though I am happy to report that the men with guns do also shoot a fair proportion of one another. The white night-crow in the dark, and all the birds that arrive in darkness flee in terror from Greek village electricity, and it is to be hoped that they are still somewhere far off in their wilderness, further and further into the dark. They are like Robert Head and Darling I suppose, whom Giorgis tracked down in a Virginian forest among overgrown footpaths and the ruins of villages, to the cawing of rooks in the distance and the hooting of their abandoned car, in a hut where they lived with the works of Plato and Aristotle and a small garden for cannabis and potatoes. They were old disciples of his from the other end of the world, and Giorgis is a romantic man. Later they paid him a return visit, and tried to live by selling books in the Greek villages, but that was not a success, and now they are lost again in their unrestrained forest liberty, as enviable as the birds maybe, but with as many hardships. They 'flee our approach, our feverish contact fly'.

We went into Pyrgos that day to the post. The estate does have a post-box, but no one I met knew whether post was ever collected from it, and it had a battered, dishevelled appearance. In the town there were huge shoulder-high bushes of dark-red geraniums that smelt overpoweringly as you brushed past. We stopped at a cloth shop which used to sell toys, which was still exactly like what shops of that kind were in Ruislip in 1938; it even had the same smell. I do not know what the toys used to be like, but Giorgis used to play there for hours as a little boy, because his father's *zacharoplasteion* was next door. All I know about that is that it had a wonderful array of bottles of coloured liqueurs of many improbable colours, set out on towering shelves behind the counter and never disturbed, most of them emptied by the poet in youth and filled up with water. Off we went by bus from there to Katakolo, passing many new houses of unbearable architecture: the Greeks do love ugliness if they can afford it, they have a naive passion for it, like the French. Hagios Iannis, which was hardly more than a name and some thistles, has a square now, and near the sea sprawls the low, grey, sinister bulk of what appears to be a building designed to win a prize from concrete makers, a refrigerator factory with no windows. It is like a picture ripped from some modernist architectural review of 1960. The locals marvel at the horror of it whenever they pass. We saw a big herd of a hundred sheep though, and nearer the sea-shore the houses are jollier and more relaxed. There is a small colony of sand martins' nests in a little cliff which Seferis used to call the Cappadocia of swallows, because it was like the mountain caves of the monks.

Everywhere was a reassuring noise of chickens, but at the bakery appeared an English tourist family who did not look reassuring at all. They were dressed for a picnic, and worried by everything, with two gloomy boys trailing after them, one with a ball which he bounced and the other just loping. They all had the kind of floppy hat which it is impossible to wear with an air, and they were too hot, and perfectly middle class, and did not seem happy so far from their island. Normally I am very pleased when I see any English abroad, but these ones with their fair hair and sufferings gave me the shivers. Giorgis bought a local paper that reported him in Kalamata with brief but sonorous praises and we bought three pounds of fish: that is, we tried to buy one pound but were per-suaded to buy two with a third thrown in, mostly the delicious little soles of the bay and one large *loutsa*. We sat long over our ouzo, conjecturing what mountains must lie beyond the mist to the south, then home we went to lunch with our light-blue plastic fishbag, to eat fish and huge clementines with their leaves on, and cheese and bread, both very fresh, and to drink wine from the cellars of heaven, from the barrel. It was a wonderful morning, all in all. The sea was perfectly blue and elusive, but far more intense than the sky. Mitsa had found a four-leafed clover in one of her flowerpots.

I remember that we discussed the appalling noise of a dozen or more cats in the yard which sometimes tried to invade the house. There is a Greek proverb about the screaming of the she-cat when the tom-cat makes love. It is used of yelling about one's rights when one is not in the right. That evening we went out to a tavern at Vola, which lies towards Olympia. We went with Christos I think, but we could have gone with anyone because although again there was no bouzouki the human noises were more shattering still. The food was still more amazing: veal like a wooden table, an omelette of unbelievable crudity in which a huge lump of very salty ham nestled, delicious small olives as sweet as currants 'from the hill', with a lot of very good pinkish wine from the barrel. We got to bed at twenty to one, I woke at dawn to cockcrows, which were magnificent and varied, then slept again at once until half-past nine. On that morning Giorgis told me limericks he had made up in Greek, as good as Lear's. The day was cloudy but our expedition had the force of a revelation.

We went by taxi to see a poet who is an ex-Communist working as a dentist in a nondescript town to the south called Sacharo, on the main road. I have read his poems since, but at the time I had never heard of him: the first impression was of a pleasant man in a pleasant town with excellent taste and a quirky collector of objects as of friends; Giorgis had become a good friend of his. We went to a village they both knew well and I had visited with a vaguely topographic interest that had faded away by now even from memory. It is one of four or five towns including Phrixa, all buried in the hills south of the Alpheios, more or less opposite Olympia. I remembered Phrixa the best because of finding a bit of very old pottery in a ploughed field there, on a freezing cold, rainy day when I ended up riding behind a tractor, and I remembered Mazi quite well because I took my wife there, only to find there had been an earthquake and the whole village was rebuilt somewhere else. This one was Lepreon which used to be called Strovitsi. It had once had a harbour that was the lost site called Lower Samiko, where they find ancient pottery in the sand on the beaches: earthquake long ago obliterated all visible trace of it.

Strovitsi is a mountainside village with a tremendous water-source that comes pounding out of the cliff above it and spills over under plane trees and washes the roots of houses until it disappears downhill past a church with that skeletal look of poverty and lack of flesh that mark it as medieval: earlier than that was built the name Lepreon was first forgotten. There are not many visible traces of antiquity in Strovitsi, only the suspicion aroused by the abundant and pure water. Two white ducks, so quiet that I took them at first for children's toys, had a nest in the long grass. The village patisserie or *zacharoplasteion* of Mr Marangos was as we verified for ourselves the best for fifty miles or more in any direction, though his shop was modest enough. One of the unusual features of the ancient Lepreon is its size: there were bits and pieces of it high in the hills and woods, and far down the road inland. There was the place called Palaiopyrgos, the old fort, and there was Exovigli, the outer watch-tower, and there were others, some scattered among the houses and churches of the mountain village some five miles away up the road through the pine woods. Somewhere up there, perhaps when the forest was planted, some Mycenean graves had come to light. The reasons for this generous scatter are two: the abundance of water, and the hiddenness of the place. It is not a defensible fortress town like the mountain akropolis of Samiko, but a place of refuge: in a way it is typical of Triphylia.

When Pausanias visited Lepreon in the second century AD there was not much to see there; he records only the brick, that is, mud-brick walls of a temple to Demeter. Since the sanctuaries of Demeter were often at a distance from a fortified town, as the one in the second book of the *Aeneid* is for example, and many in the Peloponnese, this one has disappeared untraceably, and the mud-brick has gone back to mud. Pausanias must have come to Lepreon along the valley bottom by much the same route as we did, and climbed as far as the springs above the church. He had no idea what riches, that is, what ruins, he was missing. Lepreon had a sad story that tells us a lot about it. It may have been Homeric Arini, but let us forget about that. It lies about ten miles from Samiko and five from the sea up a lost and wooded road like a farm track. Pausanias knew that it once contained a temple of Lykaian Zeus and the grave of Lykourgos and the monument of Kaukon, so it must once have belonged to the loose confederacy of places we call Arcadian, but the first we hear of the Lepreans in history however mythical is that half of them took the Spartan side and half the Messenian side in a prehistoric war. We then hear that they wiped out a place called Triphylian Pylos, which is not easy to identify, and brought the Pylians home with them as Lepreans. The Arcadians were furious and attacked them, so they got help from Eleia, at a cost of 'half their territory', which we must assume was huge and ill-defined. They had to pay a tax of one talent a year after that to Olympian Zeus.

They called themselves Eleians of Lepreon and under that name they fought in the Persian wars of the fifth century. But on the excuse of that war they stopped paying their tax to Elis, and appealed to the Spartans to help them. Aristophanes refers to Eleian Lepreon in *The Birds*, but that buttered no parsnips and when the Spartans had fought Elis at the end of the fifth century, Lepreon turned back to the Arcadians for help in the fourth century and to the Achaian confederacy in the third. It is evident throughout this unhappy writhing that they could scarcely have any hope of independence, and wherever they turned they suffered. The glamour of Olympia which was controlled by Elis overwhelmed them, the high Arcadian mountains overshadowed them, the sinister presence of the Spartans or their long reach did little to protect them. The pitiful history of Lepreon might be reason enough for showing some interest in the people, but they lived on the remotest margins of Greek history, and in a way of the Greek world, so they get neglected. All this interests me, but what draws my more passionate attention is the story in Pausanias about Lykaian Zeus.

Lykaion is a mountain you can see from the temple of Apollo near Phigaleia, and *lykos* means a wolf. The cult of Zeus there involved the murder of a child whose dead body was actually eaten;

this happened once every eight years and the man who killed the child was called Lykos, the Wolf; he must leave his clothing, swim across the lake and live in the wild for the next eight years avoiding all human contact, then he must swim back across the lake, put on his clothing and resume normal life. There is no doubt that this eerie and disgusting ritual was really carried out from prehistoric to Roman times. All that was found the last time anyone explored the mountain was a pile of ancient iron knives and deposits of iron knives were apparently connected with the cult of Zeus on the mountains of Attica also. I do not think any of these idiosyncratic hoards has ever been published. There is no reason to suppose the ceremonious murder ever occurred far from Lykosura in central Arcadia and it is astonishing that it lasted so long even there. One would not credit it at all about the Greeks if there were any way of wriggling out of it, but so far as I could ever see there is not. There is another myth about Lykaian Zeus, which says Lykaon was a man in the golden age, who lived on familiar terms with Zeus and all the gods, and entertained them in his house as Abraham entertained the angels. He had fifty sons, of whose names diligent scholars of the subject have recorded seventy-three. Lykaon is said to have killed and offered one of his sons to Zeus, who was so angry that he killed all forty-nine of them, or all seventy-two, and punished mankind with Deukalion's flood, in which Deukalion was a hero or just man, like Noah. The story is to be found in Ovid and else-where, in a variety of versions, though no classical Greek seems to be much interested in it. But the story of Lykaon as an earthly friend of Zeus had been in my mind since I came across it in Pausanias.

From near the water-spring a road climbs steeply into the trees towards Hagioi Taxiarchoi, the Archangels who are the colonels of the armies of heaven; in this case it indicates not just a church but a village where the uppermost water breaks out from the mountain-side, just under the crest. Before you get so far, about three or four miles from the village is a rickety signpost saying (in Greek) ancient site. It is a steep place, and both Giorgis and I had some trouble getting up it; he had seen it before, but I am sure I never had. After a rather scrambly climb up goat tracks among some big piles of stones overgrown with brambles and bushes, you come to a place of larger stones, a wall which looks like a circuit wall of something like 400 BC, though such guesswork is idle, and then a steading, with a roof, a kind of two-roomed longhouse, still half roofed, with a block of cement above the main door inscribed by its owner to say three generations of his family lived here, which takes it back to the early nineteenth century, and in terms of archaeology to the age of innocence. This building is of a breathtaking beauty. About half-way or less up the walls you can see a change of workmanship where the uncemented stonework becomes modern, that is, nineteenth century. But the stones are huge, they would be terribly hard to handle, and they are really unique, like the stones of Mycenae, utterly out of proportion on this remote hilltop to any purpose they can have served. But alas, enormous size is not a safe way to date a stone.

The roof was thatched reed. The insides of the rooms have some relics of much lighter wooden modern divisions and there are small windows. The building is oriented if at all north-south, not east-west, which may have something to do with the first rays of the sun striking through a doorway as they did at Apollo's temple at Phigaleia. Towards the southern, downhill end, the two-roomed steading degenerates into a jumble, though the stones are still huge. Nearby is the circuit wall, and if you can pick your way among the chaos of wildly flowering weeds and undatable pieces of rock, you come out like a swimmer through the surf at a level plain with smaller wild flowers, where you will find the complete ruins of a fifth- or fourth-century temple. Once again I give a hostage to fortune by guessing about a date. This temple has been dissected like a fish or neatly excavated, but I do not know by whom or when.

This was a civilised building of the usual design, with fluted Doric stone columns, oriented precisely east and west. Nearby there are the stone ruins of a water-channel. The outer wall is very much overgrown. You could hear the bells of sheep in the distance, somewhere near the village of Taxiarchoi. Everything smelt of rosemary and wild flowers, which are smaller and more abundant at this height as they are on the Sussex downs. (A little further north I remember whole mountains smelling of lavender after a thunderstorm.) Here there were red anemone, purple, blue and pink pimpernel, broom, and many varieties I could not name, swarming all over the ruins. It was quiet and the air was still and quiet. You could see the new German houses on the hill below H. Ilias near Phigaleia, and a mountain I thought must be Lykaion further behind it. I never saw a better view nor a prettier place, so of course I decided that it was in this steading, with its marvellously archaic construction, that Zeus was believed to have lived on good terms with Lykaon and his animals: I could come close to believing it myself. If there had ever been a temple of Zeus Lykaios may it not have been here in a double building with Zeus worshipped at one end and his favourite Lykaon at the other?

At this moment unfortunately, while Giorgis sat happily under a tree and the left-wing poet from Sacharo was still prowling the ruins like a cat, I suffered an attack of low blood sugar, which sent us racing, so far as one can race on wobbly ankles, back to the car and downhill to Lepreon where I consumed two sweet cakes and felt all right again. But we left Lepreon with our heads (or mine) full of unanswered questions. We drove from there to eat fish at a restaurant by the sea, as peaceful and as isolated on the sea-sand as you could find anywhere in the world. We talked about poetry I think. But as for Lepreon, if I may quote my diary, 'It has vanished like a dream among its quiet wild flowers and when we left the flocks were out of hearing. Of course it was a place where gods had lived with men; Lykaon-Zeus must have occupied that steading, with its doors to the west. Date of the walls at Hagioi Taxiarchoi, which is about a mile further and higher, with stone houses? Did they bring water down or carry it up? When did it first go to feed the mills? G.P. told me of filling in a form for George Seferis in hospital, how he could not bear to write "occupation, diplomat" as if he were a twister, and in his upset misspelt it in the end; looked it up when he got home. He was our Lykaon and our golden age.'

Ovid rejected the idea of Lykaon sacrificing a son: he said it was only a story about a Molossian, not a Greek, and the transformations at the end of the story must not be forgotten: of one story or myth into another, or of the nasty reality of the ritual into a myth. The golden age is there only to contrast with all that follows, as Paradise is a story-teller's device to introduce the true theme of Paradise Lost, 'Out of the black oak oozed amber honey', but not for long, and Ted Hughes in his admirable version of Ovid tells us what followed.

> . . . The lightning had gone clean through Lycaon.
> His hair was in spikes.
> Somehow he staggered
> Half-lifted by the whumping blast
> Out of the explosion.
> Then out across open ground
> Trying to scream. As he tried
> To force out screams
> He retched howls.
> His screams
> Were vomited howls.
> Trying to shout to his people
> He heard only his own howls.
> Froth lathered his lips.
> Then the blood-thirst, natural to him,
> Went insane.
> From that moment
> The Lord of Arcadia
> Runs after sheep. He rejoices
> As a wolf starved almost to death
> In a frenzy of slaughter.
> . . . But still his humanity clings to him

And suffers in him.
The same grizzly mane,
The same black-ringed, yellow,
Pinpoint-pupilled eyes, the same
Demented grimace. His every movement possessed
By the same unappeasable self . . .
(from *After Ovid*, ed. Hofmann and Lasdun, 1994)

Ovid's poem is called *Metamorphoses*, or the *Transfigurations*, and he is a specialist in how one figure is transformed into another, how your feet root to the ground and you go long and thin and only whine, you are a reed, how you leap into the sea with a shriek so raucous with grief that you hover for ever, just above the surf, arms flung out and feathered, as a sea-bird. Looking at the view when you have clambered with difficulty on to the walls of Lepreon you cannot help considering that it is the earth, the rock, Greece itself which is constantly transformed and transfig-ured in your eyes: by the light, by day and night, by the season, by changing your point of vantage, by submitting to the discipline of a new way of looking. I found that particularly true the next day, when our amiable friend the poet from Sacharo had to go back to work, and Giorgis and I set off for another journey deeper into Arcadia. I call it Arcadia, but its boundaries are like those of a jelly fish, like those of Mercia in the dark ages, constantly altering.

Lepreon after all is less than a long day's march from the Alpheios, which is the border of Eleia, and it is small wonder that this ancient and idyllic place was constantly being swallowed up and spat out by the stronger country to the north. Yet we are told that Samiko, the huge and puzzling akropolis on the next and nearest mountain to the south, was erected (by the Eleians, it is supposed) in the late third century, and then (small wonder) swiftly abandoned. Whatever was it for? And how did it come to be named after Samian Poseidon, who had a cape on Samos though we know nothing about his temple there? Did Delphi decide on the name, and had it anything to do with earthquakes?

Any dramatic case of earthquake at that date would probably have left some indication in the written sources. My own first, hazardous conjecture was that we should look at Samian history. Samos, like other Ionian islands, teetered in and out of the Persian empire, and in and out of Athenian influence and the various leagues and confederacies in which Athenian power was expressed. But in the Hellenistic period the island fell into the hands of Antigonos One-Eye, and then of the Ptolemies: it became the headquarters of their fleet for years. Is Samiko the folly of one of these Hellenistic kings? It was the fashion at that time to build people a new city, and diplomacy may well have adopted an Eleian mask, so that we hear of it as 'Eleian': who knows? All that is left is some ill-defined humps and bumps in the earth beside the large medicinal lake, and a most putrid smell where the water comes pouring out of the rock, far more toxic, for better or worse, than the smell of Bath water. They say it is where Herakles was cured of some festering wound. On the whole I was inclined to blame old One-Eye or his admiral for the fortification of the mountain-top at Samiko, because who else would do anything so silly? Now I think it might have been Kephalonian.

We set off with Kostas, who became a close friend of mine, as he already was to Giorgis. He is a tall man but you must picture him curled up to fit into a tiny car. He is also the kindest of men, and the swiftest in action because he has worked as a local journalist in a kind of silver age of local journalism too good to last. We were to leave early, which luckily suited my mood. I felt the opening of book three of the *Odyssey*, when 'Out of his lake the sun comes diving high Into the blazing mirror of the sky'. In the end we set out at nine and came home exhausted at six, having travelled what would have taken three or four days and nights on foot. By eight in the morning and by seven in the evening the soap opera that took place at our open kitchen door, to which I was becoming addicted, was at full blast, so that I could hardly tear myself away, but the mountains called. We travelled inland north of Lepreon by Slavochori, Krestena and the Amygdalies road, where we turned left along a track to the Convent of Sepatou, a former monastery now colonised by nuns, overlooking an idyllic valley and a giant waterfall so abundant and so loud it filled your mind for hours afterwards.

The Convent was full of charming old ladies like a Convent my sister was once in near Carnforth. The wires outside were crowded with young swallows or house martins twittering above the noise of the distant waterfall. The Superior, who I understood was a kinswoman of Giorgis, was away, for which I secretly blessed heaven, because the chapel had a holy ikon attributed to St Luke, which was certainly a late-nineteenth-century botch: the Saint must have lost his touch. The whole place was dug or quarried into the rock of huge cliffs, and its speciality was towers and flights of stairs. Even its approach is steep, but sweetly scented with flowers. The others were each given a loukoum as a greeting present, but I am not allowed to eat it, and as perhaps the reader can divine, I was not displeased to leave. All the same it was a fine site, though not as fine as Alipheira, towering on a mountain nearby. All these mountain sites that the ancient Arcadians went in for were refuge sites really, which Sepatou also is in its own way. It is not surprising that the Arcadians finally saw the futility of their small, furious and stony 'cities', and came together at the end of the classical period to build their Great City or Megalopolis in an inland plain, but the fact and the known date give sites like Alipheira a special interest for archaeologists. We did not drive up to Alipheira on this occasion, all the same, though there is now a better track than there used to be. It has been said of the arts that only with the falling of night does the bird of Athene spread her wings, but the same may be said of bulldozers, which were at work; only with the death of education and of religion does the ministry of tourism get to work making roads to the remotest convents and the most inaccessible antiquities.

We were on our way to Apollo the Helper, at his temple called Bassai (the glens) where as Epikourios Apollon he reigned for centuries in the middle of nothing and of nowhere. The place had the local name of the Columns, Stous Stylous, and was found by a wandering Frenchman in 1760. The god had an excellent water source, out of sight behind his hilltop, which still has its classical stones, and he was lucky to get his temple exactly when he did, about 417 BC, because it is by the architect Iktinos who had just worked on the Parthenon. The Helper was a warrior god, but this once beautiful and lonely temple was a thank-offering of the people of Phigaleia, which is not far off, for keeping them safe in this place of refuge, and above all safe from the plague. The frieze of this temple is in the British Museum, since it was bought at auction by the British Government from Cockerell and Haller von Hallerstein in 1812. C. B. Cockerell went on to design the Ashmolean Museum at Oxford and the huge cross on top of St Paul's Cathedral. In the course of the sale, his German partner made fine drawings of the frieze sculptures to tempt the governments of Europe, one of which in its turn was sold at auction in London not long ago. Luckily it was bought by George Seferis, and is now in the Gennadion Library at Athens. It is distressing to have to record further that these fine carved stones were kept in a closed room for more than twenty years after the war, for 'study' by a member of the British Museum staff, and within a fortnight of their being at last opened to the public were left unguarded; it is thought to have been an Australian who sawed off a head and went away with it in his raincoat pocket.

Of course this is not as bad as the time just before the war when the Museum decided that the Parthenon frieze needed cleaning after its long immersion in London grime, and used a detergent which could then not be removed without severe abrasive damage to the surface. The worst harm is said to have been done with heavy-duty scrubbing brushes. Roger Hinks was blamed, but he was new and junior in his post, and had not dared to countermand the orders of the elderly buffoon who was really responsible. These things do make one ashamed, and the refusal of successive governments to put them right makes one disgusted. The frieze from Bassai does admittedly make a most interesting contrast with the Parthenon frieze, since it does seem to belong to a different and southern type. It may probably depend more on drawings done on the stone, and less on the inspiration of individual workmen, but whether that has anything to do with the remoteness of the temple site no one knows. It has a flying delicacy of line that looks far later in date than the Parthenon's noble gravity. Bassai is only about the height of the top of Snowdon above sea level, being 3,707 feet or 1,130 metres, but it is more than equally snowy. I have seen it in the snow some years ago, when it did have a special and memorable beauty of its own, and I have very often raised my eyes from Olympia to where it is and seen the mountains snow-covered. The frieze was first discovered, I believe, when a fox dived for cover under some bushes, into a pile of stones.

How much of the architecture of temples in the fifth century was mathematics, how much rule of thumb, no one knows. The mason and the sculptor were paid the same wages. But the designer? I cannot help recollecting that in the early eighteenth century the church tower of Dursley in Gloucestershire had to be repaired, and the job was done in two or three years by Thomas Sumsion. The result was admired and he went on to do just the same for Sherston Magna in Wiltshire, a few miles away. Both towers are very beautiful and look like fifteenth-century work: and both are exactly modelled on the church tower of Colerne, Wiltshire, where Sumsion was born. What do we know about Iktinos that tells us he was an architect in any other sense? And the stone? It is not true that it was carried from an enormous distance up to Bassai: that is romance. Southern Greece is made of very hard stone, much of it perfectly suitable for temple building, and we have no way of knowing where the stones of Apollo came from. We only know who stole them, and will not give them back.

Andritsaina is growing like everywhere else in Greece, but it is still a fine place. It was once the best town in Greece for eating bean soup or buying the furs of the wild foxes; it used to look like that, indeed it still does. The guidebooks complain about the roads from here to the temple, but there are only tracks, which are no worse than all the other tracks in these mountains, with the exception of this one bit of road, which must have been done over with tarmac for some official visit. Bassai is still amazing. You arrive at a large car-park with a tourist kiosk (shut) and a row of new cottages that must be meant for workmen or lavatories on the hillside. Peering over the hilltop where a ramp now ascends is what looks like a Sultan's tent, but this three-gabled, flapping shape houses the temple. Complaints were made that it not only let in rain and snow-water but somehow concentrated them on the temple, so now some lengths of old drain-pipe lean up here and there against the canvas. Inside the tent you are at once very close to the columns, but they are chained and held by heavy neck-fetters lest they might totter. The floor is now gravel to drain away the rain the tent lets in. The general effect is more pitiable than I can easily express. The other day the Greek archae-ological authorities brought together a symposium of the hundred and twenty finest world experts, and took them to see this mon-strosity to say what should be done. In the past, when the temple was shackled and tented, we were promised it would take eight years to repair. That was five years ago, but now we are assured it will take another twenty, if they decide to undertake it. No one was at work when we visited except a boy to take the five hundred drachmas entrance fee. We still do not know if the experts (at whom the mind boggles) – or is it the government? – have decided.

To me it is not only a holy place and a place of pilgrimage, now ruined and desecrated, it is the tatters of a midsummer night's dream. I came here as a young man from the lost cave at Stomio where the wildest of goddesses lived, who was made pregnant by Poseidon in the form of a horse. That is a place where the River Neda disappears down gaping potholes in the rock, the gate of Hades. The river has just come rambling with many water-noises along the bottom of a ravine as if it were heading innocently towards the sea. It vanishes and all trace of it vanishes, only to reappear not far from the beach and to enter the waters of the bay as demurely as a schoolgirl. If one explored the potholes and the water caverns who knows what one might find? From there I had climbed quite a long way, but very exalted, to Pavlitsa, the ancient Phigaleia, where I was handed over to the priest. There were hens running about that seemed to live in a building with Byzantine frescoes, and I had a late delicate lunch of fried eggs. From here I tried to go to the Styloi by footpath or mule track, but I was some fifty years too late. At Dragoi I was told one could get a mule. When I arrived at the temple it must have been after midnight; I had acquired an ancient Aristophanic character for a guide and a malevolent donkey to take my baggage. I lent my guide a bit of rope with a lasso which he gleefully put round the animal's neck, mounted, and clattered off saying 'Petraki, I see nothing what-ever'. I had foolishly given him an immense mug of undiluted ouzo as I was having one myself. So I slept in the shadow of the columns, and even the moonlight on Lykaion could not keep me awake. When I saw the temple the next morning at dawn, it was the most amazing thing in the world.

Of course one cannot allow that kind of adventure. For all I know the old man fell down a ravine as I nearly did; I remember he had never seen a torch before and was much excited by it. Nowadays there would be numerous and elaborate campers, and hordes of undesirable 'hippies', of whom in fact we saw some that day, dutifully tramping. In my day there were two of us, I think, altogether. Antiquities are now all behind wire fences, and I was just lucky to get to Bassai before the fence-makers arrived, which was some time after 1976. It is all a great pity, is it not? The columns looked so solemn and so lonely that night. What should be done? I have no superior wisdom and I do not know how to guarantee the rebuilt ruins against earthquake or snowmelt or avalanche. My own view is expressed by the old folksong about Edward my Son: 'E'en let it stand till it down fall.' But when all is said and done my hero at Bassai is Brian Shefton. He got there with a mule right in the middle of the Civil War, guided by someone I knew as an ex-mayor of what was then the tiny village of Olympia, by back ways and by little-known footpaths and sly, overgrown tracks. It was a remarkable feat and I wish I had been with him, but I was still a boy at school in England.

The path from Dragoi looked now as if it had been really dangerous on that night so long ago. A canopy of cloud was dropping spots of rain; Giorgis thought it might be snow and it was cold enough, but the snow was gone from the mountains. Lykaion looked magnificent and just the same as I remembered it: like a wolf's pelt and skeleton hung out to dry. We did not attempt the vertiginous path, and there is nothing like winding around the shoulders of mountains in a car to make one lose all sense of direction, so I still do not know how exactly it went. We drove past Dragoi, which looked a charming spot, with a white mule grazing above it. Somewhere we passed an old woman riding side-saddle on a donkey as if it were 1950 or 1850, but nowadays one has to be in mountains to see such visions. Once or twice we saw flocks driven along the bulldozed bus track, which we were following, but all the villages seemed asleep or deserted. It was as if the entire countryside had been restored to the herdspeople and the animals, and all human dwellings locked up and then abandoned, and this is to a large extent true now. People leave their houses and move to the cities, revisiting their village only for summer holidays. On the island of Kythera they come home from Australia, and sit in the squares and the cafés twanging the bouzouki, which was still in fashion when they left Greece.

We came to Perivolia (the Gardens) above that terrific gorge of the Neda which until that moment I had forgotten. It looked steep and deep and very dangerous. This brought us at last past the ancient Phigaleia, where that youth like a filleted stone herring was dug up who now adorns the Olympia museum. He is so geometrically conceived he hardly qualifies as a *kouros* at all: and yet a few generations later people who knew what he looked like were at work on Epikourios Apollon. Frazer of the *Golden Bough* was present at this youth's reappearance in Phigaleia: I think it was the only time he saw anything of significance dug up, but it was the end of his good luck because a few days later dreaming about 'sandy Ladon's lilied banks' he got terribly lost where the Ladon and the Erymanthos come roaring into the Alpheios, somewhere above Aspra Spitia. The largeness of the circuit wall enthralled us, Giorgis found several kinds of orchid and even the trees in the hedges, let alone the old trees treasured in the fields, carried loads of an amazing blossom like wild sloes. Then after some toing and froing and floundering, just beyond the war memorial where I was gazing down miles of green hillside into the gorge where I must once have climbed up, we found the spring, sheathed in its enormous fifth- or fourth-century stones, under the gigantic plane tree with the classical marbles now somewhat neatly ranged around it.

They used to be just in a ring, for the conversations of the village elders, but they will have been looked at recently by the archaeologists, who so seldom leave well alone. They were digging here last season, and we were told they found something or other, but no one remembered what. Perhaps it was a long word: it is typical of people from Athens to come here and spend all summer digging for a long word. Still, the village was the same, the handful of names on the memorial were the same family names for two or three generations just as they are so often in English villages. The church was shut and I could not see any hens, but the priest I remembered who gave me the lunch,

Pappaphanis, who was a young man then, is now about eighty and has just gone into retirement at Volos. In 1963, I sent him a second-hand Greek text of Pausanias which he wanted, but I have never known whether he got it. The spring-water was the same, though years ago they filled up the bath into which it poured for fear a child could drown in it. That was long ago, and in the reign of some Pappacentaur of priests, and maybe the disportings of villagers in water five or six foot deep were frowned upon. The villagers had put down a cement floor to avoid the splashy mud around the spring at some time in the Twenties or Thirties, but that is luckily breaking up now and going back to nature.

Beyond the spring the track headed off to Dragoi, so that must have been the way I went, thirty-two years ago. We could not delay to wander along it again, or dream of descending into the gorge again. Phigaleia is yet another site like a place of refuge, surrounded by high, silent hills. *Haults sont li puys et ténebreux et grants, et dans li vals sont li eaux courants.* It seemed a million miles from Bassai, where the Phigaleians must have grazed and watered their sheep five or six hundred years before Christ. It is curious the place should be called the glens; it sounds like a shepherd's or a mountaineer's word. To gain the opposite hillside and the prospect of lunch, we had to go back to Perivolia and cross over there, and then follow a road clinging to the cliff in case it should, though at times we wondered if it ever would, bring us down to Zourtsi, now called Petralona. I do not know why one should prefer the Slav names, but I saw that Giorgis and Kostas did too, and they are more satisfactory in the mouth. We did get a very late lunch, where the system was that a lady cooked for her own family, then served the same to whoever came, until it ran out. We were far down the valley by then, but there was a freshness about the cheese and the wine from the barrel, and a generosity about the pastitsio that spoke of the mountains. They even turned the television down for us, and down again, and finally off.

We passed along the one street of Lepreon, and I cast looks of

longing at the road sign to 'Hag. Taxiarch., 5 km', but then we
were back on the sands at Sacharo, at another café for a breath of
early evening air and a coffee. As we left the region of the high
mountains we felt light-headed but sad, like angels walking this
earth at the moment they alight here and heaven disappears.
Cloud and mist were descending swiftly, and the last sight of
Lykaion, and his last face, were terrifying: grey and bleak and
formidable, and high above us. Giorgis tentatively proposed we
could go to a poetry reading by some lady he had been asked to,
or a concert of classical music, but I refused to stir for the first and
knew I would sleep through the second. I do not think we did
anything more at all. My record breaks off and it is obscure where
it begins again. I know that my excuse for avoiding the poetry
reading, which Giorgis was grateful to hear and used for both of
us, was that next day was the formal reopening of the theatre with
a play called *Arkouda* (*The Bear*) by Chekhov. Kostas, who still has
his sources from when he worked as a journalist, entertained us as
the sea lapped the sand, with terrible news of the government
having secretly signed an offshore gas and oil concession for
Hagios Andrea to a firm in Texas. Jeeps had been seen speeding
up and down over the Pharos hill at Katakolo, with the company's
sign on them. I heard terrifying stories of the new oil-polluted,
coffee-coloured jellyfish, which leave you with a large poisoned
bump for life wherever they sting you: they poison you, being
themselves poisoned. The only means of controlling them is by
praying for turtles, which eat them. Luckily there are some in
those waters.

Finally what are we to think about the temple? It is a tragedy.
With its presence concentrated and crowded into a tent, the
whole thing seems taller than before, every column towering and
the whole construction overwhelming, but it is so simple that you
feel a fool walking round it. There are now many roads that lead
to it, the main road or two main roads from Olympia up into the
mountains, then our Krestena road by Alipheira, then the road we

came home by, which turns out to be one I had always wanted to try, because it led from the coast to New Phigaleia (Zourtsi) which must surely be connected to my Phigalei (Pavlitsa), though the old maps were hesitant, and the buses had been the merest rumours of buses, which anyway I did not much like to travel in; I had always preferred to walk or if necessary to take a taxi or a train and then a taxi. There was another route I noticed which may well be the easiest of all. If you go south to Kalo Nero, and then inland towards the Kalamata road, you will pass a small signpost to Dorio and Psari which claims to be the road to Bassai as well. I have not tried it, but I have verified it on a modern map, and it is surely worth trying. It goes by Dimandra and Kakoletri, east of the other roads. The building of a temple to Apollo on that height, on what had become the classic Greek model, was at least subconsciously a gesture of willingness to take part in history.

Coins have been found inscribed *Arkadikon* that circulated in the fifth century. The Arcadians must have been mostly herdsmen, perhaps far-wandering: there is a fifth-century Arcadian verse inscription at Olympia that calls it a place of many flocks, or many sheep, rather as Giraldus Cambrensis says of Snowdon that it would pasture all the sheep of Wales. I remember the inscription at Olympia because it is in a particularly fine script, to the south of the temple of Zeus near the east end, and also I must admit because for a time (confused by modern Greek in which the same word means an apple) I thought this must mean 'Arcadia of the many apple trees', which would no doubt be lyrical, but scarcely true of the landscape. (There are wild pears in eastern Arcadia but that is another matter.) The word is used in the *Iliad* of a North Arcadian place (II.2, 605) as well as of a man rich in flocks, that is, one whose flocks roam here, there and everywhere, like the flocks of Odysseus. I am glad to note that the same mistake I made occurs somewhere in the text of Pindar, so that I am not the first. If I am right, and grazing and the consequent grazing rights have much to do with the original vague confederation of the Arcadian highlanders, then it would follow as the night the day that the shepherds and goatherds of Theokritos, and of the entire pastoral convention in poetry, might easily have roots in the Arcadian way of life.

But the first Arcadian setting for the competitive singing of shepherds, goatherds and cowherds does not occur in any Greek poet unless in a mere epigrammatist: so far as I know it occurs first in Virgil. The Romans did have a particular interest in Arcadia, bizarre as it may seem to us. It is so antiquarian and half-crazy that it seems to me to come from the hand of Varro, a man of Etruscan blood and wide and indigestible learning, who invented for example the seven hills of Rome. He lived to a great age and acquired huge authority. The Romans in a desperate wish to attach their own mythology to the Greek myths, which had all the prestige of literature, of art and antiquity, adopted the city of Pallantion in Arcadia, an abandoned stone 'city' then but of venerable antiquity, and claimed it was the same as the Mons Palatinus, the Palatine hill, under which their oldest stories could be domiciled. That was where the Roman she-wolf must have suckled the Roman twins. They therefore remitted the taxes of Pallantion as a reward. A bronze antique female wolf was found in Italy at the Renaissance, and promptly supplied with a sixteenth-century bronze Romulus and Remus.

The wolf is interesting, because there were no more wolves in that part of Italy in that period: she was to them a mythical and foreign animal who might suckle human twins. In Arcadia there were surely wolves. I see that a guide to mammals including those of Greek lands published in 1967 included the bear but gave no importance to the wolf, yet I can remember in about that same year a wandering musician and a boy being caught by a pack of wolves in north Greece, and the only recognisable remains were a hand still grasping the fiddle. About the same year wolves chased a village postman on his bicycle in the hills near Florence. He was lucky, because in the Arcadian mountains he would not have had a bicycle. I knew a postman at Olympia in the Seventies who ran, jogged and walked forty miles a day. The wolf wandered as far south as the Theban plains in bad times as lately as the Civil War. In Arcadia it played at least a lively part in popular imagination. The door in the side of the temple of Apollo is turned to the sunrise over Lykaion, which is called by its ancient name, Wolf Mountain.

Can anything more be deduced from what little is known about Arcadian history? In prehistory they lived obscurely, and let us hope happily, among their wolves. In history they are called Dorians like other southern Greeks, and the queer relation of their dialect to Cyprus and to a mysterious element in the language of Homer (where the whole mixture of elements is to some degree mysterious) is a specialised scholarly interest that wanders away and gets lost. Until they built Megalopolis with Theban help as a cork in the explosive Spartan bottle, the Arcadians were usually in the Spartan penumbra as allies of a useless kind. We know nothing of any great Arcadian wealth or trade: indeed, they lived in the land where Odysseus was fated to die. He was told that he would not find peace until he left Ithaca and wandered until he found a land where the oar he must carry on his shoulder was taken for a winnowing fan. That was thought by the ancient Greeks to have meant the middle or the east of Arcadia: and there he died and was buried. The place really was some kind of graveyard of innocence. The Arcadians did fight, but almost always in other people's wars.

There is not much more to say of the valley which at its lower, more open end Lepreon commands, and at its upper end Phigaleia dominates, with its hidden, upper sanctuary of Epikourios Apollon overlooking Lykaion, except that such a valley was always grazed up and down by transhumant flocks, which went high in summer and came down in winter, as the flocks did in Sicily, and as they did from Delphi towards Arahova, and as indeed they still do today. The flocks have tracks of their own, they go aside to hide-outs, to water-springs and to familiar patches of grass. When they make their big moves those are at walking pace or grazing pace, but that is only twice a year, otherwise the country we had been exploring is ideally suited for the wanderings of Arcadia of the many flocks. The only other thing that we know about the Arcadians is the faint tradition that they were particularly skilled in music, but whether that means traditional music or the weak pipe or even the little drum, no one knows. Even Virgil's Arcadian herdsmen 'Both in the flower of youth, Arcadians', which alludes to a Greek epigram, is not the whole of his picture, which is sometimes in Sicily and sometimes in Italy, and mysteriously includes North Africa: but that is perhaps from a hint in Homer.

It is pathetic but I suppose inevitable that we have so little secure information about Arcadia, and most of what we do know comes from Pausanias, who wrote terribly late in the day, and who leaves us often to guess what he has read and where, and how he knows things. We have the stray information that Lykaion was the birthplace of Pan, the herdsman's god, who sees the most distant things from his mountain-top. There is a small bronze statue in the Olympia museum of him peering, hand over brow, probably at some shameful erotic manoeuvre, but maybe only for a lost sheep. The conception that I think Pan observed was celebrated at Lykosoura, and the strangest of dancing men in cloaks with the heads (that is, wearing the masks) of animal-headed gods were found there. They are only small terracotta figurines, made for the shrine where they were dedicated and not available anywhere else. They are repeated in a long frieze or border round the hem of the marble cloak of a goddess, a Hellenistic copy of an original from the same shrine, which is now in the Athens museum. The cult apparently included an animal-headed dance, which can have been no secret.

There is another story that Pan was ritually whipped with squills, for some quite unknown reason and at some little-known Arcadian festival recorded by Roman antiquarians. The whipping was done by boys but no one knows why, and whether they whipped a statue, which is usually what happens in these cases, or whether they whipped a person, and if so how hard, no one knows. Squills sound painful, but we may hope it was a statue. Theokritos mentions this obscure rite, but the variety of vegetables with which a curious variety of statues were whipped in ancient times does not really interest serious scholars, which seems a pity. It usually has come connection with fertility, in the case of Pan no doubt the fertility of the flocks. For poets of Virgil's and Horace's generation the claim to have seen Pan was copied from some lines in Lucretius, who speaks a little earlier about the eerie noise of the echoes heard by people lost in the mountains at night, and the magic echo of the distant reed-pipe of the flocks. No doubt that really is where belief in Pan comes from, and from 'those black Arcadian mountains dear to him', as Horace put it.

It is tempting to draw out the history of Arcadia into modern times and more recent folk poetry, but the truth is that those valleys altered utterly in late antiquity. The world of the *Chronicle of the Morea*, which records many details of Arcadian history in the middle ages, is to me more bizarre than the classical age and more remote than the golden age. But the tumble-down pageant of chivalry with its tinkle of ornaments and the headlong crash of its downfall would really confuse readers, as it has often in the past confused me. I am clutching the *Chronicle* lovingly in my left hand as I write, but it is simply a different stage-play that was enacted by quite different characters on the same stage.

> They sent to Kalamata and they came on the next day,
> And they found that castle feeble, they found a monastery,
> They took it and made war on it and with the sword it fell . . .
>
> (1711ff.)

These are the battles of great lords whose power centres were elsewhere, in Epiros or in Athens where a Duke reigned on the akropolis. Personally, I look forward to the downfall of these

people, when they paraded like the French aristocracy at Agin-
court, whom I cannot quite call idiots because they included
Charles of Orleans the poet, or like the Western knights who
attacked the Russians over the ice and I am glad to say it cracked
and they sank, and like the German knights who adventured into
Switzerland, and I am pleased to say were annihilated by having
boulders dropped on their silly heads. As for the French chivalry
of all Greece, they paraded at Orchomenos near Thebes, rode
their fine horses in full armour into a marsh with flags flying and
trumpets playing, and while they lay wallowing had their throats
cut in a highly effective manner by an army of wandering Catalans. But the summer came and the Catalans disappeared as water
disappears. And there was silence in the black mountains of
Arcadia.

A poem written by Mandelstam as a very young man gives the
atmosphere of the valleys very well. I have translated it and quoted
it before, but in a specialised context, and as I become older I get
more interested in this god-inhabited place, so I give it, if only to
commemorate what Virgil calls days when the Siren nourished
him, and he blossomed in studies of unhonoured idleness. Mandelstam called his poem 'Midsummer' and he wrote it in 1916.

> Orioles in the deep wood: vowel length
> is the one measure of all tonal verse:
> and on one day a year pure duration
> pours out and nature's metre is Homer's.
>
> Like a caesura that long day dawns:
> from early morning longueur's lazy weed:
> oxen at pasture, golden indolence
> won't let you draw the whole note from the reed.

I do not quite understand the next bit of my diary; it is more
puzzling than Mandelstam. It is surely about taking a shower next
morning, and the sprinkler head came off, as it sometimes did.

'Today hot water a.m., wonderful hose-shower, then it would not switch off or turn off for anything, and finally a tremendous, dense shower of rain.' We sat long while Mitsa went off to a memorial service with the in-laws, and came home laughing. We were reading poetry, some Valéry and a poem of mine, and Giorgis's translations. I was also preoccupied with the famous waterfall of the River Styx, which to my surprise no one had heard of, and no map noticed it at all. Off we speeded to Olympia, which has grown grossly and out of all recognition. It was filled with the queerest-looking people whom you see nowhere else in Greece except maybe Athens. Some of them wore large black stetson hats. Olympia, which I remember best when it was first ruined in the mid-Seventies, and earlier still when it was nothing, now has a hotel called Nomads. It is all hotels. But the good old Spap, once the only railway hotel in Greece, and in my day the only hotel of any kind at Olympia, is now shut and has been looted ('I think I guess by whom,' said Giorgis) and is waiting to be a ruin. The old museum looked shut too, but two dozen buses were parked there. The Hill of Kronos looked brushed and well-kept behind fences, but God only knows what the smart-looking 'Olympic Academy' beyond it can be. An American girls' school?

We drove on past the ancient site and ate lunch at what I remember as the chicken restaurant, heavily draped for me with memories of Takis Sinopoulos and of my wife and her son Matthew when he was about eight. The doctor had a theory that there are only two kinds of Greek restaurant, one where there is nothing and whatever you find you eat it, and the other where the owner tells you what you must eat and you must eat that. There was a terrible row once when Takis had been surprised by very good soup and ordered more. 'You don't need more soup,' he was told. 'You think I don't give you enough soup? You think I don't know what you need?' I forget how that ended. Deirdre thought there was only one kind of Greek restaurant, the kind where they have nothing, and she was pleasantly surprised by this

95

one. Mitsa even remembered exactly what Matthew ate, seventeen years ago. It is not because of restaurants that Deirdre had not come, let me add, but she refuses to sail or fly and hates tunnels. Nikos Gatsos hated them just as much, which is why he never came to England, but he also hated moving staircases; I think his very worst thing was moving staircases, I think my wife's is submarines.

Giorgis and I waited outside a café at Olympia in the road that leads down to the station, while Mitsa went off to buy some butter, which she preferred for some reason to buy here. It was a lengthy proceeding. Giorgis says that now there are cows in Greece as there were before the war, but not to graze, they live in sheds and never see the sun, like the old Express Dairy cows that were always said to live in huge tiled caverns underneath London: I met a man once who claimed to have seen these beautiful tiles. An elderly ex-mayor came up to us, he remembered me as someone who always sat in the same café for lunch, twenty years ago. That place was owned by an older ex-mayor, the one who once guided Brian Shefton to Apollo's temple with the mule; I fear he is long dead. He remembered the German column that had taken over the village after a big battle with the resistance, with orders to shoot the men and boys: they were begged off by a German archaeologist who lived here, Kunze I think. He must have known that some of them were guilty, but he swore they were innocent. My old friend had remembered the German party chiefs arriving at Olympia before the war in huge cars, which must have been a hazardous journey as the roads then were. When the war came he went to Athens and got a job as a waiter in a German officers' mess, which is how he avoided starvation. His son was an educated young man who ran a small bookshop, but now he owns a large tourist jeweller's shop. We failed to see him because he was thought to be asleep.

Now the whole main street is frankly revolting. The modest place where I had dinner every night in 1975–6 no longer exists.

The shops are full of expensive and undesirable objects. The only improvement is that the poem by Takis Doxas, a buffoon with unlimited pretensions, and a bronze bust now at Pyrgos, has been taken down. It was inscribed in stone as I recall, under a tree as you approached the classical ruins, and spoke in high terms a violent message against the left in the Civil War. Christos had dashed back to Pyrgos to fetch some fish for a present, Mitsa arrived first with her butter and some twenty-star cognac for cooking, at which Giorgis exploded, and we all went off to Lala where they had old friends. I had always wanted to go to Lala but had never been. It was near the famous battle, and I wanted to see the site of that, but it also offered a possible clue to the preoccupying question of what Pausanias means by the quick or mountain road from Olympia to Elis. For that matter how did the southern Greeks approach that sanctuary? Did they cross the Alpheios by a ford? Or a wooden bridge now quite lost? I have been there in August and I would not attempt to cross it on foot, but no doubt the dam below Olympia has deepened it. Its flood-plain is huge, and it buried the temple of Zeus ten feet deep in silt.

I have a print of Olympia made by the Victorian Brandard from a drawing by Holland of the Plains of Olympia before any excavations had taken place. The Turkish officers in their turbans cluster round the Aga's tent and there are pieces of antiquities lying about in the foreground. It looks like the ancient site taken from the bottom of the Kronion. The date of the drawing must evidently be between 1800 or so and 1824, and the only surprising thing about it is the certainty and rightness with which the site was identified: but in Rome in the eighteenth century Winckelmann's generation at least thought they knew where to find Olympia. My picture of it does look more inviting than the same area today. The Aga lived at Lala, but I had never quite understood why. It is because Lala is healthy, being high up on a sandy hill, you smell the sweet freshness up there. It is also a good place to plant cherries and is still a huge orchard really. Kiphisia near Athens was another Turkish settlement and another plantation of cherries, as the Turkish writers tell us. In the Aga's day there were two thousand eight hundred Turks who lived up at Lala, with virtually nothing between them and the sea. Lala itself ranks with Auch in Gers as one of the great unexploited, unspoilt places in Europe. I have never seen such views and prospects in Greece, and seldom anywhere on earth. Now the Aga's house survives in one room only, and that belongs to the council.

We sat with our friends looking out over the cherry trees, which were just coming into blossom. Some of the family were wonderfully ancient, a grandfather and a great-grandfather, both with bone-crushing handshakes. Discussion centred on the United States, because the father was just back from Chicago. Behind their heads you could see Olympia and, beyond that, mountain beyond mountain perhaps as far as Lykaion. The best views of all were from a chapel where we stopped to gaze from Lala hill. My problem about where was the mountain track or rough road from Elis to Olympia seemed to be simply solved. A big wind was blowing, cool but not too cold, like an English spring day. The modern road was wooded, with wild blossoms and flowers at the edge, and then dense pine forest owned by the state. I was dazed with conviction about the ancient road, though I do not really know where it lay. The few times I tried out where I thought it was in the past, it came to nothing. All the same, Lala does look like the beginning of the solution.

Then came the evening with the formal and densely crowded re-opening of the theatre, for which free tickets awaited us, just behind Mr Mercouri of the wine. After Chekhov's *Bear* came Vlachou's *Grocer's Daughter* which I thought very funny indeed. Vlachou was the grandfather of Madam Vlachou of the *Kathimerini*, the best paper. It was farcical and overwhelmed us, the company was lively and very young. It was a great success into which music kept suddenly and very successfully intruding. The piece was written in about 1890, with some jokes about language and about the army which to me were old friends from Byzantios's *Babylon*, and from that heavenly work of irony *Military Life in Greece*. Byzantios worked at the first Greek court where dialects were so thick that no one understood anyone; his play is one of the funniest books I have ever read. His other play is called *Hashish*, which, perhaps luckily, I do not remember. He became an ikon painter and decorated the ceiling of the old Saint Andrew church at Patras, in a modern Italianate style of 1850, as if Greek history had never happened. It is a strange monument that he left. Vlachou's play is now a nostalgic farce, because no one remembers that period and we all like it, yet once it must have been sharper. The Chekhov was fine too, the characters strongly impressed like the clear impressions of very old prints. There were some uncertainties of timing, as there always is with amateur Chekhov, but no one cared, because the whole show was such a roaring success. I believe it played for night after night to full houses.

About thirty-five of us dined near Katakolo. The young women in particular impressed me with their great beauty and presence: it was the new generation, and the first time I had seen or heard them. Giorgis had forewarned me but I was still bowled over. The music the men played was wonderful too: a drummer who just grinned a private grin, a wild-eyed guitarist who played himself to rest, though not to sleep and it took him hours, and a bouzouki man who looked like P. J. Kavanagh who could play behind his back. They played 'Rembetika', 'Andartika' or resistance songs, and 'Theodorakis'. It was all very young and provincial; Giorgis thought it an honourable effort. He was the grandfather and secret president of them all. The resistance songs were sometimes unintentionally far funnier than they had once been. They danced, first a girl alone, then others. There were rows of young women, one of them I thought incredibly young-looking and touching, with straight, short black hair, straight from an Attic vase painting. She told me they were all school-friends more or less, but a young lady teacher said not so: they had met in the theatre and all they had in common was they wanted to achieve something. As we left they were discussing the New York theatre this year with perfect coolness, as if it were Athens. Outside, when we went home, there were thousands of stars in the sky, and I saw them all. As we went to bed a cock was crowing bravely at the bright moon, but the chickens in the olive grove had all gone to sleep somewhere.

4 : A Poem Lived

THE roads that wandered towards the site of Elis, where the British carried out a survey once that produced an embarrassment of riches, or if you prefer to think in a mythical way, where Herakles was called in to clean out the Augean stables and used the river to do it, bury the traveller deeply in the unspoiled Greek countryside: by Lala to Neraida and Persaina, Mouzaki, Koutsochera and Ephyra, or by Pelopi, Barbasaina, north by Chemadio, and Thalames and Krioneri. But all that is in Eleia, it is more enchanting than Arcadia but it is not the stony heart of southern Greece, the country of the wolf-cult which tails off to the south into the homeland of the vendetta, where the villagers built rival towers separated only by lanes, in order to batter one another to bits whenever occasion called.

We sat one morning in the Eparcheion, the café in the shade of the Cathedral where the old tower of Pyrgos (the *pyrgos* of Pyrgos) used to be, which was the seat of the *Eparchos*, the provincial governor. There we drank orangeade, since they say it is dangerous (and I believe them) to drink anything stronger without little nibbles of prawn or boiled egg or olive. We talked on that fine morning of the national poet, Solomos, and the family feuds by which Giorgis explains his undoubted eccentricity. The inheritance was disputed because of his mother whom the old Count Solomos had married on his deathbed, but she then insisted that her son by some other liaison should share in the family money. The case went to Corfu, and when it was decided against him, the poet Solomos never went back to Zante. He never went out without a brand-new pair of gloves, being of course a contemporary of Beau Brummell. He drank only Zante wine called Verdea, very wisely in my experience, but in the end they say eau de cologne, which he claimed did him less harm than the doctors. He was after all a contemporary of the Black Drops that ruined Tennyson's brother, so no doubt he was right there as well. But this rather grim picture of the old man does not take into account the light verses and the visits he lavished on English ladies in Corfu, which are under-emphasised by Greek writers out of perhaps an anachronistic sense of patriotism. There is not a lot known about the colonial ladies of Corfu, except a disability: that they could not pronounce the word orange, Edward Lear says. Some called it oynge and some called it awnge.

A friend of Giorgis's turned up who wrote extremely able, flinty poems, who had known Nikos Gatsos all his life; he was called Kostas Panopoulos. He was a fund of information about Nestor's and Homer's Pylos: he thought there were four places all called Pylos, and renewed in me a nostalgia for the crazy learned literature of the subject, on which I had wasted hours and hours once. A kind of drunkenness overcame me for the old, crazy articles, one by an archaeologist of supreme dottiness who could not go for a country walk without discovering Homeric monuments. Kostas had all that at his cheerful fingertips. After lunch he carried us off to beyond Kyparissia to a mad, quite isolated stucco palace or fort, built obviously by a lunatic. He called himself Harry Fournier or Fournarakis, but he had nothing to do with *Le grand Meaulnes*. He was a Greek American who had expressed himself by building on the lonely seashore a white Gothic castle with balconies and turrets, and a huge Trojan Horse containing a library of universal mythology, and a great number of more than life-size plaster statues of some naivety. It was very mad indeed. There was a Tour Eiffel, and a shrine to 1821, and maybe the horse was a horse of Poseidon. It had a fine aristocratic domelike rear and a large tail, but the builder is dead and the library was shut. I do not know what books it contained.

In Kyparissia we called on another of the literary lecturers we had heard, who was a colleague of Kostas as an educational consultant or inspector, and wanted to write something about Giorgis: we had to deliver to him a large wad of typescripts and photocopies and new poems, because he intended a complete book about the poet. He was at least as clever and obliging as before, certainly, but I was becoming dazed with the literary life, and was grateful when we raced off uphill to the castle and the old akropolis where I got so prodigiously bitten by mosquitoes in 1963 that my whole face swelled up and I reached Pylos like a pink balloon. Now the castle was enclosed, there were two water-springs under a vast plane tree, one dry, the other tapped, and a lovely Turkish inscription. The ruins of a bath-house had been there once, but they were swept away a year or two ago, lamentably enough. Now chickens lived in the pretty house of the Edwardian poet Palamas, the Greek equivalent of William Morris. One side of the lane was stepped and cobbled, and the houses looked lovely as they fell to pieces. In that house Palamas wrote his great *Dodecalogue of the Gypsy*. That upper town is perfect now, but it will not last long. Kyparissia seemed full of ruins and the ruins full of cocks crowing. The sunset is supposed to be unrivalled except at Santorini, but for us it was swift and yellow over Zakynthos.

Kostas and Giorgis swapped folksongs to one another as we drove home through the trees, and the headlights picked up the yellow blossom of the mimosa. Then Kostas told me the tale of Professor Pezopoulos's daughter, whom Nikos Gatsos had wooed and won, to the fury of her papa. The Professor would therefore not admit Nikos to some exams, so he went off and worked for the radio instead and never went back to the University of Athens. He had a close friend then called de Georgis, who like Nikos was a cane-carrying dandy, who in the end became the Greek translator of

Beckett (or was it Joyce?). They had been rivals for the lovely daughter of Professor Pezopoulos, but Nikos had won, I am glad to say. At one stage her father is said to have had him arrested for a night or two: Takis Sinopoulos knew the details of that part of the story, but now he is dead. The whole incident seems to emerge from a world of folksongs, because that was how I heard it, or just because that was how it was.

I knew that soon we were going to Zakynthos. We had been going there ever since 1963, when I first heard of the carnival comedies that then included interventions by the audience, who shouted out verses impromptu, and the actors replied in verse from the stage. But that was the end of a tradition dying out, like that of the Cretan *mantinades*, couplets composed impromptu and sung after dinner. I have heard that done with enormous panache, but now you must go far to hear them. In the last twenty years or so, Giorgis had been to Zakynthos a number of times: it was the offshore island for his part of Greece, scarcely more exotic to him than the Isle of Wight or the Channel Isles. This time we were determined to go there together, as we had always promised each other. Later, I might go to Kythera, though that dream was beginning to dissolve. But for this or that reason Zakynthos was constantly postponed. Giorgis wanted me to stay with a friend he had there, and not in a hotel, and the friend was in Paris, but she would soon be home. She had an ex-husband who had remarried and had more children I think, and now suddenly committed suicide, which had upset everyone. I did not at first take much interest in this story because it was unreal to me then, and I cannot remember the ins and outs of all our arrangements: since Giorgis had taken charge, it was best for me to be passive.

There were only a few things I seriously wanted and one was to visit the grave of Nikos Gatsos. I had laid out this book in my mind as a long series of poems or songs for him, like a procession. He was one of my oldest and best friends, in Greece or anywhere, a magnificent and lonely poet, who on his own and by passion as a very young man had cracked the problem of how to write modern poetry in the traditional and popular language. That is something translation can scarcely convey. His one great poem was *Amorgos*, the name of an island, by the way, that he had never visited. The mastery of Greek that he showed in that poem, and in his translation of *Blood Wedding* by Lorca, *Matomenos Gamos*, is what George Seferis meant when he told me that of all Greeks he envied only Gatsos and deferred only to him in his mastery of his native language. I have heard Lorca's brother confess that in certain lyrics Gatsos seemed to him better than the original. He was truly a great poet and the most admirable of men. When he died I did write a lamentation for him, but I will not repeat it here.

The story of his life is a very strange one. I knew he was born at Asea, near one of those ancient hill-forts or places of refuge with which Arcadia is dotted. It was dug by the Swedes before the war, and Nikos as a little boy used to go up to the site when they were working and crouch beside them and watch what they were doing. I knew little about his family except that his father had kept an inn of some kind, a *khani* or place to rest and to feed and water your horses, somewhere nearby. He was fond of his mother, who lived with him in Athens, and bitterly distressed when she grew old and died, which happened in my day. After that, for a long time he used to go to Asea once a week by taxi from Athens, upright and white-faced with some flowers on his knee, leave them for her and then go back to Athens. But he loved Asea and at times spent long, idyllic summers there, coming back with extremely funny stories; I remember one about the village policeman investigating a hoard of rusty weapons of war that some member of the resistance of the Forties had buried in their garden and never retrieved. Nikos must have gone by then as a student to Athens, where he was taught by the great Veis (sometimes spelt Bees) who had a complete knowledge of the local antiquities and traditions of every village in Greece, and would greet every new student with enquiries about his local haunted well, or whatever it might be. He published nothing so far as I know but a snowstorm of pamphlets, which ought to be collected.

Nikos was a smart and handsome undergraduate with an eye for the girls. He carried a stick then. But the war came and he was called up; you had to go and collect your uniform and a gun, before anything else happened. A few days later he returned to the office and handed in the uniform and the gun, which he viewed with evident distaste, and told the clerk he would not be needing them. That was that: it was a gesture of pacifism with which the bureaucracy did not know how to cope and he was left alone. Later, he wrote *Amorgos*, which is the nearest he ever went to explaining his position. He starved during the occupation, sold his library which he most bitterly regretted losing and spent days gambling for a shilling or two on the pavements of Athens. That was an obsession he never lost; it was the nearest he ever came to having a vice. Sometimes in the summer he would spend three weeks at Aidipsos or somewhere similar where there was a casino. He wrote no more formal poetry or virtually none: some charming lines to Seferis on his birthday, a poem about a medieval knight and a few more translations.

And of course his songs. About those he could be really gleeful. He rejoiced in unlikely rhymes of the kind Gershwin used. He had a flair for them and a genius for singable lyrics. They were never published in books in his lifetime, though I had some on the yellowing sheets of an old magazine that featured them once for a Christmas issue, and I had learnt some by heart. He became popular beyond the bounds of popularity, and, in spite of the drains of gambling and charity, he became rich. He lost one chance of great wealth one day in August, when his musician, Manos Hadzidakis, who was also probably his closest friend, begged him for a few lyrics at once for a film. It was blazing hot, the air-conditioning in Flocca's, which was his afternoon café and place for interviews, had probably broken down, as it often did: in those days that was the only air-conditioned café in Athens. Nikos begged just for once to be let off and assured Manos he could supply the words himself, which he did, and Nikos missed a world success that might well have made him a millionaire. The film was *Never on Sunday*.

He put something serious, and seriously considered and intended, into his popular songs. I had realised that, if only from one we were able to commission from him for a television film about Greece in 1975. His words were about the crucifixion, and it is apparent from the selection of his songs published after his death that he turned to religious themes, which of course offer an immediate contact with traditional Greek language, towards the end of his life. The songs as a whole are beyond praise. They were printed with the title *Blow Wind Blow* in 1992 by Ikaros for his niece Agathi, whom I remember some ten or twenty years ago being taken about by Nikos extremely young, rather like Cordelia being shown round Athens by Lear in a good temper. Nikos saw the proofs, I understand, but not the complete volume; he died in May of that year. He had Parkinson's disease, which we might have guessed many years ago, because his hands shook or shivered slightly a long time before he died.

Meeting Nikos Gatsos was one of my first objectives in going to Greece in 1963. He was already at that time famous by word of mouth, and outside Greece he has perhaps never been famous in any other way, except that his fame by rumour has greatly increased, like that of Socrates. He was a wise man, a capable and rather negative diplomat, immensely learned in poetry in many languages and personally deep. I knew *Amorgos*, which I admired then as I do now, boundlessly. I think it is one of the greatest poems written in any language in my lifetime. I had heard rumours of what he was like, a little from Philip Sherrard but more from Dom Moraes and from Henrietta, who admired him as much as Dom did. Philip published the first translation of *Amorgos*, and I remember in 1963 seeing a new version in typescript by Keeley, but I had never, I believe, seen the original text until then; it was a very rare book, though since that year it has been reprinted many times. And yet I knew a very few lines of *Amorgos* by heart in Greek before going to Greece. They must have been quoted in Philip Sherrard's *Marble Threshing Floor*.

To meet Gatsos, you simply showed up at Flocca's in the afternoon and asked for him. He always sat in the same place, in the far corner of the first room, presiding benignly over a collection of girls and young men who adored him, composers and literary people. I remember among his Greek regulars a retired ballet star, later a theatrical director, who looked like a leopard and yawned away afternoons, a lawyer who became an MP, a novelist and so on, but he knew absolutely every Greek writer as if he kept files on them and could characterise them to the bone. Of his foreign friends, who came and went of course, I remember a daughter of the Israeli General Dayan, a Latin-American model of great beauty who was more than once the cover picture of *Vogue*, and an American poet of my own age whose life was tragic. He was homosexual and settled in Crete, where there were mushroom clouds of scandal above his head, but I think he was as innocent as the purest water. Unfortunately he gave up poetry to write novels, turned to film-making and had all but dried up altogether, or come to the end of his resources, when suddenly he died of untreated appendicitis in 1983. He was my fellow-disciple twenty years before that, on that apocalyptic night of wind and lightning on the akropolis, when Nikos said, 'There is a game you know, we used to play, when Elytis and I were young men, and surrealism was all the rage . . .'

I thought at the time that the way this game works offered a clue to how all poetry works. I still think it does so, but not maybe a very useful clue, or anyway only a clue you have to be a poet to follow. Nowadays they say we are all poets, so perhaps it is worth repeating. It is a version of the old game Consequences: one person secretly writes down a question, the second person an answer, the third a comment. When the three are all in some queer kind of unconscious contact with each other, which means it is best not played from cold, but after dinner as we played it that night, the question and answer and comment take on an amazing relationship like the play of static lightning. I remember What is the drumbeat of retiring time? Loudly, slowly, and in the strictest time. It is only a game, but it is surely very queer. Personally, I went on to write a long poem that took me two years, leaving out every other kind of connection; I do not now believe that was a wise course, but it may have been a necessary one for me.

Sitting at Nikos's feet, I tried to educate myself as a poet. He, meanwhile, claimed to have dried up. My American friend Charles thought Nikos did write, but secretly and maybe something un-writeable, something further over the edge than *Amorgos*. Drying up is a peculiar process and it often has simple, everyday causes. Dom Moraes was scornfully ill-treated by English critics in the mid-Sixties, went home to India and stopped writing poems for seventeen years. I first knew Dom in the mid-Fifties, in Oxford, which was when I was first beginning to fumble my slow way towards love, let alone towards the harder realities of poetry, which were like taking a grip on a rope as you slide down it. He had been a real poet for four years or so, since he was fifteen. I had been scribbling verses since I was ten, but I was a much slower beginner, not ready to publish a book for another three years. Even then I had never attained the devastating simplicity of Dom's early poems, and I envied him that.

> 'Dying is just the same as going to sleep,'
> The piper whispered, 'close your eyes,'
> And blew some hints and whispers on his pipe:
> The children closed their eyes . . .

It is the hints and whispers that make this poem so eerie and its beginning so ominous. One can see the story will end badly, like Wordsworth 'droning away the snow, our old disgrace'. When I first met Nikos he was like a cascade of the most refreshing snow-water, and the experience stopped me from writing poems, but kept me hanging about making experiments in poetry for about eighteen months. Only a certain crassness enables one to go on: or there are certain poets sneered at by the others who are so wet they never can dry up: and I have served for a lifetime in their battalion.

Nikos was sweetly encouraging, but he was a severe critic, like one of those angels taking his axe to the root of the tree. He could impinge a writer in a sentence or two without malice, but like blowing a smoke-ring, and I often thought that conversation with him was like a long August journey in some provincial railway train. Only when we were alone it was almost exclusively literary: about the aesthetic quality in Éluard which he thought a weakness, or about Spanish and Greek folksong, or about Dylan Thomas who aroused his curiosity, or about the nuances of English words for a wood or a coppice or a forest. I sent him once a book by David Jones which surprised him and he liked it: it was a triumph ever to surprise him about poetry, though he purred and grinned to strangers like a tabby-cat. To look at as a young man he had a startling resemblance to Paul Celan, but as he grew older his white forehead reared into an enormous dome, and huge black rings developed under his eyes. He could have been a Frenchman or maybe a Turk, but his name was Italian (from its Greek spelling) and his blood apparently Greek.

Although he had dried up, in that he very seldom attempted to write formal poetry any more, yet he knew exactly the value of *Amorgos*, and there was nothing dried up about his conversation. The reason for this must be that he calmly and gently used the tears of angels and muses, and what Lorca calls *duende*, in his popular songs. I have some reason to think that he knew the value of those too: he was secretly gleeful about them, proud of their professionalism, and in the end he allowed the book. But I remember one hot afternoon at Flocca's when there was an absurd happening called the strike of composers. The radio or the government had attempted to ban some song for reasons of political colour, so all the composers were to forbid the use of their songs on the radio. Mikis Theodorakis and Manos Hadzidakis were to meet at Flocca's to shake hands in front of the cameras, though to do so they needed two separate tables side by side. Nikos sat in his corner making jokes, one of which was, 'I have been on strike as a poet for forty years, but no one has noticed.'

He was buried in his village, where he had always felt at home and happy. Like Edward Lear he had never married, perhaps for the same reason, because by the time he was rich enough he felt it was too late. I do not think he was ever paid properly, except maybe by his record company; his publisher would not on principle pay a poet, however many editions he went through. Nikos's heart was in Arcadia, but after whatever result education had on him, and then the exile to Athens of his student years, he sought out the president of the students' Arcadian society for precise information and suggestions about local Arcadian words. That was at the time of *Amorgos* or *Blood Wedding*, but those are not dialect poetry: certain words have a naive or provincial ring, but every word is immediately intelligible at one reading or hearing. That is his strength in language, a kind of iron-wristed tact and a mastery (in a tongue that then had no proper dictionary) of very wide resources, from every level of that tongue.

Giorgis had known him and admired him, and had treasured his praise, but was rather tongue-tied when they were first introduced, which was late in the day: I know all the same that he treasured Nikos's praises and regretted having not seen more of him. I saw him so much because I frequented Flocca's in search of him in the afternoons. One of my happiest memories of him is an earthquake-smitten evening in a recording studio, when the singer who was scarcely out of school had brought with her a small white dog on a red lead and Nikos took charge of it while the girl did her singing in a plastic box. Nikos wandered around with an inane grin, introducing the dog round the studio. Giorgis was as anxious as I was to visit the grave where Nikos had gone to ground at last. His Zakynthian friend, who had suddenly materialised in Pyrgos, wanted to come as well. It would be fair to say Nikos was loved and respected beyond the bounds of his acquaintance. I had caught the infection from Dom and Henrietta before I had ever met him, and I shall never know such a master again.

> . . . Therefore, young men, with the wine in your mouth
> with kisses and with green leaves in your mouth
> go down, be naked in the water-streams
> as the woodworker tracks the grain of the wood,
> and as the adder from the barley gardens
> comes out with fury in her superb eyes,
> and as the lightning threshes out our youth.
> Do not laugh, do not weep, do not rejoice.

That is a fragment of *Amorgos*, of which the best translation is by Sally Purcell, and the most easily available by Keeley and Sherrard in the Penguin *Four Greek Poets*. The lines I quote are from a lamentation I wrote for Nikos, which is in *The Rags of Time* (1994). That poem gives a vignette of how I imagined his village to be before we went there: it was not quite so poor as I supposed and the road where the inn was does not really go nowhere, but the thin blossom of the mountain pear and the dry thunder in the stone mountains are right, because they are essentially Arcadian landscape and Asea is certainly that. As for his songs, they are as light as feathers and untranslatable. Here is an attempt.

> The northern star goes out
> and the hill rises
> the circling river of light
> in heaven surprises.
> The children are asleep
> under the fruit tree
> I kiss their eyes and drop
> a tear down heavily.

The train has gone now
and you have gone now
gold honey of wild bees
gold honey of wild bees.
The train has disappeared
and you have disappeared
to an island of peace
to an island of peace.

From the summer you have taken
in your tiny hand unshaken
that low star to which I waken
and gone to another country.
And after dreams I run
for you my only one
water that will not run
in springs so freshly.

The train has gone now
and you have gone now.

I translated this at random from one of his earliest songs; it is made
of nothing at all but an idea of music, and I have never heard its
music. It gives no idea of his funniness or his power, nor of the
young man Orestes flying at nightfall like a bird to the darker
trees, or the mysterious chorus, 'they whisper and his brothers
weep for him'. But there is not and never was anyone else who
could write lyrics that flowed and sang as they flowed, like his. It
is true that in a world with so few great composers Greece has
been spectacularly blessed since 1945 in Hadzidakis and Theodorakis with their enchanting gifts, but also in having Nikos Gatsos,
who never ceased to be the beautiful ruins of a very great poet.

All the same none of us knew quite the best way to get to Asea,
so that we were luckily forced to use a map; this is something that
Greeks seldom do, except for the crudest road-maps, because

good maps are even rarer and more recent than good roads. I suspect even so that Asea owes its place on the maps to its name as an ancient site. On my map it appears once on the main road, once a little way north of the road, with capital letters and the sign of an ancient temple (which it has not got), and once as a simple village on a different road altogether. We set off by way of Epitalion, the village where Takis Sinopoulos was born. His family house has been pulled down to make a square, where a man was selling enormous Alpheios fish from a box from the back of a motor cycle. T. Sinopoulos Road is a queer little back alley between houses that must once have come out at the doctor's back door. Still, one must not complain, because Byblos Street in Athens where our friend the novelist Iannis Tsirkas lived, on the edge of a wood somewhere behind the Hilton, has now been renamed Iannis Tsirkas Street, but it has only four houses in it because it ends at a cliff. The way to Asea turned out to lead by excellent roads. You turned off the southern highway before Kyparissia as if you were taking the new, quicker route to Kalamata, but after the long, straight drive to a point near Hagia Florina you turned your back on Messenia and headed uphill into the Arcadian mountains towards Megalopolis.

We had gone right round Lykaion and Lykosura, where the grizzly cult was based, and the games of Lykaon used to be celebrated (there is no doubt they were proud of the old wolf-man in ancient times), and came out at Megalopolis, in sight of the cooling towers, like the ones at Didcot, which for thirty years or nearly have been such a landmark of the central Arcadian plain; only their beautiful pink and white stripes have faded a little. After a difficult meander through the suburbs of Megalopolis, past the football stadium and some enormous garages, we came suddenly on a disquieting monument to two hundred and forty innocent Greek hostages who were shot there by the Germans. These smaller mountains were quite high in the end, about a thousand metres, and from them we swooped down on Asea, and the road to Tripolis. Further to the north lay Mainalos, the mountain of Virgil and of pastoral Pan. It means Mad Mountain, a condition said to be caused by the nymphs in lonely places, and possibly cured by a local mountain river: but where ritual and practical belief become entangled in saga, where entertainment takes a fatal precedence over mythology, one had best abandon the trail. Athens has a mad mountain of its own, and a famous cave where madness was cured: but this is Trellovouno, which the romantic modern Greeks say is because of its crazy colours at sunset. In fact its ancient name was Hymettos, and the Italians in the akropolis in the middle ages called it Monte Imetto, which became Monte Matto, and was retranslated into Greek as Trellovouno. Mainalos is a beautiful word, and a beautiful mountain which I wandered over in the past looking for the tracks Pausanias followed: just below it lies the Arcadian Orchomenos, the southernmost place in Arcadia according to Homer. He ignores towns such as Asea and Lykosoura as the empty grazing grounds of poor shepherds.

Lower Asea trails an unlovely length along the main road. You pass on your north side the deserted *khani* of the Gatsos family, the small inn building or shop building which might have been designed by Prince Albert. Twin flights of steps lead up to the front door and below them lies a dark, arched entrance probably for barrels. On either side of the front door at the top of the steps, which is a blue double door, are the two windows, plain with eight panes each. It is a small and moving piece of architecture, once white and picked out in blue, and tiled. Behind it and to one side there are bigger, low, rambling buildings which once must have sheltered men and animals, for which there were also large yards. The impression is that of a very small, nineteenth-century Russian hotel, like the *khani* of the Pasternaks at Odessa only more austere. The frontal view is purely neoclassic, although without columns or pediments. It was admirably designed in its day, and it is still a rare and beautiful wreck to encounter. It is quite silent now and wholly deserted. The only café left in the lower village is a run-down-looking establishment, full of nothing and empty whenever we passed it, which must belong to a cousin, since the proprietor's name, E. Gatsos, was over the door.

The four miles or so uphill to Asea itself were extremely pleasant, except for a rather raw new graveyard on the first hillside. The village itself is settled comfortably in a saucer of hills, with bright green crops in every direction on the hillsides except for the background, which was a small mountainside of glittering stone scree. Somewhere up there lay the ruins the Swedes had dug; their remote quietness was their main defence of course, until in the warlike Hellenistic period Megalopolis was founded. Inside the village near the war memorial was a shop that showed signs of recent activity; it said it sold everything, and was run by Barbadimis of Akourastos: old uncle Simon the Unweariable. He was not there and the village was almost completely deserted, but I did spot one very beautiful, old-fashioned house nearby, and that turned out to be Nikos's. It was quite deserted and the garden was overrun. The doorway was one or two storeys off the ground, with solid wooden outside stairs to approach it, but there was no one there: only at the foot of the stairs there was a rank of tall, very fine, white irises in bloom. The place looked like what it was, a good old substantial house in the country, where an innkeeper or a farmer might live; it had a court for animals and a rough orchard, in fact it was not without a certain ragged or austere grandeur. The windows were tall and shuttered.

It had long been abandoned as the whole village had. We met an old man of seventy on a tractor, who reckoned he was the youngest man left. The villages are going out like lights, he said. We did see two little boys all the same, being delivered by car from school, but there were only the two of them. Not that they minded, they were happily engaged in bug-hunting and long running games as if this were 1920, not 1995. All around the village it was spring, but there was a huge quiet. We took the lane, which was a track really, leading to the cemetery, and on into the fields. It was a pine wood turning suddenly to cypress when it got near. On the other side, nearer the village, was a field of spring wheat, with some red anemones round the edge on our side. You could hear the faint dang and dang-dang of a sheep-bell from an old ewe in the yard of a small stone hut higher up towards the mountain. The cemetery was an elegant old place, with its own white chapel and a long, sheltered bench for sitting out. There were some old family tombs and plots, two monumental family tomb houses of marble and a plot behind the chapel where four or five of the Gatsos family had their tombs together. The oldest was born about 1860 and I think he was Nikos's father, more than one of the old ladies had lived to be over ninety; one was aunt Aphrodite, of whom I remember hearing, one Dina, who married, and beside them lay Nikos. I had nothing to leave him but a little wild rosemary. It was a very peaceful place.

We found out in the village that Nikos had once had a crippled brother and it was remembered that for a long time he used to bring flowers to his mother's grave, without any kind of show. It was an extremely correct and old-fashioned place. Each of the two bells on the chapel had its own dedication and its notice. Nikos must have gone away to Athens before he was twenty: and long before that he must have gone to the grammar school ten miles away or more, in Tripolis. We did see the name Gatsos over a shop in Tripolis, which made us wonder whether he boarded with cousins in the town as a schoolboy. That does seem likely, as there were no buses before the war to serve a village so remote, and no regular carriers. In that case he suffered the illusion of living in two worlds, as I did as a boy, of which the chief disadvantage is that you seldom or never make real friends at home, and few lasting friends at school. No doubt Nikos was a strange little boy, and to some degree must have felt cut off from his roots at upper Asea. I was extremely glad to have seen it: I could not have imagined it, or invented such a beautiful place for him to be brought up: even the memory of it comes to me like a gift.

It was easy enough to get from Asea to Tripolis, but once we had got there we were plunged into farcical frustrations about getting lunch. The first problem was an unnerving system of one-way roads. Then Giorgis sent Kostas our driver off to find a place or information about one. When he came back Giorgis had already asked a lad, who assured us that lunch was to be had in a certain suburb. We got there, found a grand and horrible eatery among pine trees, explored for a place said to lie behind it, but that was shut, drove on to a village and youths with billiard cues came and stared at us as we were told that was shut too. We went back into the heart of Tripolis, passing the little notice again that whispered in my heart Archaeological Museum, it was late and we were hungry, but we were determined. I see I have forgotten to mention a restaurant that said Open but was not and a frightening chicken place on the Champ de Mars where the owner was apparently mad. We drove three times round the Pedion Areos (Champ de Mars) opposite the law court, and by three quite different routes around the intricacies of the one-way system, before at last we discovered a place to leave the car, and walked the two hundred yards or so to the restaurant Kostas had found the name of in the first place. It looked highly unpromising, like a Swiss chalet, and probably shut. Some more experienced traveller than me has already said that when things are at their worst in Greece, suddenly you are consoled from an unexpected direction, and that is what happened.

The place is called the Park Sale, which means Parc Chalet, or Chalet in the Park. The cooking was the best in the European style I have ever encountered in Greece outside Athens (and there rarely). The wooden walls inside had been hideously overdecorated, but we were too tired to care. All the same it was strange to see a miniature balcony without room to stand tucked in under the roof. We ate a salad which arrived masked in a pink sauce, but contrary to our low expectations it was delicious: even Nikos would have approved of it. Then I had steak with mushrooms,

Kostas had canelloni, Theodora had a pilaff, and Giorgis had a huge pork chop with a pepper-and-wine sauce. The wine we drank was from a grape called moschophilero, which tasted like the secret ingredient in New Zealand Sauvignon, its smell was dry and fresh at once. The whole bill came to about five pounds. On the way home Giorgis slept happily, while I tried to write a poem about a mule and the moon, and how it swam away to Zakynthos; I think it must have been in Greek. We passed a very robust old lady with five goats on individual leads, an old man with three of the same, which looked quite enough to me, then an old woman side-saddle on a big donkey leading a smaller one with a string, but going where? To her olive trees? It was a mystery.

We did not quite get home. We went and sat at the café on the beach near Sacharo, with our feet almost in the water; there we sat with Vangelis the dentist, who gave me an excellent poem he had written me, and his wife Maria fresh from Italy, who told us all about the hellish sufferings of taking a child from Ancona to Florence via Bologna, which were new to her. She was impressive on the subject, but I did not think it fair to complain that you cannot go straight through the mountains from Ancona, you have to go round. We argued a bit about the diplomatic languages of Europe, which were in the news because the French wanted to reduce the number, and to start by excluding Greek. This typical bit of French bloody-mindedness annoyed Giorgis as well, and my attempt to foresee the hell of having to learn Serbian, Polish and other imminent languages as well as Portuguese and the rest fell on stony ground, while when I truthfully expressed my own longing for all foreigners to stop talking English at once, because we are happy to learn French, I was scorned. Nikos Gatsos always said if he were dictator the first decree he would enforce would be to forbid the Greeks to learn foreign languages, and I suppose Giorgis has a not dissimilar view. I suppose what I really think is that the French position is appalling bad manners, but I do see their point.

It was half-past eight in the evening when we got home, and Mitsa had begun to be anxious. Even two or three white iris Theodora gave her did not really mollify her. I had stupidly said when asked one day that I liked calf's liver, so that evening we ate large lumps of tough liver called calf's liver, but not 'milk-calf's', which you have to specify. When I asked if that was easy to find, since at our village butcher's in England we never see it, Mitsa replied happily, 'They don't sell it, they keep it for themselves and eat it at home, like we used to do.' Her father had a flock of forty cows, and Giorgis's father used to buy all his milk from them, for his *zacharoplasteion*. A television interview was beginning to threaten. I had agreed to it out of politeness but hoped it would never occur. Alas, it was going to be next day at five in the evening, because on the day after we were really going to Zakynthos with Theodora. Meanwhile Giorgis was going to spy out a hotel for me, because soon Charis would be coming home with his fiancée from Athens for Greek Holy Week and Easter.

Titos Patrikios whom I never met, who had given the lecture on Giorgis's poetry at the town hall, that building of such terrific grandeur given to Pyrgos by Latsos, was the son of two National Theatre actors whom Nikos would have known, but I did not. The theatre was part of the worldly life of Nikos, like his choice of restaurants and the way waiters idolised him and were terrified, where he swam swanlike and confident and I of course could never follow him, yet Nikos the Modern Citizen, the Parisian or New Yorker, had been an essential aspect of him. Patrikios had been (unlike Nikos) a left-wing Paris sociologist, who had been to prison after the war for belonging to the wrong splinter of the resistance. In France there was not much resistance until 1943, but in Greece it had begun before Greece was invaded and before 1939, against the local fascist dictator Metaxas. Patrikios, whose name pleases me anyway because he sounds like an Irishman, had been sentenced to death by the Germans. He spoke on tape of the modern phenomenon of poets who do not write striking lines that we all remember, or even single poems, but an oeuvre, poetry. I had heard something similar said by John Berger, and in another sense from Nikos Gatsos, and had thought it true. Now when I heard it on a tape of Patrikios I thought that what had died with Nikos had been somehow a world.

Titos mentioned Photos Paschalinos, who was killed at about thirty for sheltering English soldiers. He was to me a new piece of the Greek mosaic, and I was glad he was a good poet, though I do not suppose Nikos had ever heard of him: his book was extremely rare until Giorgis had it reprinted at Pyrgos.

> I have known some young people in the provinces
> who live without purpose but quietly and to the full,
> they do not know a lot they are not learned in love
> and some of them really never went to school . . .

> . . . Inside their shops they never stop working
> and some work hard and long and without mirth,
> but whatever you tell them, they won't understand
> the meaning of this life, the joy of the earth.

His poetry is a monument of Greek pre-war provincial life, of the rise perhaps of an intelligent and articulate middle class, and I suppose of a Marxist view of the provincial proletariat, as seen by an intellectual who was one of them. As the poet was silenced there is no arguing with him. The casual mood and the easy flow of his sentences put him in place as a disciple of Karyotakis, an admirably sour and abrasive poet before the war, when that was most needed. He is just a little like Larkin, but the same variety flowers out of his tough-looking provincial roots. The poetry of Paschalinos is as light as a flower, it might never have been noticed, and yet one does not forget it as one may forget the poetry of equally admirable human beings.

There was a doctor for example who called at the house, an excellent children's doctor, a paediatrician. He came with his hands full of poems, while I was drawing lilies, which reach a certain stage in Greece two months before they do in England, when they are irresistibly drawable and virginal. His parents were Asia Minor refugees in the exchange of populations with Turkey in the Twenties, and his father shepherded a few sheep, on Mitsa's father's farm, with eight children in one small room: now they are all professors and so on, all of them have money, only the doctor has this incurable wound, that he bleeds poems without end and to my mind quite unmemorably. Perhaps it is a clash of cultures: I had an Arab friend who swore to me that every schoolmaster in the near and middle and far and furthest east wrote poems, none of the poems were memorable but none of the schoolmasters could write prose. It sounds a happy world in a way, as far as it goes.

The television interview was fraught at first. We could not find a taxi, or the right building, which turned out to be next to a ravishing ruined neoclassic library building with weeds growing out of it. Then we could not find the right floor, but we got there in the end, and the journalist turned out to be an elderly one I had known for twenty years or more. He and a single cameraman took the interview with a couple of wobbly cardboard columns to suggest the Parthenon and the Elgin marbles. It all passed off very easily and we returned to normal life, past the ruined library and an equally ancient and ruinous grocer's shop on the other side of the street, past the brand-new library; we picked our way over some surprising obstacles made of cement, past stacks of motor cycles, to an ouzo in the square. There were a few big bangs in the square, the first of many, because Easter was coming, but otherwise central Pyrgos a week or two before Easter is just a slightly livelier Chipping Norton, with more motor bikes and bars like Italian ones, and more polite converse. That night we watched a Russian film about gypsies which Giorgis had on tape: the views of the steppe were spectacular, the horses were fine, but the Greek translation was unimpressive and Giorgis fell asleep and I do not remember the end. I wrote in my diary that those people, with their intensely erotic stares, were really less good than the horses, who were much more erotic as well (this view is dangerously subjective no doubt) and 'the film, which had much music, did seem very long'.

I was certainly still dreaming that evening about Nikos Gatsos's village. It was as if a quest was over, as if I had tracked him down, and yet he was still laughing at the idea. Someone had told us how he had given Nikos the Arcadian dialect word bitteralmond, and yet there in the poem you could see him call it the bitter almond: surely Nikos was right, surely in a way it is even obvious he was right? There are similar choices in the Dorset dialect poems of the adorable but wildly eccentric William Barnes, and in a few daring dialect poems of Hardy and of Tennyson. One cannot claim as a foreigner to have the same sense of what works and what does not as so subtle a poet and so fine a judge as Nikos. One may say at least this: Nikos wrote his great early poem *Amorgos* for Greeks and in Greek, and it is about all Greeks, not in Arcadian or for or about Arcadians exclusively: 'a little wheat for the festival, a little wine for memory, a little water for the dust'. It was that single line more than anything else that hooked me: the simplicity of it, the sadness, and a kind of frugality or poetry which it has, even a kind of human wisdom.

I have already said my own goodbye to Nikos in verse. Before I had seen Asea, I imagined that like the souls of our predecessors his soul has flown west into the sunset; it was there that I said my goodbye to him. The verse is mine but the images were from Inuit art, from the snows of Canada.

> The falling sun whose yellow hair half seen
> spangles the sea-water's unlighted green
> dives to the west and limit of all things:
> the murmurous air remurmurs with swan-wings,
> midnight draws on the suffering spirit

to where world-wandering seas dumbly repeat
the infinite purgations of the waves:
to the mind's ocean, where the ice-cap heaves
his mountainous white crest to the snow star,
and music and all voices come from far.
The friend of man is ice-cliffed, or owl-faced,
and the slow horn-beaked raven is the priest.
It is into that country we shall go,
and when we have been sprinkled with that snow,
and come to where pure suns swim in their west,
our soul shall settle on a place of rest.

5 : *Zakynthos*

I HAD been focusing the slow, inaccurate machinery of my mind and reading on Zakynthos for what felt like an age of the world, because I was conscious of having gone to Corfu for the first time on a sudden impulse years ago, and ever since then I had been catching up on things I should have known and done and seen. Corfu came to me as a complete dream I suppose, because it was already in the early Fifties Lawrence Durrell's island, then much later his brother Gerald's, and it had taken me time to break out of that dream. In the same way a hundred or two hundred years ago, you would have been subject to the still more compelling dreams of Byron's Greece. Only W. M. Leake, the archaeologist and professional soldier, was tough-minded enough to brush that aside, and he was Byron's contemporary. He had an adventurous time too, carrying orders signed by Nelson aboard *Victory* to British ships to help him, and collecting notes of what naval timber was then standing in Epirus, and an eye-witness account of the Souli campaign written by a Greek but in Latin.

Timber brings us back to the problems of Zakynthos. The truth is that practically nothing is known of the island in antiquity and whatever ruins may exist rest undisturbed in the earth. In historical times, Zakynthos dodged and weaved a little in the constant attempt to find powerful protectors. The only authority on prehistoric Zakynthos was the formidable Miss Benton in 1932. The Augustan

Strabo said it was a fruitful place, and encyclopaedic Pliny in the *Natural History* wrote of its harbour town as productive and magnificent. But Homer says it was wooded, he says so in a line three times repeated in the *Odyssey*, copied in the Homeric hymns, and translated in the *Aeneid, nemorosa*, forested. The line is 'Doulychion and Sami and forested Zakynthos', and it does not have to mean more than 'windy Troy' or the 'helm-crested Achaians'. In fact Zakynthos rises to a great height and we have no evidence that anyone ever deforested it: who knows? To Homer it was only a smudge on the horizon, a remote member of the kingdom of Odysseus. Yet as Giorgis wrote in a haiku,

> Zeno observed,
> Place then does not exist.
> Do you think that is true?

It is only the most dubious kind of help to be told that Zakynthos was once transfigured to a colony in Spain where it was pronounced Saguntum by the Spanish. Wretched Pausanias, to whom I am bound by loyalty, tries to tie Psophis in Arcadia to Zakynthos, but Psophis is far inland, and his argument, which was no doubt inherited, was a piece of sophistry about place names. I feel an urge to call it psophistry. It is also Pausanias who assures us that the name of Samiko comes from the temple of Poseidon on Samos: are we to believe him there? What about the city stormed by the Romans that gave its name to the Homeric Sami, in 'Doulychion and Sami and forested Zakynthos'? That Sami is a name for what we know and Homer in the *Iliad* knew as Kephallonia. Might that not more easily be the origin of the queer Samiko on the coast of Triphylia which is under the sea-sand now? We do not know the date of its destruction. We must take these things as we find them, and Zakynthos also as we find it: the southernmost landfall except for distant Kythera, home of Aphrodite and the seals, of all the Ionian islands, which belonged for about four hundred years to Venice, raided by the Turks, 'liberated' by Napoleon, and administered with some pleasing idiocy but more shameful cruelty by the English for the first half (roughly) of the nineteenth century. In Zakynthos we get no help from history and none from archaeology.

We would get much more help from archaeology on Kythera, where the poor, storm-swept island was a crucial link between the mainland, that is, Sparta, and Crete, whose mountains are visible on clear days from the top of Kythera. They have dug there in the last few years, to find the material links in the bronze age in which archaeologists delight, and some evidence of the nasty ritual cannibalism of those times, so it is thought. They have traced the use of exported Spartan stone, and discovered a fine little bronze scorpion, on whom the learned mind will no doubt linger long. It put me in mind of the little coiled snake found at a site called Lissos in Crete, half-buried in a feast of shepherds at Easter, who were going up into the mountains when I was there: the snake was inscribed Asklas and the site had been an early sanctuary of Asklepios. I shudder to think what a scorpion might be thought to cure.

We have no such news of Zakynthos, only a few words of a song that Korydon sings in the fourth Idyll of Theokritos: I praise Kroton, he says, 'and Zakynthos is a lovely city, and so is the Lakinian shrine that faces the dawn, where Aigon the boxer ate eighty loaves all on his own'. The temple had a wood and flocks, and stood on a cape near Kroton, still named Nau after it. There was once some connection between Kroton and Zakynthos, if only a link of sympathy, because they both issued coins that showed Herakles strangling snakes nonchalantly with one hand though he is a youth in an armchair, not in his cradle, and that image usually signified an alliance against some Hellenistic tyrant. No one can offer any convincing explanation, and we will do better to resist any temptation to link the coinage to any real or imaginary event in Zakynthian, or for that matter Krotonian, history. The herdsman Korydon was just quoting a popular song, as he had boasted he was able to do. He would never have seen Zakynthos, and the oldest Zakynthos anyone knows now is the white and pinnacled town by the sea painted by Edward Lear, best known to me in the superb coloured print he made which I see every day. *Zante, Zante, fior di Levante!* He rather hated it, I am sorry to say, after the grandeurs of Corfu: he particularly disliked the mercantile complacency of the currant merchants; he said he could not help thinking of those heavenly vineyards as so many desserts and mince-pies and Christmas puddings, laid out in fields.

The sea was as calm as if we had been carrying the dead body of Arthur Hallam. We drove to the quay in a cloud of dust, and waited there for Theodora, whose guests we were. She was having lunch with an old school-friend, Stathis, who turned out to be the Captain of the enormous ferry. Stathis was a tall, fair-haired, Nordic-looking seaman, with the personal authority that goes with rank at sea, but with a sweetness all his own. I think he was rallying round to console Theodora for the death of her ex-husband, he had been a childhood friend and we became a foursome on the island, which they both loved with a consuming passion, something far beyond patriotism and more moving. Stathis and Giorgis had never met before that day, but with Theodora the Captain was on the intimate terms that come from long friendship, although there had never been anything between them, nor was there likely to be since Stathis was married, with children.

Zakynthos is not twenty miles from the coast: indeed she is longer than she is far away, and with a population of thirty thousand twenty years ago she was not overcrowded. The big container lorries on the ferry alarmed me needlessly. All the same, there has been too much building since the earthquake, which was in the Fifties and catastrophic, and now the plain five miles from the harbour town, and the hillsides that overlook it like an old opera house, have filled up with the English. Every island has its own plague of tourists, but this one has for some reason the

English. In the wicked, colonial days there were only seventy English, and now there are more like seven — or can they have said seventy? — thousand in the summer with their pink thighs and their dark glasses and their golf club and their horrible little sailing boats. Other places have the French or the Germans, but the English haunt the ghost of those Ionian coins with Queen Victoria's head on one side and the lion of Venice on the other. But the lion of Venice which the Venetians call the Cat is really an antique bronze Chimaera, part lion and part snake, so that the lion on the coins is not the lion of St Mark, as I believed as a little boy, but a boring, elderly English lion. This year they even appointed a vice-consul. Let us hope he does more for them than the awful Mrs Brooke-Papadopoulos did for me when I was arrested from a Brindisi ferry at Kerkyra: for all she cared I might be languishing in a torture chamber of the Colonels to this day, but luckily that little episode did not last long, and I trust she is dead.

The setting out was easy enough this time, and the view of the castle at Chlemoutsi was fine, although it did not last long. But the shunt backwards and forwards into Zakynthos harbour was alarming, with people's honey eyes masked in dark glasses. At Kalamata admittedly I saw a spectacle shop with two big windows both exclusively full of dark glasses, and there it seemed appropriate to the far south, but here it was as if a racehorse were suddenly wearing them. At the same time, just before we landed, I heard a horrendous argument about new conditions of work imposed by the ferry company: which at the time I understood, and was on the Captain's side, but I made no note of them and now I have forgotten. They are curious, these conversations at sea, sometimes with ships far away and usually quite casual. Once in the Adriatic I heard a ship yelling for help: it was sinking with a cargo of cement that had got wet, it can scarcely have been much bigger than a barge, but we listened calmly and did nothing, because the whole breadth of Greece was between us.

We were hardly out of our ship when we were into the Captain's car and sightseeing. We whizzed to a field of really huge olive trees, planted where the people used to meet for the great local festival of Saint Leipios. They had grown to be really enormous sometimes, bigger than anything I had ever seen on any Greek island. It is certain that the Greeks, and the ancient Athenians in particular, noticed and adored ancient trees. They were proud of the olive on the akropolis which must have been Mycenean, and a survival from the Mycenean palace there. The Athenians had a list of the most ancient oak trees as well, and their most honourable assembly of old men went every year and held a picnic under each one in turn, fulfilling various rites demanded by law. Pausanias notices with veneration the oldest plane tree in the Peloponnese and I think the oldest vine, which almost incredibly survives to this day: it is the size of a swimming bath with a young chapel under the shade of its branches, if they still put out any shade. Yet the nineteenth-century Greeks took some time to start writing in praise of old olive trees. The first poet to do so was Richard Monckton Milnes, the friend of Tennyson, who refers to the silver glistening of the Cathedral-like branches. It is a Wordsworthian idea picked up when he was at Cambridge no doubt, where Wordsworth's brother was the Master of his college. An ode to the olive was circulating in Greek soon afterwards, but I have never seen it. The national poet Solomos yields only his translation of a few lines of Homer, with the bodies of athletes *glykolamporizontes*, or sweet-gleaming, from their rub-down with olive oil. These olives on Zakynthos turned out to be all over the island and deserve a special pilgrimage.

Speeding down a green track soon after we came to an old aqueduct: some of its arches were pointed and some round, so maybe it was Venetian or even Byzantine. Zakynthos has always belonged to whoever could control it by sea, and the Venetian local aristocracy took root there. So far as I know, after one nasty slave-raid early in their occupation, their control of the Ionian islands was undisputed, though the Turks had attacked Corfu as well as Zakynthos. The aqueduct is a thing of wonder today, half drowned in wild flowers, in weeds and flowering bushes. From there we went as far as Porto Roma to the north of the island, past many queer-looking English houses and shops, with even queerer-looking notices, to come to rest at a shut tavern on a grassy hilltop overlooking the clearest of clear blue water: the weeds had been neatly piled up by storms on to the beach, but beyond that you could see the bottom for hundreds of yards out into deep water. We saw the house of Kolokotronis, where he stayed before he set sail for Greece and started the War of Independence. The British did not approve of this anarchic action against the established rule of their Turkish neighbours, so the house was protected by rumours of ghosts to keep people away, and by upper windows for hot oil and shooting, in case of real interference: the house was a fortified tower really. I was pleased to think, as Giorgis was, that when Kolokotronis landed on Greek soil one of the small armed party who met him was Giorgis's own great-great-grandfather. Another of the party was an ancestor of Mitsa. Giorgis had a great-uncle in the next generation who was a lord of many herds, and used to come with his animals once a year to Pyrgos with his gold-mounted pistols in his belt, and set up his tent in the great square, and do business. It was a world surely not unlike that of the first senators of Texas, who set up their wagons round the senate house at Austin, and sat on the fences laughing while the prison burnt down and the fire brigade were unable to put it out.

We passed English houses of some grandeur, though I do not know who chose to live in them. We heard of a happy professor from Glasgow with his wife, who proudly showed a wonderful piece of embroidery they had bought from an old family, which in fact was Chinese and made yesterday. To be honest, we saw no embroidery for sale in the entire island, even in the remotest of cottages, as good as what you would see in the Congregationalist Chapel at Frampton-on-Severn. Admittedly the Chinese do not make the collie dogs on hassocks with their lolling pink tongues, but otherwise they have cornered the market, and not even the Greeks do flowers now as well as us, nor were they ever quite as good at those pathetic one-funnel steamboats from the Frampton–Sharpness canal.

We slept that night in a friend's house, Theodora's was being repaired and Iannis did not seem to mind. His rooms were amazingly like Giorgis's or the Doctor's or those of any friend of theirs, full of modern art, some by friends but some posters from European museums, all in excellent taste. Yet it belonged to a man without any high degree of education, who was the son of an old-clothes man with a horse and cart, a roundologist (*gyrologos*) as the Greeks call him. This house was near the old ghetto, and close to where Theodora was brought up. *The Garden of the Finzi-Continis* in Greek was by the bed, and a small seven-branched candlestick in the living-room, but that had no meaning except that Zakynthos has always been good to its Jews: in the war they were hidden and none were betrayed, and when Theodora and the Captain discussed if any were still alive, I observed that they did so in terms of their first names. The houses are of great grandeur with gardens and breathing space, even in town, though the earthquake of 1953 had of course made a difference. Still you could see all around you the relics of a Venetian colony, the long colonnades outside the shops, the frequent squares and sometimes the wonderful neo-classical architecture. It became obvious where Pyrgos got its good taste. Everywhere lemurine kittens played at hunting and being found in the long grass: they were not wild. A few cows were grazing. I was introduced to *paximadia*, not the rusks of Cretan monasteries of the same name which you have to soak in water, but a kind of currant cake or biscuit which must be what Garibaldi's army were carrying before they sat on them or whatever, so that they were transformed to the Squashed Flies of the English nursery: the original is now to be found only on Zakynthos, and Theodora was a severe critic of which kind was best. It is sad if one must believe that Edward Lear never discovered them.

The Captain was off to sea again and a change of cars was taking place, so I was dumped, not without relief I dare say, in a bookshop that I wanted to see. They had no books about Zakynthos, and none exist except those by the slightly doddering old amateur Oikonomou, a man with the soul of an antiquary as I have, who spent his life producing many tomes about his native place, improving as he went along. That is not such a bad lifework after all. There was a nearly new moon that came out then and it seemed an omen, because that shop, which was called Theoria, turned out all the same to be a treasure-trove of books. It was there I first saw the new edition of Solomos, in one very big volume, too heavy alas to carry or send, by Alexiou, most brilliant of editors, whose Cretan books and *Erotokritos* I have. They sold wonderful books, some of which I am still cursing my folly for not buying, some of which I bought. When I could find nothing even about the churches of Zakynthos, the lady in charge pulled out an illustrated booklet about a study of them by schoolchildren and gave it to me. It turned out to contain the most thrilling information that none of the four of us knew anything about and Oikonomou also missed. Let it wait for its proper place, because at that moment I just simpered and said thank you, without realising what I had been given. Thank God I got the lady to sign it: she was called Vicky Apostolatou.

There was still light enough to go up to Solomos's monument in the evening air. The view was pleasant but it must once have been better, because some Greek American, of the school of Harry Fournarakis but with more money, had just built an imitation, not quite exact, of Jefferson's Monticello on the opposite hill. I have long been an admirer of the original, but this thing is a real pig for grossness. The terrace where Solomos's monument stands carries two quotations from his verses, one moving enough, but the other a kind of Christmas-card verse. It is curious what a difference those few miles make, but I suppose it is really the years and not the miles that make them, between Solomos on the lovely leaping light whose gleaming beams, or whatever, and dear old, dour old Ritsos with his sufferings and his Communism, whose monument is Monemvasia and the sea, and who wrote of the light in the mountains during the resistance: 'There is no water, there is only light.'

We came down by Foscolo's house at the corner: it is fair to say that if Solomos had gone on writing his poetry in Italian he would never have much outdone Foscolo: a few obscure verses in the *Oxford Book* would be his memorial. But his reputation goes on climbing. 'Porphyras', as Alexiou has printed it, makes far better sense now, and George Seferis's intuition that a great poem underlay the ruin has been confirmed. Solomos once had several houses in Zakynthos, but his principal one, which appeared to be a pleasant Regency sort of place, was locked and guarded and newly fenced in. The nobility never really got on with the people in Zakynthos; the register of their genealogies in the Libro d'Oro was gleefully destroyed in a populist rising, and although Napoleon abolished all ranks and feudal rights whatsoever in so many words, in 1805 his reign was over, and in the early thirties, I am sorry to say, the English restored all inherited titles, whether local or Venetian. It was one of the more amiable of their acts of misgovernment I suppose.

The castle still has its lion of St Mark over an inner gateway, but he was shut away for the night. We peered up at the strong walls and down at Lear's view of Ithaca, only that the bare hill opposite is not as bare or barren as it looks, and the town no longer sprouts that wonderful multitude of white rococo minarets, which were not minarets really but bell-towers, and now are dust. It must have been the most entrancing place in the world in its day, which probably was between Trafalgar and 1840. When it was Byzantine in the middle ages it was a poorer place, but it has shared the decline of the West in the last hundred years, I mean of course the architectural, topographical, physical decline, more slowly than mainland Greece, and even in 1953 when the earthquake struck, the Zakynthians, surely alone among all peoples, calmly proceeded to rebuild the whole place as nearly as they could exactly as it was. So the bones of it are perfect, and I noticed only one grossly modern hotel in the main square. It now takes a connoisseur to tell the difference in date between the genuine survival preserved by a miracle, like the Bank of Greece in that same square, and the pink-and-white library opposite which is newly restored, colonnade and all. All that has gone is Lear's path that leads downhill into his picture from the girl in the olive grove; it disappeared in a landslide in the earthquake, so now you must follow the winding route of what must once have been a donkey track.

We ate at a restaurant called the Arekia, with Maria who was a close girlfriend of Theodora's, and the Captain, but not only did he have another hour-and-a-half trip to do, he agreed to travel the same sea yet again late at night to take someone's parents from Zakynthos to the site of their sons' motor smash somewhere near Pyrgos. The Captain reappeared the next morning looking as dazed as you would expect, but he had slept a few hours in a cabin on the ship. The restaurant was very surprising. It was small and decorated with pictures and prints, including a good one of a shoot with dogs, and a terribly bad landscape of Lear's view. In fact it turned out they knew nothing about Lear, no one we met in Zakynthos had heard of his view of the island, not even the galleries or librarians. They did know all about the view which they said was Sergeant's. He is spelt anything from Sergeant to Sarjint, and he was a travelling English artist who did some copper or steel line engravings of this island and probably painted it some thirty years before Lear's visit. I did not much like his work but his album has been reproduced and it is an excellent witness to how the place once was.

The food was ordinary but genuine. But the truly amazing

thing about the restaurant, which is named after the local habit of singing impromptu couplets, was the noise, which really was incredible, and all produced by three or four singers, one very old and gloomy, one a fisherman, all barrel-chested basses, who reminded me of the Spanish composer and Civil War general Gustavo Duran, who used to say with approval of such singers that you could see their back teeth. Indeed he told me once of a poem of mine that it was the first time he had seen my back teeth. When the idiosyncratic music was over and we were on the pavement, the darkest and most barrel-chested of all of them was disappearing up the cement stairs of a flat, when suddenly from sheer high spirits he roared out some favourite chorus in tones to set the dolphins leaping with fright.

The next morning we woke slowly, but with pure eyes and clear heads, and wandered across the road to the shop for children's clothes run by our host of the night before. His father wandered into the sunshine under the arcade where the shop had a better entrance, chewing a biscuit (*paximadi*) and nodding a good morning to everyone who greeted him. It was a lazy and happy start to the day. Giorgis sat at a school desk which was part of the decor of the clothes shop, having sat in just such a desk as a little boy before the war. The town was like the nicest town in Italy, or a favoured region of Paris itself, with its shadowy arcades, only it had a seaside prettiness and sunniness of its own. We went to the art gallery, where my diary is incoherent with enthusiasm. I do remember two or three magnificent bronze-age pots and a few bits of marble tombs, one with two miniature columns and a little pediment, sheltering a relief carving of a naked man on a rock staring out to sea, and just the prow of a boat approaching. Is it a drowned sailor or a fisherman with hand to brow, staring for a shoal? Why is he sitting on a pile of rocks? Most of the gallery is full of ecclesiastical art, the loot really of the earthquake churches. There were five hundred in the city of Zakynthos alone, and the working people were divided into guilds; the barrel-makers for example had their own, and so had every trade. Each one beauti-fied its own church; the system was much the same as it was in England until the end of the sixteenth century, and an important key to the system of welfare, of apprenticeship and of taxation. It has been studied best, I think, in a book about the charities and foundations of Venice.

That gallery contains the little ikon where the Friendly Society took their oath up by the castle in a chapel under the noses of the British garrison. This society is the famous alliance to undertake to restore Greek independence by force of arms, which succeeded in the war of 1821; but I seem to have been more impressed by Jonah and the Whale: 'Eighteenth-century Jonah with bell-tower smoking like factory chimney. Whale a dragon-dolphin, grey and dirt-blue landscape, deep blue sea.' What I think was most striking was the twists and turns of Greek painters in the Venetian tra-dition, and their constant regressions to the wilder waters of Byzantium. Kantouris for example was a 'Venetian' painter who liked to incorporate his cat. He was a priest, because he had been in youth a satirist, and someone threw vitriol in his face, so he could never go about in society again, or so he felt. Kantouris painted Saint Luke painting, and I wondered whether that might be a self-portrait. But the most memorable discovery was not among the Veneto-Cretans or any of those late, formal Saints who are almost merely Venetian: it was a painting from the only place in the eighteenth-century churches of the Greeks which was still awaiting proper decoration in the eighteenth century.

This was the balcony for unmarried women. I have heard of those balconies in synagogues, and it is well known from the plots of operas that the Sunday expedition to church was fraught for Christian girls, because it was the only time your lover could spot you or your prospective bridegroom or seducer could measure you up. I have known a woman who never left her house and garden in Albania except for church, until suddenly one day she was married off to Manchester. The balcony for these unmarried women is not usual and may well have been an innovation in Zakynthian churches, where it is not universal by any means. Unless I am mistaken, the decoration of these balconies on the island is unique, though there is a Canaletto procession of the Order of the Bath at Westminster that recalls the processions of Zakynthos. The easiest example to see is hanging above the entrance desk of the art gallery and this may well be the oldest: it is by the early-eighteenth-century painter Ioannis Korais. They all represent what the Greeks call Litanies, that is, grand ecclesiastical processions, either of a guild or a parish or both, with the ikon carried under a canopy as the Sacrament is carried by Roman Catholics.

There is no proper study of these very beautiful depictions, though for their landscape and townscape art alone they are of the greatest interest: I do not know which is more fascinating, their witness to a former appearance of buildings now utterly altered or to the appearance of the people, of all classes of a society now dead and gone. Two were reproduced in the booklet from the Second Zakynthos Highschool (1994) which I was given. In the Korais, grandeur predominates, the priests are numerous and splendidly robed in yellow or rose or green with embroidered stoles and silver-knobbed staves, some are embroidered all over like flower-gardens, they look as high-minded as the Fellows of an Oxford college in procession. The military guard of honour is in red tunics with red stockings and black boots and huge black hats, the tunics have fine embroidered emblems and gold piping so that they must be a sort of guild. Their wigs are full-bottomed affairs and they hold enormous drawn scimitars of polished steel that reflects their red uniforms. A boy trots beside the priests, singing from a book. The canopy-bearers appear to be lawyers or judges, one has very long linen or silk bands over his black gown, another, which is certainly a portrait, wears his black gown open to show the same red uniform as the guard of honour. People are staring out of all the windows in the green- or yellow-stuccoed town houses, and small wonder. The last of these remarkable long images of processions is illustrated in the same booklet and it seemed to me more improbable and more striking still, but we got to see it later, and it is really far stronger as a work of art than its illustrations.

At the bottom of some stairs we found the marble plaque of a gentleman called Samuel Stranis from 1812, looking exactly as if it were in Christ Church Cathedral: his family were friends of Solomos and the hill where the monument is still bears their name. I think it was the vividness of the men in the processions that aroused my curiosity about these outmoded aristocrats, and the curiosity increased at the Solomos museum, which has the poet's inkwell and tobacco jar and his Ariosto and his manuscripts. The papers do not look at all easy, and the other possessions are moving only because they are so ordinary: I no longer smoke a pipe but an Ariosto of that size is just what I have been looking for. Downstairs they show you the tombs of the poets, Kalvos and Solomos. The room is marmoreally gloomy and intended for something close to worship. Solomos gave money for the War of Independence, Kalvos died a poor man in Louth, and was brought home within my memory by the help of George Seferis: he will rest more easily in Zakynthos, and between them they are the link between the Greek tradition as it was in the eighteenth century and the way it has flowered now. At the door of this small museum, which was opened just for us at lunch-time, is the wooden figure-head of a ship. She is a mermaid four or five feet high with one hand catching at her wind-blown hair and the other clutching the tail of the dolphin or dragon she is standing on, to cover her lower parts. She is a spirited design, from the galley *Judith*, one of two volunteer ships from Zakynthos that fought at Lepanto in 1571. Chesterton would have liked her and so did I.

The Verdea wine that Solomos favoured turned out to be excellent, and I shall not drag the reader round all the sights of the town, either the green beard of trees on the castle mound, or the alarming cannon pointed straight at whoever enters the main door of the library, the ikons in the Solomos museum (where Sergeant is to be found), or the way the shadow falls across the square by St Mark's Catholic church. Solomos was a member of the Ionian Academy of Kerkyra, an offshoot of that peculiar university run by Lord Guilford in a toga and a laurel wreath, which did not alas long outlive him. That was the only common ground where Lear and Solomos might have met, had the painter known a little more Greek. Lear came to Corfu only to try to comfort Lushington for the death of his brother at Malta, whom everyone, including probably Lear, had loved much more; when Lear had followed the judge to Corfu and learnt Greek, the Greek poet had just died, but by then he had taken from the mouths of Cretan fiddlers, often blind, who sat outside the doors of the wineshops in the sun, the style of Greek folksongs and of the *Erotokritos*; in that popular poetry slept the seeds. Then home he went to a bottle or two of Verdea and wrestled with the possibilities of the Greek language, which it is fair to say he transformed and extended in his poetry beyond expectation. Where there might have been, would have been, a break in the tradition of Greek, there is a vigorous and sappy stem.

Our afternoon's excursion was into wilder country past the church of Phaneromeni, a lovely small church inside the city, near the corner where a Saint was born. It was completely rebuilt stone by stone to look as it did in the eighteenth century after the 1953 earthquake. We drove out among olive trees, up English-looking lanes drowning in flowers, skidding to a halt now and then while the Captain leapt out for various myrtles and wild peppers and bright miniature gladioli like the wild flowers in Cornwall, but of the most vivid red. He gasped like a boy at the contrasted colours of green and the weaving of light and shade on the vines and the olives: it was a new-created world on that day, and the spring light made the mid-afternoon like perpetual morning. We climbed up into the hills at Machairada, the church where popular revolution broke out before the French revolution, when the Libro d'Oro, symbol of the Venetian shackles, was destroyed. It was a beautiful place with a fine stone tower of many storeys and a balcony and windows so that you wanted to live in it. The church itself was full of elaborate gilded woodwork, which is the Zakynthian speciality, and lit by a huge chandelier. The pictures were unashamedly Venetian, the Princesses finding Moses in the bull-rushes for example, with pyramids and a black servant with feathers in her hair. The crossing of the Red Sea had a Roman drowning in a tidal wave, a wonderful thunderbolt striking and a rainbow flashing in heaven. The church courtyard smelt deliciously of its bitter orange trees.

From there we made a determined onslaught on the village of Skoulikado (Ear-ring?) by many twists and turns and villages, and to find the priest, who was young and modest and working in his garden. He opened the church for us to see the balcony painting by an Italian schoolmaster called Nikolao Visconti, whose work is otherwise quite unknown. As a schoolmster he worked at Katas-tari, which is another village nearby in the hills, and that is all we know. An inscription tells us that 'This procession (*protzision*) was done at the expense of Doctor (*Dotorou*) Ioannis Bios of Kerkyra (*Korfiati*) for the Virgin at Skoulikado, Aug. 23, 1828'. It was the Octave of the Assumption. Someone called Spyridon de Biazis has noted that a number of the faces are portraits, including Visconti, the Doctor and Hector the Kephallenian, who is hitting someone with his rod, and it is said that everyone recognised an old woman called Perliro. The painting is not straight like one by Korais but convex, like the swelling box of a theatre, in this case a screened gallery for young women.

The procession is led by banners, white cross on red ground; at this stage it looks like a revolution, with the boys with candles straining forward and just one white cross banner on a blue ground to recall the Greek flag. The people look exalted but the landscape is skilful and realistic. The priests and their attendants have a more operatic appearance than the earlier ones, the little boys are charming, both the well and the badly behaved. The most impressive bit of painting is the nobility or gentry in a group. They are the only example I know of portraits of this social group at this period except for paintings of meets or court paintings which are never as good. The formidable black sobriety of most of the coats, the whiteness of the linen, the chaste tones of the other coats and the haircuts would make one think they were a crowd at some Duke's funeral or dinner at Trinity, Cambridge, in Tennyson's first year, were it not for their long white candles. The women follow them in another dense group. In the background stands the church as it once was, in its full rococo glory. We were told it was destroyed by earthquake and had to be rebuilt later in the century. The canopy covering the priest who carries the ikon seems to be borne by the grandest of the gentry. The welcoming committee greets them arriving at the church, which is probably the same procession in miniature, all there was room for. But it is the solemnity of the faces that impresses, their concentration. Someone is flying a red flag with a white cross from the top of a cypress tree. In spirit this is a million miles away, and yet physically the young men might almost be the solemn-eyed youths who gallop their horses on the Parthenon frieze. It is certainly a most beautiful monument of art, and a staggering insight into the prosperous and civilised society of Zakynthos as it was in August 1828. How Byzantine the faces are, yet how modern, how very Greek.

We were all equally impressed by the balcony painting. Perhaps somewhere an analogy will turn up, in the theatre or a church or a synagogue. The rest of the church is impressive too. We saw an ikon of the 1830s or so that had an early renaissance clarity and more of the true quality of great painting than the original from which it was apparently copied, but of course it was unsigned. The church was lit by two candelabras of cloudy glass and two of bright brass. There was a throne with a giant, overtoppling canopy

of elaborate woodwork like a galleon come to rest. The bells in
the tower were Venetian, as the Greek guns were in 1821. The
only puzzle about the usual tale in the Ionian islands, that all iron
had to come from Venice, is the ironwork of certain balconies:
but after all Nauplion, where Greek-cast iron normally comes
from, is no nearer than Venice by sea and a more dangerous
journey round Cape Matapan. It was with regret that we left that
remarkable little church; the priest and his brother zoomed away
in their van back to their patch of ground, and we plunged into a
deep surf of flowers: broad green and white thistles, goat-horns
barely showing, glimpses of cows and even of the sea.

We descended on Halykes, a beach with a quay to the north
beyond Katastari, where I am told the English swarm and go
bright red. From here we took to the hills again, not just the low
crest above the harbour where the pretty churches are with the
rococo bell-towers, but we traversed the island, through a world
of mountains, stone huts and dry-stone walls. You could see the
evening sun stroking the hillsides and probing the deep valleys and
mountains as he descended. We came down to a village of great
beauty, much more Peloponnesian in feel, to a plane tree, which
is a rarity in Zakynthos, and then to the hugest, oldest olive I have
ever seen. It has split into four trees, but its circumference is simply
gigantic: it must be easily more than two thousand years old. At
Exochori we passed a field with twenty wells, all private, so that
every family excavates and owns one: naturally there is plenty of
village chatter in this field on washing day. Then with a sudden,
unnerving swerve in the dark up what was not quite a track, we
came to rest in the shadow of Theodora's house, among wild
flowers as if the rocks themselves had chosen to flower. The
Captain uncurled himself from behind the wheel and sniffed the
sea. It was faintly glimmering to the west, towards Italy.

Complete silence, not a sheep-bell, not a wave. Simple and
intense colours among the rocks, that was all. We had just passed a
herd of sheep on the road and they were silent, even the dogs and

the chickens of the mountain villages were utterly silent. The setting sun played with huge shadows, but the highest mountain on the island, which we had just crossed over, was only about the same height as Nikos Gatsos's grave at Asea. There were not many neighbours to this lonely house, maybe two hundred and twenty-five at Exochori above us and sixty-five at Campi below us, but one or two workmen dropped in morning and evening for a chat and a glass of whisky if Theodora was there. They were pleasant and cheerful men like people in isolated villages in England, but their values were not the same as ours: 'They're not half dead like us,' said one, 'there's hundreds of them up at Exochori.' He brought in some twigs of judas blossom, and argued stubbornly with Theodora over a coloured snake, an *astritis*, a viper, the most poisonous of all, he said, and the most highly coloured. She could not bear it to be persecuted, but he had missed it anyway. I think he hoped for the excitement of a general snake-hunt on the hillside.

It was hard to do anything but sit at a window. The wind got up next morning and cleared a mist, and the view of a little grassy hill or two was of an Irish character, yet there was no doubt there were vipers in the furze and no foxes. What I was anxious to see were the local seals; there are three at the moment, much studied by a French girl for fear they may die out. But I think the truth is, unless you find where they breed you can never really be certain how many there are. Why should they frequent that nasty island of Mykonos? Perhaps they actually like what passes for music there? The remoter caves of Kythera or Antikythera sound far more likely. The Greeks are at least equally excited by turtles, and the other day I was delighted to hear that a tourist plane from England was stranded at Heathrow because Zakynthos allows no planes to land in the dark during the turtles' breeding season. Apparently what they do is pop their two hundred eggs each into the sand of certain eastward-facing beaches, chosen many centuries ago, and when the numerous eggs crack open the little turtles scurry to the sea by dawn light to find parents and breakfast. But they think any really bright light is dawn and they make for it, and loud noises terrify them, so the Zakynthians shut down their aerodrome altogether until the sun is well up.

That was a fine house to spend a little time. Giorgis wuffled about in his luggage and found some special sausages Mitsa had sent to Theodora. I dived about in the library and discovered a procession on a balcony by Koutouzis of 1766, restored alas in 1865, in St Dionysios by the harbour, and an olive tree bursting open into six trees, no less, at Skinaria, photographed by Oikonomou in volume two (p. 247). I am sad to say he also refers to that magnificent painting by Visconti as 'popular work of the later nineteenth century', but he does notice more ancient columns than I had done.

> I will go to Koukesi:
> Twenty houses you may see.
> And in the middle Bratis's hall
> Which is waiting for a fall.

It has plenty of ancient columns and cavernous barrel-entrances and outdoor steps and upstairs porches, in fact it was a more magnificent version of the Gatsos house. The Captain remembered it well. The Loudzis house at Kato Akrotiri once had a porch with six columns for that matter. Meanwhile Giorgis was writing a poem about a dream of a train going abroad. But that did not excite me as much as the fact that in 1953 an inscription turned up in the ruins of a church that commemorated 'The whole city called Chandax in the famous island of Crete, being under siege by the godless Saracens, in 1657 . . .' Chandax is Heraklion, and this was sent out with written prayers, obliterated now, and hair cut off, to the Virgin of Episkopiani. Twelve years later in 1657 the city and the island fell, less than a hundred years after Lepanto. Here I find a note of a query, 'Where was it we saw a row of Saints and Christ in niches like cardboard cutouts with the hands bent forward in high relief, as Cimabue's do and they do here on crucifixes?'

For lunch we had the magnificent red wine of Exochori, octopus cooked in it and served hot, just as Giorgis's mother used to make it, and sucking kid from the next hillside, with the best-smelling salad of tomato, lettuce and dill. I learnt then the unlikely etymology that *Arekia*, the Zakynthian form of improvised couplets, are so called from *all'orecchio*, in your ear. If that is true they have undergone an amazing magnification in our restaurant, of which Sicilian opera is a thin shadow, and the full-bearded roaring in church is a demure imitation. The biggest noise of all starts at midnight of July the thirty-first for the festival that begins August, when every church bell on the island peals. The songs, as the night and the feasting go on, do sound a touch drunken but people sing from table to table, as they eat what sounds like samphire, chewed raw. Even the Saints in this island have a robust, primitive quality. When Saint Joseph arrived headless from Crete he was simply rebaptised as St John the Baptist and took over his feast. There are Saints like St Thyrsos and St Phrissos (Phrixos?) it is better not to enquire into. Giorgis maintains there is a Saint Anempodistos, the Unstoppable. Theodora has notes on Zakynthian blasphemies, some of them preserving the names of Saints otherwise unheard of. 'I **** the cassock of ****.' Later in Pyrgos I found a prim-looking guidebook to Zakynthian blasphemies, and I must admit I was impressed. 'I **** the heavens and the earth and the universe.' 'I **** the mosquito net of the holy Veronica.'

The landscape gives you the sensation of being luckily left alive in the background of a Lear water-colour, but the white cross on the headland does not mark anything Christian, nor even as I had vaguely supposed was it a Christian take-over of the Mycenean tombs that were found there. It is where fascists used to throw stubborn resisters over the cliff edge, or is it where the resisters threw the stubborn fascists over the cliff edge? The first was likelier, and in that case the myth was barefaced and characteristic: there are nooks and corners of Greece where the only product is lies, and these are of a marvellous elaboration, like the ecclesiastical woodwork on Zakynthos or the gilded poops of the Venetian state barges, and the *Book of Kells* and the *Odyssey*. I was studying crosses: but those I liked best were the starkly, geometrically ornamented iron ones from the last century in a few overgrown graveyards, with a wrought-iron halo and an iron half moon for the name, which swiftly washes from the dark iron like chalk from a blackboard. In the same book of photographs by D. A. Zivas that records these crosses is a section of tall towers in the fields made of straw and reeds held together by fantasy, that used to stand in the vineyards to guard them at night. I have found them described in early Christian antiquity. They were three or four storeys high with primitive ladders to climb them, and Giorgis said they were usually near a tree, to hold them up. Giorgis has slept in one, since they survived in Eleia too, and Stathis said the young used to make love in them, but you had to be lightly built.

> Prospero upon his island
> Cast in a romantic form,
> When his love was fully grown
> He laid his magic down . . .

The lines are from one of those poems written in Lawrence Durrell's personal springtime as a poet, just before and during the war, which have about them, in spite of the large number of scattered Greek place names, a peculiar peace, a kind of silence, almost an awe before the landscape. It is from *Cities, Plains and People* (Beirut, 1943), which contains many lines I have always remembered, because they were my substitute for Greek travels between leaving school in 1948 and getting there at last in 1963. The first line of this poem recalls Virgil's autobiography at the end of a *Georgic*: 'Once in idleness was my beginning.' There are wonderful lines later about the yellow Emperor and his 'veins like imperfect plumbing', which I read now, and the poem ends with two more remarkable and lovely stanzas about Prospero falling asleep on the seashore at the open entrance to his evergreen cell. The sequence was first published in 1946, just in time for me, though it took me five or ten years to discover it.

There was one more photograph in that book which meant something to me personally: a splendid, really a superb baroque window, with an ensign in stone, probably of the donor, and a solid door, to the old Jesuit house of studies on Zakynthos, or as I suppose they would have said Zante, which fell in 1953. There was an unexpected innocence almost amounting to idiocy about those eighteenth-century Jesuits which pervades their lives, all their enterprises and their voluminous controversies, so that it is not surprising that they were attacked by the modern monarchies and efficient ministries and treasuries of Europe, and finally by the bumbling old Papacy itself. Few of them perhaps were like the aged Prospero upon his island. They accumulated the finest collection of coins in Palermo or Naples, and of sea-shells in Brittany or Paris, they introduced gas to Preston in Lancashire and their processions (unrecorded alas) in Latin America included costumes of coloured feathers and live pumas or leopards from the jungle, and great salvoes of fireworks. Those things were only the culture of the age no doubt, and we have no modern equivalent, but two or three hundred years ago, there is no denying one might have had a nice time in Zakynthos, stupefied by piety but finding loopholes here and there. No loophole for secular love all the same, and no poems like Durrell's.

That evening we went down to the sea and inspected the alarming height of the cliffs, three or four hundred feet sheer above the water; later we saw the little court or yard of each house, and the wreath of palms for Palm Sunday stuck in a cranny above the tiny village church. Nikos the gardener sent two large carnations for Giorgis and me from his own greenhouse, to wear on television, but luckily the interview was only on the radio, with a disc jockey, so our self-consciousness was not projected, except that I made Giorgis blush and stumble because I was asked what I thought of him, and I said he was one of the few skilful and great poets alive, and I was very proud to have known him.

> They say there is a mirror in the desert
> and if you go and look in it
> for one second you will see
> your true face
> the shapes you altered as the years went by
> the chasm of your self.

> But I have been and I can tell you
> there is no mirror there at all.
> The desert is the mirror
> and you will not get to see anything.
> It blows out there, it goes on blowing
> your face is quickly ruined like the sand
> you lose your eyesight,
> and you will never see what you once were.

The musical quality of the original is irrecoverable in my version, but the poem, which is a new one, has an attack, and a clarity, and it haunts and terrifies. I liken it to certain terrifying and truthful lines of George Seferis, or to the brief and bitten-off poems that Kavafis sometimes wrote. We climbed up the mountains fast by a good road, by the ting-a-ling of goats and dong-dong of sheep in their families and tribes, past the magnificent tower of Koilomeni, an octagon crowned with stone flowerpots and a ring fence, that rests on an ornamented square storey too tall to be a cube, pierced with four double arches and surrounded with an iron balcony: then three more tall storeys to the ground. Stray flowering weeds grow high up in the stonework and the eight niches of the topmost storey display the emblems of the Passion: the skull to indicate Calvary has an alarmed expression as if it has looked into the desert mirror. The eight corners have each a herm but I doubt whether they are portraits. From the way it sports with light and shade this tower must be called baroque, and yet there are rococo touches about its rich ornamentation. All the same it lacks a spire, which the Greeks call a pyramid, on the roof, it was restored if not designed in 1892, and the entire church is late eighteenth century. As for its title *Koilomenou*, this is a church of Saint Nicholas, and if this queer word does not mean 'in heaven' as in the Latin *coelum*, no sensible suggestion is available. There is a monastic ikon inside called Our Lady of honey, or the Bee Virgin, *Melissiotissa*.

Giorgis knew a fine palace in a back street of this village, like a palace in Vienna or Naples, now restored and guarded and barred. In fact it was distinctly uninviting: when it was more ruined he was lucky enough to get inside, but it has undoubtedly been done up for sale, like a Christmas turkey. It was built for the retirement of a general under King Otto of Greece, who I suppose was a Bavarian with neoclassical tastes, if any, and no intention of being disturbed by the populace. Such a big building must have an inner court, and some shabbily pretty outbuildings were scattered around it, but it had only a Habsburg kind of handsomeness, I felt cold at the sight of its bulk and was relieved when we swooped downhill through the plague of unpretentious modern houses in the plain to our radio studio, where the disc jockey had a motor cycle loaded with vegetables, and spoke of a German wife and a daughter who was a professor of archaeology in Germany. I thought him the liveliest and most charming of men. We were interviewed about one another, and to my alarm about Kalvos, but Giorgis luckily could quote him. I could only say he had the sea in him, but Giorgis added at once, 'And the waves, and horses.' 'Horses, and horses of the sea, white horses.'

When we were free of this duty, Stathis took us careering around the lights of Zakynthos, a huge Happy Easter sign where the Colonels used to spell out their messages above the city, and his own ship, all outlined in lights. A bell-tower like a lighthouse was picked out with white bulbs like St Peter's itself, that St

Sebastian of buildings, leaking and dripping light from every part, outlined in pinpricks of light. We drove up to the castle gate, which used to be a walk as he remembered from youth, of about an hour. There we halted behind the red lights of the Happy Easter sign, and looked down on that other world of the docks, and the still unexplored world of the streets. I think there had been some idea of eating at the top, but the places were all shut, so we returned fortunately to our old restaurant, the Arekia, which was dramatic, I think because of an English family who were guests: it might have been an engagement party with the owner's family. The place was theatrically festive, the songs ear-cracking and acted out like opera. One man had a baby in a pram, but no one seemed to mind. There was a table near the door of old and poor Greeks, one was blind, one was tight and wore his flat cap throughout; a new singer was introduced who was not as clever or professional as the owner, but a gorilla of a man with a voice to match, very pleased with his audience and his reception. He replaced for a time a doleful little fellow who seemed to have stepped straight out of *It Ain't 'Arf Hot Mum*. Madame scuttled here and there, the boy waiter negotiated the pram, one man sat alone in despair all evening.

The songs they sang were beyond praise and belief for what I can only call their genuineness. They would not have been very different from the repertory you might have heard in Zakynthos a hundred years ago or more, and those that were datable seemed to me from about the 1840s. They sang 'Xanthoula', a song by Solomos, set in his lifetime and sung in taverns then, a lyric made of moonlight and sea-spume, a piece of nothing, and yet its persistence has a historical interest, and I have never heard it out of Zakynthos. They sang *Arekia*, the half-traditional and half-impromptu couplets, and a song about a wicked huntsman and a wicked nun, and the old song, though younger than the others, like a Neapolitan boating song, called 'Yialo, Yialo' ('the sea, the sea'). Then they sang an alphabet song and a days-of-the-week song, by no means in their first youth. The song I liked best, and which Giorgis and I both found unforgettable, was quite fresh to all of us. It was a ballad set to or adapted to an old Zakynthian up-anchor song which is a vigorous and jolly tune. The chorus was a 'goodbye to Zakynthos, goodbye to Kerkyra, I shall not see you more'. It was about some prisoners in chains, 'and they put them on a steamer, a steamer, a steamer' (*vapori* was the word) where they were fed on biscuits, 'and took them off to Kerkyra, and hanged them by the neck'. No amount of searching afterwards discovered it in any book. But when was it written and what was it about? I very much fear, although at the time I argued other-wise, that it belongs to the British colonial period: soon after the days when Cartwright painted Lear's view from exactly the same spot, in 1828, but long before Lear's visit in the Sixties.

The first steamboat to enter the Mediterranean came out in the Twenties to help the Greeks towards independence: it was a marvel of the seas under Cochrane, but its boiler blew up before it ever got into action. By the Thirties they were becoming a common enough sight; this one sounds like a member of the British fleet, no doubt in the Forties. The Greeks hated and resented hanging, because the Turks were great hangers: they hanged a Patriarch in Istanbul in the 1821 war, and they went on hanging Greeks from the old Venetian *pharos*, the slim, tall, ruin-ous tower at the entrance to Chania harbour, into the memory of old Cretans who remembered it in the 1960s. King Otto brought an executioner with him from Bavaria, but the common people got rid of him by refusing to sell him bread or to do him any service whatever: he was boycotted. The Germans revived public hangings in the 1940s to everyone's disgust, and of course the silly English still thought it the right way to treat assassins in Cyprus ten years later.

We went home through rain showers and very bright moon-light, a mysterious and beautiful drive past sleeping Venetian villages with preposterous bell-towers, past the dim gleam of woods and the scarcely discerned shapes of the hill pastures, and then the sudden, swift arrival that never ceased to surprise me. We got up late the next morning and explored to the northwards, keeping quite close to the west edge of Zakynthos as long as we could. Our first stop was the favoured and sheltered but now desolate site of the monastery of the Anaphonitria. This had been a solidly fortified abbey, and the gate-tower, now serving as bell-tower, beetled above us. As we pushed open the creaking door, a hen entered first with that portly and portentous waddle of the fattest old mother hens. The cell of St Dionysios was here, the seventeenth-century Saint who was Abbot and is now the patron of the island as Spyridion is of Kerkyra. Dionysios was sainted largely because as Abbot he confessed his brother's murderer who came to the Abbey door, and instead of pursuing the vendetta like anyone else, smuggled him down to the sea and got him away in his Abbot's boat.

Over the arch of the gateway below the tower grew white iris, tall and cool and beautiful. Inside there were roses, three churches all of different sizes, and a vast abandoned open-air wine press. Beyond a pedimented gateway the Abbey lands and groves and fields and farms and gardens stretched for miles, but inside the great court it was still a place of perfect peace and silence. Venetian insignia crumbled on the Abbey wall, and only the smallest church, the family chapel of the Flambouriaris family, was cleaned and tended and open for business. Over everything hung the toppling weight of the Abbey tower, speaking of an older age of the world when this was an outpost of Byzantium. That great empire which took so very long to crumble to dust had controlled southern Italy and reached as far up the coast as Ravenna, where the *exarchate* or governor's palace is still standing. The sea has receded and the ships have gone: Saint Apollinare in Classe was once a harbour church, since *Classe* meant the fleet, and the written records of the Ravenna colony go back to the seventh century. I do not know how far the Abbey of Anaphonitria goes back, but its legends are fifteenth century. If as I suspected it is older still, the truth probably lies deep in the dust of the deeds and charters of abbeys that are kept in the cellars of the Palace of St Michael and St George on Corfu. But no doubt that tower really is fifteenth century, in spite of its weighty appearance of antiquity.

We climbed by car over what was scarcely a track, between fields where there were unlikely clumps of garden flowers at the roadside. Suddenly we came to a cultivated garden or grove of olive trees and onions, with the outer wall lined with little roses and buxom deep-red geraniums. We were looking for this place, which the Captain had wondered about for years; he wanted to find those tall purple wild flowers, wallflowers, which the Greeks call *violettes*, there had been a lot of them growing out of the stones at the Abbey, but here they were cut down: he found only one yellow one, but his face was transported with pleasure at it. We went on for miles, and came on other planted flowers, a lily in a wood and the remains of gardening near St George of the Cliffs. But here (where they are preparing a hostel) we found ourselves in a storm of shooting, all intended for the little pigeons called *trigonia*. They are migrants and they had just arrived: indeed we had seen the first one or two near Theodora's house. But this was a fearful barrage. It was like a shoot at Chatsworth. Small wonder that the convent was tightly barred and shuttered. A stray dog found a bit of bread intended as bird-lure and went away shame-facedly on his own to eat it.

So down we went by fields and weeds and flowers and ploughed fields and village views to Volimes. This place is really three villages one on top of the other, more or less continuously so that you feel hemmed in, but once you sort out which is which they have great charm. We halted for a woman selling embroidery from her house, but it was all rubbish, and the only bit that did look all her own work was a kind of long-stitch embroidery of dull purple daisies, such as one used to see as a child in the milkman's house: I have never liked it as a style, and this was not at all cheap. The arts may be hell, as Larkin remarked, but the crafts are much worse. There was one extremely strange thing about Volimes, which was the church of Saint Paraskevi, Saint Friday, that is. It was founded in 1584, and the bell-tower built in 1683, but in 1733 it had to be rebuilt, and in 1953 the whole thing, bell-tower and all, disappeared so that they survive now only in photographs. There was until 1953 a procession painted on the women's balcony. It has now all been rebuilt and the people are extremely proud of it. But what I take to be this new, restored church is precisely the village church of Skoulikado as it appears in the 1828 painting by Visconti. The windows and the doorway are exactly the ones photographed at Volimes. At Skoulikado they tell you their church must have looked as it does in Visconti's painting 'before the earthquake'. From the one church to the other would be a mountain walk of five or ten miles, and the dedications of the two churches are not the same, so we should rule out a procession between the two churches. I am sure this is just a puzzle and not a mystery, but it is a bewildering one. When we were in Volimes I did no more than glance at the church, so I discovered the anomaly only just now, and I can see no solution, unless Visconti was a portrait painter who simply copied his landscape and the church with it from the painting at Volimes? Or can this balcony painting have been rescued from ruins in 1953 and exactly fitted Skoulikado?

One never gets to the end of anything except time. We ran downhill to Korythi and the Papal island of Saint Nicholas, which used to be a monastery and so the Pope owns it to this day. It would be worth founding some ichthyophagous and slippery order to keep up the good tradition. We did our best, by having a large and most unexpected lunch at a restaurant that looks out at the island. A little further toward the north tip of Zakynthos lies a grotto to which tourists are taken to see the seals. The Captain assured us that to stink like a seal is proverbial in Greek, and Giorgis supported him, though Theodora had never heard of it.

My hypothesis is that since the ancient Greeks used rennet for cheese-making that came from seal-liver, then the man in Theokritos in the seventh Idyll who stinks of rennet is thought to stink of seal, and that this queer idea, since seals do not stink, comes from a scene in the *Odyssey*, where they do stink most vilely. So I was thrilled that the superstition lives on in Greek. I have smelt whatever there was to smell around baby seals, and been close to fully grown ones in the sea, though always in Scotland, and was never offended by any stink. Perhaps they got their name here on the island of St Nicholas, because they are called *monachus monachus*. Homer just supposed they might stink because of the cheese smell, I assume.

About five miles from the harbour town suburban development begins, with all the devastation you could imagine to the lonely sea-beaches. At Saint Dionysius in the town we found two priests or monks singing away at full blast, in voices that at least summoned up a distinct memory of the *Arekia*. I noticed, and so did Giorgis independently, that they were singing the office like cantata, with a dramatic sense that you felt might at any moment burst out into the full flower of Italian opera. It was most enjoyable. The famous procession painting on the balcony was rather in the dark, and I could not make it out properly, but you could see it had a fine calligraphic sort of rhythm to it with a crescendo in the middle. I did not go to visit the dead body of the poor Saint, since I felt embarrassed. Giorgis has been in the past, but his taxi-man told him then that everyone in Zakynthos lights a candle here if they have business, and then they all spend the rest of the day blaspheming against him, which they do (as we said) with an extraordinary ingenuity, quite untroubled by bashfulness. There were crowds and crowds of candles alight that afternoon, and I did dare to light another two or three. There were a lot of worshippers and two little cherubs of twelve in red silk holding candles came purposefully out of the sacristy as we were leaving.

We had to race to the quay as the rain strengthened, though

luckily they cannot leave port without the Captain. The rain, as it turned out, was merely the prelude to a rough evening. She rolled and swooped and bucked and cow-kicked as if she enjoyed it. A coffee-cup slid and broke on the bridge and as the weather got worse Stathis became calmer and twinkle-eyed. We were told the weather promised to get worse still tomorrow. So we said our sad, swift goodbyes, and Zakynthos began to fade, to wither into the state of a happy dream. I thought of the city with all its colonnades, and of the great library of the Roma family where now only an old woman survives to hold the fort, and she has to be locked in by a servant every night for fear of burglars. That is near the lovely little church called the Blessed Virgin of the Angels. I suppose true civilisation begins now only with those villages untouched or less touched by earthquake. New houses sprawl across the plain, but old ones nestle among uncropped vegetation, unpruned and elderly trees. Zakynthos and Kerkyra I'll never see again.

We got back to Pyrgos in the rain and the dusk, passing the same lonely trees and small woods that we always did pass, and often in failing light, and a few rivers and the little vineyards barely sprouting green leaf. It was what they call wolf-light, *entre le chien et le loup*. I felt as if I had been away from Pyrgos for a year, and now Giorgis dropped me at the Pantheon hotel and for the first time, I suppose, since I had left England I was alone. In England it was Easter Sunday, so I knew Deirdre would have got home from Cornwall, where she had been for about a fortnight. I managed to telephone her successfully: now that I am old I feel almost ashamed to be so in love, for fear it may be an imposition, so the phone call was a great relief. I saw Charis too that evening, still looking about eighteen, and when he smiles younger: in fact my language with him was mostly not Greek but only looks and grins. He had arrived home on Saturday, so it was as well we had gone to Zakynthos when we did and Mitsa had him to herself for a day. But my head was still full of the island, the yellow-headed wild parsley in the north, the Scottish kind of landscape up there and the olive trees split into four like the one at Exochori and surely two thousand or more years old. Someone, the Captain, I think, had told me a pathetic story, a folktale or a song, about a girl who was sold for a bunch of parsley. I wrote down her name in big letters, indeed I may have been writing a poem about her: she was called the *Selinopoulemeni*. But I have quite forgotten everything about her. I just remember where we were in the car, as far to the north as we got, near Skinari below Karythi, with the yellow heads of the wild parsley under the walls beside the road.

It was a long time before I stopped dreaming about the strange variety of that island, and it has remained unique; I have never known a place like it, or at all like it. It was a play within a play.

6 : The Storm Passes

ZAKYNTHOS had meant little to me, though I remembered the horror of the earthquake in the mid-Fifties, until I saw it as a tantalising tongue of land from the Lyra as the sun went down. I had known it was the birthplace of Solomos, but I had never grasped quite how singular a society it had been. Its beauty I had recognised only through Lear, more than twenty years after that beauty had been devastated in 1953. It has been for me just one of the many cloudy islands, the many shifting silhouettes in the sea, that lay between Odysseus and home. There are said to be a thousand Greek islands that are inhabited, and I am sure there are some hundreds of British islands, Orkneys, Hebrides, Scillies and the rest, seal sanctuaries grazed by goats and places inhabited by the most innocent of the Irish. There is something in common between us. Now I felt a renewed hunger to be going home, like Du Bellay in his triumphant sonnet to his friend Dilliers.

> Je voy (Dilliers) je voy serener la tempeste,
> Je voy le vieil Proté son troppeau refermer,
> Je voy le verd Triton s'egaier sur la mer,
> Et voy l'Astre jumeau flamboier sur ma teste . . .

But that poetry is too full of life, too gambolling and cavorting and jolly and vigorous for a big modern ship: it requires something before 1860. What strikes me now as amazing is how Solomos, an early-Victorian Greek gentleman after all, a writer of Italian literature in impeccable neoclassic taste, could turn himself into the fountainhead of modern Greek poetry that he became, and hold a serious conversation with the poetry of the renaissance: because the *Erotokritos*, which I was now rereading for the first time in years, is essentially a renaissance poem, with the same intimacy and charm, and full-bloodedness and vigour of Du Bellay on his journey home. It is as long as an epic, and a story Shakespeare, who did not live quite long enough, would have relished. It has naturally been misunderstood in many ways in every modern period, even by Kalvos who was dismissive, and by all those scholarly Greeks who fought for one language which everyone should speak and learn at school. You see their problem in the Babylon of Byzantios: while the English were falling in love with dialects as Tennyson and Barnes and Hardy did, the Greeks were fighting for the life of the one Greek language that existed only as an ideal, and did not become a reality until the army with compulsory military service imposed a kind of Peloponnesian compromise, and then the wireless nailed it in place and the television, I suppose, began its decadence.

Solomos had an extremely finely tuned ear for poetry, and it was because he could hear the poetry in it that he became so devoted a servant of the modern Greek language. Giorgis, when we talked of this, was more inclined to think the clue was in his mother, who spoke demotic Greek. But however that may be as a psychological truth, I cannot believe in the neoclassic gentleman cut out of marble in whose breast the native language of Greek poetry was mysteriously struggling into life. The poetry seems to me primary. Maybe that is because it was so to me as a foreigner when I began to learn modern Greek. The prose was on the whole deadly unattractive, and the prosy poetry in the late-Victorian and Georgian modes in Greek gave me a belly-ache: I understood nothing at all then about the genuine problems of the unification of the language. Only recently have I begun to notice how much excellent prose there really was, and observed the increasing difficulties of the language problem in English education, where just the same types of mistake tend to be made as the forgotten and dishonoured generation of pedantic Greeks used to make.

One should probably begin with the folksongs. I see that Giorgis gave me a collection for New Year 1966, and signed it under a poem I then translated, 'In an apple, sweetapple, heavy apple tree . . .', and I was still translating from the same book when we came home from Zakynthos.

> An apple on an apple-tree far gone,
> that's the unmarried when her time has come.

> I can't dance in the middle mother, I can't sleep in the shade
> make my bed in the kitchen yard, make it in the trees,
> and let the blossom drop on me and apples at my feet,
> and let the almond scatter bitter almonds at my head.

These poems have a certain realism and a sour zest that I find in Giorgis Pavlopoulos. Or to take another of these poems, where I have slightly adapted a rhyming word here or there though in a manner that would have been quite acceptable to the singers.

> They sit under the plane tree in the cool:
> they wash and shave and look in the glassy pool,
> they see their beauty and their young courage
> Demos takes one look and the men take five
> and the proud Kostas he looks fifteen times,
> he sees his beauty and his young courage
> all for his pride, all for your young courage,
> and he does not go home at night or to his kin to rest,
> he waits high in the hills, high on the mountain crest.

This is a folksong in the sense that any song may be: there is something eerie about it because of what is left out, and I have confused it further by leaving out the word 'robbers' or outlaws, which these men are, so it is assumed that they will die young, as the word I translate as 'young courage' implies. This is not great poetry, but it is part of the art of popular communication. Was Demos older or just uglier than the others? The plane tree and its little pool have a resonance, and so does the crest where the young man waits. No woman is mentioned and yet they are in mind, in the consciousness of the listener from beginning to end. I mention this folksong because it has a certain irony normally thought to belong to more sophisticated writers: in fact it is the quality of the thing as poetry that arouses one's interest, however simple the elements of it, however conventional the game may be that is being played. About this I think Giorgis and I agree.

That first morning in the Hotel Pantheon I was woken by a blaze of light, and since my room had a big balcony I went out on it to see the amphitheatre of hills that lies just inland from Pyrgos, including a clear view of Frenchman's Leap, *Frankopidima*, to which some long-lost romance must have bequeathed a legend, probably in the fourteenth century. I went up there once with the Doctor on one of his strange, brief jaunts from Pyrgos: there was a monastery we did not enter, he just wanted to clear his head of fumes and get the feel of the place, which I do not think he had visited for many years. He told me a wonderful tale about the Leap, which I have now forgotten, and am certain that he made up and embellished in the tradition to which he belonged, that of one of Shakespeare's more sympathetic comic characters. Once in Athens when I was going to climb up the akropolis, he said, 'Only been there twice, and once was with a girl.' My balcony at the Pantheon looked down on a curious junkyard (but all junkyards are curious) on a flat roof-top over a motor-cycle shop. I decided this was really a store or supply dump for the shop, but one day someone climbed up and opened two large packing-cases, from which a pair of killer dogs emerged. On another balcony, higher up and more expensive, lived a young Alsatian who played or longed to play. His game was pulling on a rope, which was bound to bring down a canopy, and possibly the whole building in the end.

Giorgis and I went to the library of which he was President to look for Zakynthos folksongs, but we found nothing like the one we wanted. We did find the blasphemies I have mentioned, including the disreputable 'I **** the chalice of Saint Sophia', in a series of pamphlets called *Flowers from Zakynthos*, recently printed but apparently collected as a lifework. One becomes in the end far more interested in the man than in his collection. Giorgis had some work to do at the library, so I had quite a long time with those blasphemies and queer names for Zakynthine flowers and so on: the kind of material that ought to be computerised, though I discover in myself a depressing tendency to cross-reference it, particularly if it has any connection with the classics. Did the ancients blaspheme in the same way, or is blasphemy a relief reserved for monotheists or for monosexual societies?

Charis came and fetched us with his car, and took us off to Korakochori near the sea, where I had lived for a month or two once with Deirdre and Matthew, not long after getting married. The same sweet old couple were still there, looking exactly the age they were twenty years ago. A few new fences had appeared, and the place seemed neater and more prosperous; but the flowers were exactly the same, the vines were in fresh leaf, and the mulberry where we used to have meals, criticised by a tree-frog, still stood, although it seemed nearer the house than it used to be, so perhaps they had built a new porch, but that was all. The old lady vanished back into her kitchen, where something was boiling over, muttering blessings just as she had brought down on us the blessing of Saint Demetrios to see us through the snows of Yugoslavia, safe home to England. That snow very nearly caught us, it breathed down our necks at Nish and crowned the crests south of Croatia. We got to Salzburg in a freezing fog and drove all the way from there to Munich and far north of Munich through bare forests outlined with frost and icicles. Luckily my wife is a first-class driver.

At the far end, the northern end of Hagios Andreas bay, the slow chewing and crunching of the sea has broken down the rock barrier, so that what used to be a rocky and skeletal arm of the bay is now a rocky island. We looked out at the blue sea and the long foam where the waves seemed to be attacking the bigger island of Tigani itself, and Charis could see Zakynthos beyond it where my ageing eyes could no longer make it out. I felt reduced to the permanent post-prandial middle age of Auden, who says somewhere of lakes that 'even reciting their names' gives him some comfort, but I am torn between the refrain 'Goodbye to Kerkyra, goodbye to Zakynthos', and the determination that sooner or later I must explore Kephallonia, and rescue Kythera from Baudelaire and de Nerval: Kythera enters European poetry as a myth, in a sea-mist of romantic sentiment; I prefer the clean bit of prose that Durrell wrote about in one of his last books.

We took the car up what was once a rough walking track to Katakolo. The flowering hill beyond Pontikokastro seemed on that morning that it might be the most beautiful hill in the world. Admittedly the intrusive fences had made headway, and small wonder, if they are intended to keep off the 'hunters' who massacre migrating birds, and who now have an asphalt road of their own. That is alarming because property speculation follows tarmac at once, manipulated in the first instance by people like those we encountered that day plotting what trees to fell (quite illegally) around the old Italian blockhouse where they imagine some sumptuous bungalow. What used to be the wooden house of Danil the painter, a local boy who lives in Paris, is now on a road, where once it was a charming and small shack, lost in a wilderness. The Swinburnian cliff-garden of another friend where you would meet quails in the long grass is now an olive grove, wired against the hens next door I suppose, or against the shooters and, as Giorgis called them, the other *maskarades* who now come up the road in their suits. All the same, it is still the most heavenly place, with glimpses of the sea, possessed by an enchantment like the places of childhood, which of course to my old friends and to Charis it is. The cistus used to grow thigh-deep, perhaps it still does, and there are pear trees gone wild from the gardens of forgotten generations.

We descended by the smooth regrettable road to Katakolo, where we hunched over our ouzo in the sun, eating snacks of fresh octopus and a mess of shrimps cooked in cheese. The sun danced up high and the sea glittered contentedly: but Charis said of all that sea where Alpheios runs out, as far as Kyparissia, the sea has gone dead and filthy, so that only Kyllene remains for swimming. He is a sea creature and would know: indeed I had always thought he would have to marry a mermaid, but a fisherman's daughter is near enough. He seldom enters the fouled waters of Hagios Andreas now, though for old times' sake he does sometimes swim out to Tigani, that innocent little island where there were the graves of Christian fishermen with crosses scratched on their pagan plates. The plates were all made wholesale I believe, in Asia Minor, where a factory using slaves in about four or five hundred AD had wiped out all rivals to its thick red wares, but the sea of nearly two thousand years has coloured them a deeper purple. And now as we looked up even Pontikokastro was deep in greenery.

Charis did his best to explain to me his adventures in probability theory, and how to forecast how many raindrops will fall on the surface of the earth. Tennyson's tutor at Cambridge would have been wide-eyed, since he wrote a gigantic work of scholarship on the operation of the tides and what moved them, in all oceans and seas. Darwin was most impressed, but I do not know who else had read it. Charis would grin with pleasure and look up gratefully at the sky, whenever he saw 'one of my raindrops'. In the hour of afternoon sleep, a dull gleam of ochre and white and yellow and saffron houses hemmed me in, the swifts were screaming above the road when nothing else stirred. Belltunes and the broadcast chants of church music echoed and re-echoed for Greek Holy Week, rebounding from the dark bulk of Frankopidima. I remembered another story of the midnight bells of Zakynthos: another night when they ring all over the island is on the thirty-first of August, for the opening of the shooting season and the crash of artillery that must follow. The only relieving thought is that no bird ever nests there now, they are all migrants and in danger perhaps only for one night.

Later we went out to Olympia, just for a ride in the evening, and took the surprising modern road up Drouva: I knew Drouva in the past as a small, secret village where the sheep and goats lived who came down through Olympia every morning and ate all the flowers at or near ground level in the hotel window-boxes. There was a sandy track that led up there where George Seferis had climbed one day in 1962 with Giorgis. He had written a poem later based on a fantasy they had elaborated together about the Centaur priest Pappakentavros, and the nymph or dryad Pitys (the fir tree). He often wrote lighter poems like that: I well remembered the last, written after a walk he took with Giorgis and me on a hilltop near Sounion where he wanted to see an ancient landscape and I had promised there was one. But what he wrote then was 'On Gorse'; it is a terrifying poem. The poem he wrote with Giorgis is published now, in a neater, stronger version, but I treasure a copy of the looser, more casual bit of verse he first wrote, which Giorgis wrote out for me in 1963.

We went up to a hotel called Europa, but it was crammed with tourists and tourist buses: the development was devastating and the expensiveness of all the new, illegal constructions did not redeem them. We had meant to stop for half an hour, but we did not even get out of the car. We sped down the hill again past the deserted railway hotel where perhaps the bees may still buzz in the tall jasmine as the garden falls into ruin, and descended on the Queen Amalia Hotel, the nearest modern equivalent to that elderly and dignified Spap. Queen Amalia's had plenty of tourists but it absorbed them better; it had bees, frogs in very good voice and a lot of wet foliage. It even had the same manager who had been in charge of the Spap Hotel twenty years before; he was our old friend, so our hearts rejoiced to see him. What was even more to my own surprise was that the vast indoor spaces in which the architect had specialised were decorated with a tapestry (1964) of great, autumnal beauty by Ghika, a thing of sheer majesty, and a number of paintings by old Moralis, whom I had always admired in his austere way, who was Ghika's friend. There was even one of those paintings of matchstick men that were once so fashionable, by Gaitis. It is important to be reminded what excellent contemporary Greek painters there have been and are. My favourite was Nikolis Ghika, Giorgis admired Tsarouchis most. Tsarouchis was more in the tradition of the procession paintings of Zakynthos, and those haunted, haunting Byzantine faces. The pictures in the hotel were better than you would have seen even in a public gallery thirty years ago. Even the dry toasted grass and thistles in a pot were in a new and better taste than hotels used to exhibit.

Ghika was born in 1906; he was an aristocrat, and by the twists and turns of the Byzantine aristocracy he was a Romanian nobleman; his father was an admiral and a fiery politician whose verbal onslaught gave one of his enemies a heart attack in the senate. The Admiral cannot have been an easy father, and Nikolis, who was the sweetest of men, must have been an awkward spider-shaped boy, as well as a passionate artist. He took off for Paris at sixteen in 1922, and Cubism became his second nature, not the kind that flourished among exiled Russians but something rigorous and real. Partly it was Greek light, the rigour of it and the sameness of near and far, or as Seferis said, the small image of a rock and a few trees building itself up by repetition over and over again into the sky. He always envied Picasso, no doubt inevitably so, yet he could do and see what Picasso could not. He was, as John Craxton said, born with a naturally searching mind, intelligent, human, inquisitive and daring, with a towering dignity and full of fun. There is almost too much to say about him here, but when he died last year, something seriously important had gone. His sense of form was almost too strong for the art of painting, but he had a sense of what painters call poetry that equalled it. I have a simple sketch he gave me once where the gummed part of a large, unused envelope serves as the sky; it is just a scribble of a few houses on an island, Syros I think, but it conveys an extraordinary and lasting satisfaction, so that I smile whenever my eye catches it as I go downstairs in Gloucestershire. He used to stay on the southern edge of Cumbria which is or was the northern, ragged edge of Lancashire, just under the moors. When it was cold he would be at his easel in his overcoat, tranquilly drawing or painting the views through every window while it snowed outside. There is no ghost I would prefer to see.

Giorgis had never taken the jump of becoming a professional painter though he had come close to it, I believed. He told me how some friends had put his pictures into a competition when he was a very young man, and he had done well enough to be one of twenty painters chosen for a grand public exhibition in Athens, out of eight hundred competing. At the time he was furious and withdrew into his privacy and secrecy, to develop as he must. There may be some analogy in this with his bashfulness about his poetry, which it would be fair to say he has now overcome. Now even his paintings are all over his own house and other people's houses. It was really George Seferis who noticed him and drew him slowly and gently out of his shyness. He had written an essay about that poet which I too thought resonant and memorable and wonderfully unacademic, in a collection called *For Seferis*, some years before the Nobel prize.

That night we went out to a restaurant, with Christos and his son and Charis, where they welcomed us in spite of its being Holy Week. We ate a rustic feast of toast made with oil in the oven, and chops, which produced from Christos the dictum that chops like women call for fingers. His wife and Mitsa had been left at home to their devotions, about which they had formed an alliance. Christos, with his black hair and flashing eyes, turned out to be half Zakynthine, but he did not like those islanders. He said they were not straight, they have too much imagination, they are *fanfarones* and liars; he agreed about their ballad singing and their blasphemies, that was all. If there is some truth in his view, then that may be why they have produced no great artist since Visconti? And why they have noticed even him only in the last four or five years? Poor Visconti never returned to Italy: we do not know that he ever went anywhere; he seems to have lived and died as a village schoolmaster. Towards the end of this meal, Charis was telling me about the disorganisation and disgrace of the University of Lesbos, Samos and Chios, where he had taught once. Then he got the giggles about every chop being a sin, little or withered or fat as it might be.

In the fresh morning sun I began to explore Pyrgos for myself. The town revealed old buildings that were more moving than I had thought, and more moving for the Greek writers I had been reading, Papadimitrakopoulos for example, and of course the songs of Gatsos. Some were grand and dirty survivors of wars and earthquakes, some were that austere and oddly flowering baroque of the 1880s. They might stand alone with one overtopping pine tree, with rose-coloured walls and tall white pilasters (that one belonged to a pair of elderly brothers who had been currant merchants, near the station for Katakolo) or any shade of yellow or ochre. A house might wear its sold pilasters or its cast-iron Nauplion balcony with the heraldic birds rather as a fisherman might wear a rose behind his ear. Or they might have smashed windows and a dishevelled air, and lean upon other buildings, as men in the streets leant up against buildings and smoked. The men wandered about a good deal, but the women were all trudging sternly with bags: their playground was elsewhere. The people in offices and banks were relaxed, but as curious as squirrels over the new English fifty-pound notes. The shops in my street sold wreaths of purple and white artificial lilies (and what a purple) and pink and white plastic carnations under cellophane. I suppose they were for Easter like the wild flowers they use as brushes in southern Russia, 'to sweep away the dew from the eyes of the dead'.

I was much taken by a gangster shirt, black with a thin, bright-green line, but I did not dare buy it. Orange trees were for sale in the first bud of their profuse blossoms, and the freshest of palm trees leaned up on the walls like desperadoes. A lady crossed the road from her place in the shade to stand in the full sun and stare at me, in the hope I might buy a palm tree. We saw all kinds growing in gardens, though mostly at Katakolo, rather as if the sea favoured palm trees as it apparently does at Penzance. There is a touch of the exotic about palm trees all the way from Torquay to Palermo: it is very queer. In a side-street every morning I noticed a long queue of police cars doing nothing, and a crowd of out-of-work-looking men, just hanging about outside offices.

Charis told me I was wrong about the pink house: it was neither the house of two brothers (but I am still convinced it was that) nor the former Achilles Hotel, but the house of an engineer who worked at winemaking. I know there were two of them, with separate doors, and they looked like two old gents in Bath, each making off, one furtively to the betting shop but the other firmly to play bridge. As I sat in the foyer of the Hotel Pantheon over breakfast, reading the *Erotokritos* with increasing enjoyment, though I found it like Spenser's *Faerie Queen* in that it encouraged dozing off, I noticed some fellow-guests dressed in bright-yellow jerseys. They seemed to be Dutch and little by little as they passed again and again they were stripping off more and more of their clothes, until in the end they were as festive as Easter chickens in bright-yellow vest and stockings and skin-tight black shorts. I could not make them out, nor was there any use asking the porter, who was my friend, because he was blind, but later in the day we saw them all at once pelting along the homeward road to Pyrgos on racing bicycles. Either it was a tip-and-run visit to Olympia with no time to dismount, or they had set off in the wrong direction. A lesser mystery that confused me for a time was that the younger son of Mr Kalamatianos was a friend of the younger brother of a boy who worked at the hotel: they sent one another greetings. Thus are the small binding threads of human societies drawn tight, I suppose. The fact is that most people in Pyrgos knew one another.

Off we went to Olympia to the museum, past what must be the house Kunze lived in during the war. The dig house is more privately placed: I have not been there for twenty years, since the days of Mallivitz, but at present I had no wish to chat to the German archaeologists or even to the Greek ones with whom Giorgis is great friends. Their newest triumph is a very subtle new restoration of the Victory of Paionios, which does indeed look masterly now in a way it never did before. This work was done by the sculptor Stelio Trianti, whose wife was the chief Greek archaeologist at Olympia, and I knew about it from the magazine *Alpheios*, which I had been sent a year ago because of a poem, but its effect, which is of amazing freedom and of lightness of rhythm as if she scarcely touched the stone she stood on, is not easily conveyed by photography. As she stands now in stone in the 'new' museum, she is incomparable. As we wandered through trees in bud and a smell of cow-parsley to the museum, I was preoccupied by one of those sharp reminiscences that only smells can conjure up, in this case a sudden memory of boating at school, the oil on the boats and that river smell in the hot, wet early summer of 1947: something I had never thought of before or since. Giorgis was getting more and more fed up with the cattle-like droves of Germans who were being lectured everywhere; he ended up by doing an impression of Charlie Chaplin doing an impression of Hitler and being handed a glass of water which he poured down inside his trousers. That cheered us up.

We liked the museum more than ever; the pair of us even got in free as members of the Greek Society of Authors. The museum was much as it had been, but my memory is bad and some things have been added, so there were plenty of surprises, at least for me. The two great pediments of the temple of Zeus, the restoration of which is a work of supernatural patience and skill by the Germans by the way, seem to raise questions about meaning I can no longer answer confidently, but I am sure their beauty and grace offer a resolution of a kind, probably the only resolution. They do not have a beginning and an end as Homer or even Pindar has, and one can or must move about in them unconfined by time, which is a loss of the artist's perfect control of course, so we may miss the story he intended to tell: I think that with these vast objects I often do. What I am sure of is that the elderly crouching character is a portrait, probably of an artist, not of a priest or prophet. At any rate he is the only one who understands everything, and he does not look happy.

But it is the smaller finds of Olympia that are the most thrilling: the Ganymede being carried off to heaven as stiff as a statue by the god, the *kouroi* from Phigaleia and from the Lyra at Hagios Andreas, of which the second is at least a bit more normal than the queer provincial shape of the first, then the huge cowface of Hera like a pastoral dream, or like Ovid's 'gods are half oxen, oxen are half gods'. The eighth-century Assyrian bronze of Greek animals and captive women dressed in feathers continues to puzzle me. Greek religion and mythology offer no key to the simplest questions about these women, and there is nothing at all like them anywhere else. Are the women African? What are the feathers? I have always been fond of the little Pans in this museum, but there is just one little bronze figure of Zeus to compare with my favourite searching Pan: his left hand is casual, not stiff with muscles and discipline, and his thunderbolt is like a lily to thrash the storm-clouds: he is not exacting ferocious vengeance, just a playful revenge maybe. I had almost said that is my kind of god, but the reader will correct my words to something orthodox. I saw many old friends, mostly goats and horses I admit, and a composite group of bronze lions eating deer that Charis relished. My best friend of all is the little eighth-century lady riding side-saddle in one of the tiniest of bronzes. As for the Paionios, Giorgis said his friend agonised for six months before laying a finger on it: and the result showed it was worth his while to delay so long.

It dates from about 420 BC, but seeing it you think that the story of art ended about then, technique drove out love as it always does in the end, until there is nothing left but technique. The best age for art on this hypothesis would be the sixth century BC, or the time of the Homeric hymns, when philosophy was fragmentary and science still more so. This is a captivating view of things, and inside the museum I can almost believe it. Yet the place contains very little really from that long history of two thousand years, though the best of it, even in the fifth century BC, is vigorous and cheerful and unblushing. The huge exhibition rooms give the impression of a tiny frieze of masterpieces running round them, with crowds of sad-eyed uncomprehending people staring their way dutifully along. I drew nothing, though much tempted, and rather unkindly refused to be photographed in front of a statue with an almond tree behind, giving the excuse of having no wish to blaspheme the gods. We fled into the car-park, where Giorgis did his Chaplin and we all felt better.

Away we went past the hill of Kronos, which we dutifully circled. Kronos's lap was full of white cistus and yellow gorse, and the field in which he stood was full of cow-parsley. By this time the cranesbill was beginning to be over. We stopped at the dam by the gravel works to admire Alpheios in his spring strength making waterfalls and cataracts, with swarms of martins or swallows that looked from above as tiny as the midges they must have been pursuing. We passed through Alpheiousa where the railway bridge is, which Giorgis said used to be a famous place for breeding donkeys. It had the old name Polatsa (I think he said) and the people there still looked like Egyptians. Indeed they do, and Ibrahim Pasha is held responsible. How curious and how terrible all these stories are, but there is no doubt of what he did to this part of the Peloponnese. I know of no place except Ireland where such a terrible history is so vividly remembered.

This back road on the south side of the Alpheios, which it crosses to the left side at the dam where the river is strongest, comes out just south of the Alpheios bridge near Giorgis's house. It passes just under the glens and the still rather hidden valleys and steep little hills where Xenophon, who lived nearby in exile from Athens under Spartan protection, used to hunt. He was genuinely a good huntsman, in days when that was the pursuit and competition of the aristocracy, and of course because it was early in the day, game was still abundant. If you compare Virgil on dogs in the *Georgics* with Xenophon on hunting, you will see what a chasm may yawn between two authors not far distant in time. Virgil does know, probably from Greek poetry, that hounds can make a wonderful, ringing noise almost like rooks in the distance, but he thinks the usefulness of the mastiffs which seem to be the only dogs he knows is only that they will deal with Spanish footpads, who may steal up on you from behind, should you be out walking in Spain. Xenophon really loved the hunting, which was varied, in these foothills of the mountains, but his place of exile was also carefully chosen, like Voltaire's hide-out on the Swiss border, in case things should go wrong for him in Sparta, as they did in the end, and a return to Athens should be a useful move.

Until the other day, even the identity of the small piles of stony ruins here and there in these hills was disputed, the old Kastro temple at Mazi and the small one near it uncovered in the Sixties belonged to Athene, so the idea that it was Xenophon's temple to Diana of the Ephesians is now in disgrace, and the Skillous where Xenophon lived is lost again. Maybe it was Makrisia. Personally I am interested in the site (never excavated) where an old woman from Mazi found a fourth-century bronze deer in the Sixties, and sold it for a pound or two to a travelling dealer from Athens. That was before the earthquake at Mazi; I was in the village a year or two later, but I think the old woman was already dead: she was a herb-gatherer. The deer was not more than three or four feet high, but she sounds as if she belonged to Artemis. Whatever moralists or legalists may say about the old herb-gatherer, I am sure Xenophon would be pleased that the bronze went to her; it is only a pity she got so little for it. In 1985 Mrs Trianti published her doctoral thesis from Saloniki; it was an admirable and most useful publication of which Giorgis luckily for me had a copy. She produces a Makistos inscription to Athene, which at least nails one name into place. There are rather wild arguments about an Artemis bronze in Boston, which is Lakonian work and has a Lakonian inscription on it, but it was perhaps stolen from the overspill of objects from Olympia itself, like the Persian golden bowl, which is certainly Olympian and also now in Boston. There is another lost place called Epeion, which Xenophon says was somewhere between Makistos and Heraia. Mrs Trianti imagines that could be near the queer little hill at Aspra Spitia shaped like a Christmas pudding, but that is what Pausanias calls the Tomb of Koroibos. So there is plenty still to be ruminated in this corner of the world.

Giorgis told us with a modest commentary from Charis the story of how in the middle of the boy's exemplary school career he was summoned as parent to hear a serious complaint. Charis at the time was fourteen and head boy of his class, but some of its members were tough citizens, and when they all went off on a day-trip under a master who was a theology instructor of twenty-three, they armed themselves somewhere with concealable quarter bottles of whisky. They were showing these off in a boastful spirit on the bus, and the theologian confiscated the lot. Their last halt was at Patras, where they refused to get back on the bus unless they got their bottles back. Charis was employed by the others as an official ambassador to try diplomacy, and he did put some clever arguments in favour of compromise, but they landed him in the hottest of hot water. His punishment was commuted in the end to carrying the canopy, or one quarter of it, over the ikon of Saint Demetrios during his school Litany or Procession. He was proud of this adventure and thought it just as funny as his father did. We went that same day to fetch wine for the house, which is best fresh from the barrel. To my surprise we went to the back door of what looked like a private dwelling-house, but it was a tavern all right, with nine gigantic barrels in a big shadowy cellar of a room. We tried to photograph them but I think it was too dark.

Mitsa was getting more preoccupied and more furious with her fasting, which it was apparent was making her ill. She did promise that next time she would ask her priest about it, but at present she was determined to go on to the end. The atmosphere became frenzied and I refused an invitation to go with her to the Cathedral: I was tempted, but memories of old embarrassment and boredom stuck in my throat and I could not do it. This was not the first Easter I had passed with Giorgis, and I still recalled with horror the special entrail soup, which is white and I suppose made with guts boiled up in cream, that I had to face after the fast and the night office. Luckily I had blushed over it enough the last time, so Giorgis had promised I need never eat it again. My excuse was an allergy to hot milk and most white foods, which was accepted as normal if a little queer. The truth is that in addition to that I found the folklore repugnant: they spend all Friday discussing the crucifixion in horrendous detail, with the big moment the 'unnailing', then they spend all Saturday elbow-deep in the guts of slaughtered lambs, which having most elaborately disembowelled, still fasting, they cook up into this horrible concoction that at last in triumph they eat. It is also true (luckily for me) that nowadays I get too tired to stand these night watches and night feasts, so I was excused.

So in the early evening I made a long exploration of Pyrgos and found it to be about the size of Clitheroe nowadays, but in quality more like Preston. Meanwhile the people were gathering, devout and furious, at their Cathedral. Small wonder they let off bombs in the public squares, and it used to be fire-arms as well. Small wonder they used to batter hell out of a figure of Judas. Mitsa is a patient and sweet-tempered lady but as we came towards the latter end of that week, I detected a glowering in her eye, in spite of her fondness for us all. On that night we went to Hagios Ioannis, and then Kostas drove us up some impossible lanes and dirt tracks and back paths to see a friend of Giorgis who was an artist in the usual European sense of the word, an obsessed surrealist. I never found out his name, though very many years ago I had bought a lot of postcards of his work at a gallery in Athens.

He was a friend of the poet Nikos Karouzos whom Philip Sherrard used to admire so much. Karouzos was not easy to meet, though I did see him once or twice at the Brazilian coffee bar, where the poets met for coffee, Elytis blushing and stuttering, Antoniou with his deep sailor's boom, a tattooed ballad writer called Kavvadias, and more writers than I now remember. That was where Elytis and Gatsos met Henry Miller on his first morning in Athens. Karouzos felt wronged because his own books of poetry did not sell and he was poor, but this meant he lived on two bottles of ouzo a day, and after he got well started on that diet his circle contracted to be very bohemian indeed. This artist was a surrealist of the Sixties, a brilliant painter of hallucinating reality like Tsarouchis, but his room was very full of things, like the one where David Jones lived on the hill in Harrow. Like David, he had an oddly youthful grin and an excellent eye: he had bought a boat painting from Kalymnos with his last fiver which would now surely cost thousands and be worth it. Like David again, he got himself entangled over epic subjects which he worked at for three years or more, and he was now changing to become a writer. He was a most enchanting man, though David was one of the greatest artists of this century and he was not that.

But I liked the fact that he had a brush with the Bishop of Tripoli because he had an exhibition there in memory of 1821, including the Blessed Virgin with a musket in one hand and her son in the other. He was also the best Greek photographer, having trained in America. He lived half the year in this shack, and half selling his wares in Athens.

It is amazing what skills lurk in the fingers of the Greeks. Giorgis had enjoyed showing off this friend, for whom he had a special and reserved affection; I think he liked that grin, hidden in that beard. At heart Giorgis is an innocent, frustrated bohemian. We went on to more skill, this time the cooking at the Paraktion: the menu was ordinary, chicken fillets and mushrooms in rice, and then fruit in honey, but the cooking or preparation was remarkable, though the wine also was ordinary and bottled. The moon came up huge and haunting, low over the houses like the moist and floating ghost of a Cheshire cheese. I am told there are thirty-five possible dates for Easter in the present state of things, and no doubt this moon was a signal for one or the other; I think the Roman and the Orthodox churches like their quarrel over this matter, they like it to be slightly magical, as if the right moon came popping up out of a cauldron stirred by his Beatitude or his Holiness.

The next morning a workman in my hotel was polishing the tall glass doors. He had been oiling them and now he was clearing up. He told me he had been a *mastoras*, a master-craftsman at motor maintenance whom the directors of a German factory had tried to lure away. When he left the army in 1975, he had bought an old Plymouth taxi and restored that. 'It was a *tank*,' he said with great pride. Swerving to avoid a child, they had unluckily hit a house and knocked it down. Was anyone hurt inside? No – well, knocked down maybe. The entire corner of the street went. He now prefers the Triumph as a car. He has a squadron-leader for a customer who 'says he likes them to *fly*'. The old blind servant listened to all this with evident approval. He is almost completely blind now, but he tells me the doctors say one must never lose hope and I am oddly comforted to hear it. As for Giorgis, he still had his trigoni feather picked up on Zakynthos at St George of the Cliffs, which was due to be an ingredient in a poem against hunters. On this day the white cliff of Frenchman's Leap was very clear, and would be for the rest of the summer, I suppose.

For some reason I dozed on my balcony into the late morning. Both Giorgis and I were very tired by now and felt the pressure of circumstances more than we had done, what with Easter imminent which made a car less easy to borrow, and the small-town life of Pyrgos. On this actual day Giorgis had to attend a press conference at his library for the launching of a book about Pyrgos under the occupation by Pavlos Sinopoulos, a younger brother of the poet, who can hardly have remembered any of it as he was a little child then I believe, but had certainly read or heard a lot from Giorgis and his elder brother the Doctor: at least that was how I understood the matter. The weather was hotter too, and when I went to meet Giorgis in the great square, I bought a copy of the book about the train to Katakolo, with the feeling that that was the only Pyrgos I aspired to understand. Pavlos's book had not yet arrived in the little shop, which was one of the two central suppliers of newspapers to the town and also a kind of small-scale free public library. It smelt of the piles of fag-ends left by heavy smokers, and it was where I usually met Giorgis.

In my diary I noted blackly that 'On my balcony it is blazing hot now, at about half-past ten in the morning, yet it is queer to imagine how this sun will in time transform all Greece to a desert of toasted thistles. Saw a dappled mule yesterday. I think, as at Exochori on Zakynthos, they are very few now and kept mostly as pets, so prettier coloured ones which used to be rare have come to predominate.' I had begun to repeat myself in this task of journal-keeping, and the truth was I could scarcely last a month at it, after ten days I flagged. I went to meet Giorgis and Pavlos in the square with the editor of *Alpheios*, 'who is going to interview me. I am getting used to this life and had better be careful.' It is useless to give that sort of wise advice to oneself: one might as well relax. For lunch the others had bean soup which looked delicious and I am sure was, but I was given specially cooked flounders, which I felt bad about; Mitsa's eyes were upon me, full of love and disapproval.

Next day Charis's girl would finally arrive from Athens, so this was our afternoon for merrymaking in his car. We chose to go back to Lepreon and the village higher on the hill above it, which was to us unexplored. It was an easy enough route to find it, the road steep and dark in the Gothic gloom of the pines. The place lies in a fold or amphitheatre, as Asea does, with the steepest scree of the mountain above it. It appeared to be on the spring line; you could see the water breaking surface at several points on the hillside with a purity and abundance that in England, or rather southern England, one never sees nowadays. Someone in a fragment of a comic poem sáys that the traveller reaching Attica in antiquity used to know where he was by the taste of the water-springs, which were all different, and I am sure it was so. I believe I would still know the taste of the trickle above the small ruined fort at Phyle, and an old shepherd told me there were a dozen springs in those mountains all with different tastes, any of which he would know at once: he may have been romantic or boastful of course, who knows? Now they empty Welsh springs into English rivers to keep the levels up, so that the people will not notice their manipulations, and the smell of sewage and of chemicals so dear to the heart of governments and of industry will not cause comment. In Hagioi Taxiarchoi there is no such problem yet.

The houses are stone and traditional and of great beauty and mostly abandoned. The school is a fine stone building but closed down now: there are about a hundred and fifty people left alive, but those we saw were extremely old. Yet the purity of the wind, the brilliance of the light, the glitter of the spring pastures and the generosity of the water made the hillside like paradise lost. As for its antiquities, the people deny all knowledge of them; all the same there were several places where you could persuade yourself you observed some traces of more ancient building, whether in the curve of a threshing floor or the foundation of a rock chapel. We did not explore thoroughly, though one could pass days at the task very happily. There were fine springs at a lower church and others high up in the village, and in that cup of the mountains where the houses lay they were sheltered and seemed a favoured and a blessed place. The temple site a mile or two downhill must have been visible for miles and commanded a distant view, and so did the queer little sentry tower that had once stood on an outer bastion of the mountain, where the rock rose up in a lonely parade of defiance between the hillside road and the valley floor, inland of the modern lower village.

That was a curious natural fastness even today, overgrown as it was. The only way up was a precipitous climb worn smooth and muddy by the flocks. At the top there were deep water cisterns, so it was meant to stand a siege if necessary. It was a dangerous scramble for me, but Charis went up and surveyed the miserable ruins and photographed them. This meant he was out of hearing, and Giorgis who was left at the very bottom feared he had disappeared down a hole. I was sitting on a rock at a particularly steep turn of the path where I had decided to go no further. I thought Giorgis might be having a heart attack, since he began shouting for Charis (who could not hear him) in the voice of desperation. This alarming little incident made it clear that more dangerous adventures would have been a mistake, but a glass of the cold water of Lepreon brought Giorgis back to normal, and little by little we all recovered.

We did see the temple site as well that afternoon; it is possible that we did too much. We went to the left round the Mycenean-looking steading and found a far easier if less dramatic route to the temple, which in the course of two or three weeks had changed its wild flowers for a fresh coverlet of new species. The trouble with the lower route to the right, which you will naturally follow if your first intention is to explore the ruination that lies beyond the steading, is that you must keep your footing on unstable stones which are largely overgrown by luxuriant flowering weeds. It is a heavenly place, and on this day the views, particularly from a perching-place Charis discovered on the most distant bit of boundary wall, over which I somehow contrived to peer, were more magnificent than before, and the distant mountains blue and rocky and lunar, at least as I now recall them. Yet I wrote in my journal the next day: 'sun blazing in a kind of blaze of light as it came up, sky blue but ground everywhere steaming with white mist, you could see only the outlines of the hills. But the mountains and hills at Lepreon whenever the sun came out were more beautiful and incredibly, richly green, inviting you like a deep bed to lie on.' I think that must mean a storm-light that shone on the hill opposite and on the valley bottom, and the blue mountains were towards Arcadia, far up the valley. The sun was red-gold and sank swiftly into a low band of purple cloud in the other direction, and that night we dined with the staff of *Alpheios* at Katakolo, which was rather as I imagine dinner with the *Edinburgh Review* would have been, for better as well as worse.

Next morning it was time to send a huge parcel of books by post to England, to avoid carrying them. This had to be done at the post office where Giorgis had warned me I would need supervision. I went alone though, and was lucky, because if you ask for them the authorities will sell you two or three kinds of cardboard box, and the biggest just fitted. But I had come without my glasses, and the old chap in charge could not believe in the simplicity of my address. What is Green? Is it a road? What is your number? When I despaired of this and tried him with St Catherine's College, Oxford, he thought that was worse, because no English postman would know where Oxford was, let alone the College. Still, we reached an agreement, and he was extremely good-tempered, and the parcel very cheap and very swift.

Charis and young Kalamatianos picked me up and swept me down a street with a real stuffed deer and some hunting shops, and the huge face of a record dealer grinning naughtily out of his door, like a tremendously exaggerated and laughing caricature of Nikos Gatsos. We dropped a message at the house of Mitsa's aunt, which I was glad to see. It opened on to a tiny garden, private or public was not clear, with two large and flourishing banana trees about five feet high that were expecting fruit at any time. We found Mitsa at home as usual, with her hair in striking poly-chrome curlers, pink and blue predominating but all glittering in the sunlight. I was pleased to discover that formally speaking I had fasted at the *Alpheios* dinner, having eaten kalamaria, which the church says have no blood, and nor do shrimps, so you can eat them both. And barnacle geese, no doubt.

Christos whisked us all off to Olympia again, because I had expressed a wish to walk round the ruins, and had thought of doing so in Holy Week. This did not work out to be quite as long or as brooding a visit as I had planned, but Christos and Giorgis went off for a coffee, while Charis and his future brother-in-law were left in charge of me. Charis is the discreetest of men, and the brother-in-law young and charming, so we just went for a walk around the ruins which passed off quite well; but there are more strings than there used to be keeping you to the path, and any-where else was left uncut or overgrown, so most of the monu-ments were invisible as well as indecipherable and only the great set pieces of the wrestling school outside the sanctuary, a great square of rough grass between rows of columns defining it, and the temples of Zeus and of Hera, were as deeply satisfying to the imagination as ever: Hera for its grace and Zeus for its weight and power, and the wrestling school to my mind because it is the only convincing monument surviving anywhere to what occupied such a lot of time and energy in the antique world.

One might add the entry to the stadium, but there is a touch of youthfulness about the wrestling school: one cannot imagine the brutal bulk of the professional wrestlers of later times in it, there is something lighter about the pillars that recalls the cricket pavilion and the grass at school, I suppose. I wish we had the practice stadium as well, but that has been partly eaten by the river and partly lies under the road and the car-park. I once found a bit of its stuccoed cornice lying in the water under the riverbank, with the coloured paint still on it. I imagine it is in a cupboard somewhere; otherwise the colour would disappear in fifty years, as it all but has done from the terracotta Zeus with Ganymede under one arm in the museum. The only buildings with decorative plaster to be preserved at all are the Treasuries of the cities of Greece, in a long row like a modest version of Pall Mall, but they do not recall the chapels they once all but were, only the banking establishments they fast became, and so I suppose it is fitting that banks have in the modern world taken over their style of architecture. The line of sacred treasuries ended in the institution that interests me most at Olympia, the oracle: I fear that Delphi overshadowed it. Maybe Olympia was too political a place and it was the snarling and greedy political side of Olympia, a place where money talked and deals were struck, that stretched out a paw and ruined Lepreon and all Triphylia until today they seem mere poetry and birdsong. Olympia has been punished with its mockery of the origins of the games and its millions of tourist coaches and its nasty hotels and idiotic shops. The pleasure-seeker should arrive by train in winter and stay at the Queen Amalia Hotel, and cast a benign eye on the ruins from the abandoned bee-infested garden of the Spap Hotel before plunging in among them.

Before it was dug, when only some bits of Byzantine wall were sticking up out of the ground, which now we would be keen on knowing more about, but the professional archaeologists swept them away in the nineteenth century in order to reach the ancient level some ten feet or so underground, the whole heath-like area was called the elbows, *ankones*, from the elbows and corners of stones sticking up out of the earth. I do not think this means the elbows of statues, though it includes those; it probably means the stray bits or useful corners of buildings that might be used as anchor-stones for small boats, hence Ancona. Still it was easily recognisable as the burial ground of some ancient sanctuary. Now it looks much as it did twenty or thirty years ago, and I found the same problems buzzing in my head when I peered at it again: the water channels, for example, which were everywhere, the huge ash altar which was a vast construction of the puddled ash from sacrificial fires sacred to Zeus. No one knows exactly where it stood and it is hard to find room for it.

'Deep wild flowers and grass had drowned everything but the giant catastrophe of Zeus. All that work buried and forgotten, signs of recent excavation, strings everywhere, otherwise the same.' The work I was doing was to start by becoming familiar with every inscribed stone and seeing how the zones could be divided by period. It was a simple enough preliminary task, but laborious since it included reading the stones. 'Old problems of the ash altar and so on stirred like old toothaches. The temple before the fifth century now buried under Zeus, of which we know nearly nothing.' Its entry was not far from the oracle of Zeus. 'Mechanics of the hippodrome starting gate.' I knew how queer that was from Manilius who describes the movement of the constellations in a poem, making sense at last of the description of this elaborate machine given by Pausanias. I had been delighted to discover that Frazer had written an essay late in life making exactly the same comment, but by now one might expect some help from archaeology, though I had not observed any: yet it must be twenty years since they found the famous starting gate for the racing horses and the chariots.

The beautiful church which had once been the workshop of

Pheidias where he made and decorated the statue of Zeus with his chips of glass and his tiny tools in a little pot that said 'Pheidias', was overrun on this particular day by some cheerful Australians who were not sure what it was. In its day that statue was said to be exactly the Zeus of the *Iliad* shaking his hyacinthine locks; it was said to have added something to human religion. Who knows? The idea we have of the divine is terribly cloudy, and since the renaissance has now played out its hand, the god is no longer to be looked for in realistic human form: but the Greeks had no renaissance, that is what separates them from us. In the Cathedral of Le Puy in Velay, on the route of pilgrimage to Saragossa in Spain, where a Roman marble tomb that was assumed to hold the relics of Saint James had been found by peasants, there is a wall-painting of the Four Liberal Arts, each one enthroned like a Muse or Virgin, and each with a scholar or professor to accept her inspiration kneeling at her feet: that is the renaissance. The four ladies are not really liberal and surely not the quadrivium taught in universities, but they are painted in the fifteenth century, and of impressive beauty, they are exactly what we call the fine art of the renaissance. Yet they are named Grammar, Logic, Rhetoric and Music. That is, they are pure medieval skills, and as for their attendant scholars, Aristotle is listening to Logic, and I do not know who the others are, but I do not expect any of them knew Greek. And I have come to the point where I no longer miss the renaissance in Greece; I prefer the traces of that innocent country which survived in this place for the eight hundred years since 1204, when Constantinople was looted by the Crusaders. As for the picture at Le Puy, of which I have kept a postcard to inspire me for thirty or forty years, I can only say, as greater men have said before me, '*Utinam essem bonus grammaticus*': 'I wish I were a good grammarian'. Once I aspired to all four, but logic and rhetoric have a limited usefulness, the theory of music is beyond me, and I have deep doubts about grammar.

We left Olympia by the Nymphaion of Herodes Atticus, a giant tribute to the genealogy of the imperial family that was also a public fountain in which doubtless the rainbows once swam: but I do not mind so much about not being a skilled Roman genealogist, though I am sure it might cast some light on poetry. Augustus wrote poetry: epigrams and the start of a tragedy about Ajax, but he wrote it in the baths and said that its suicide was by the sponge. Our friends awaited us, and once again it is time to cast away the ashes of past time and face the end of Holy Week. We were among small cottages with roofs like straw hats too big for them, made of reeds. At Pyrgos, when we got there, I found a bit of waste land just opposite the station. It contained, nestling comfortably and all but overgrown, a large, abandoned bus. Near that were two or three tractors and a number of ploughs, some utterly dejected, rusted, ruined, others less so, all of them among tall, untrodden grass and bushes. Huge old warehouses had sixty windows all smashed, and there were old houses abandoned since the last earthquake, once the pride of the south Balkan nineteenth-century baroque, but now only glum and handsome like Spanish dignitaries with bad breath.

There is no doubt I was much stirred by seeing Olympia again, as much by the larger questions about it as by the fascination of the details and the unknowable things. As a festival it must have been a remarkable scene, but as a presence I am deeply suspicious of it and of the ancient Eleians in their mountainous lair. Athens was an attempt to have a city like a perpetual festival, and although the Athenians lived in tiny houses, that blinding white vision of crisp marble hung perpetually over their heads. What was out-of-season Olympia like? Of a remarkable grandeur it appears, with plenty of political and magnificent buildings. The commercial area is still unknown, because it lies towards the Alpheios under ten feet of mud. It must have been full of Eleians, but is it not queer that they have left us not one single intelligible work of literature in their peculiar dialect, not one poem? Perhaps even the herdsmen who took flocks up into the mountains and down again sang in Arcadian.

7 : *When Thou Hast Done,*
Thou Hast Not Done

GOOD Friday in Pyrgos is a daunting thought. Indeed to me that day has been a daunting prospect as long as I can remember. When I was a schoolboy it was a stage in the marathon of stages, of rites and ceremonies leading to Easter. They were almost unintelligible, but some of them were enjoyable, for instance the music of the dark offices, and the splendid lights and colours of the imitation tomb, a special altar crowded and overwhelmed with all the flowers of every garden in the village; only Good Friday was utterly grim, the food was horrible and the priest and the choir banged their books on their pews for what felt like five minutes like children in a furious temper. I think they were simulating the thunder at the death of Christ or the tearing of the temple curtain. In the course of ages everything had come to be celebrated at the wrong time or on the wrong day, just as things are among the Orthodox, and the wartime blackout, when there were no night services in my day, made confusion worse confounded, just as the reformed services have confused and puzzled such persons as myself. I liked the endlessness of the Saturday night ceremony in the old days, though circumstances had moved it to the Saturday morning. But when it was at night and the Resurrection followed, a certain excitement was generated even in the meek London suburbs, and that dramatic moment the Greeks had always treasured. It was like a sudden showerbath in the mysterious waterfall of the River Styx, up some inaccessible, unimaginable mountain.

They marked it in Athens with a salvo of gunfire, and I like the story of the British anthropologist who asked a farmer why he was firing: the answer was 'How else would the corn grow?' One of the most impressive spectacles was the Epitaphios ceremony which represented the burial of the dead Christ, usually a lifelike embroidery of a handsome and nearly naked dead man, which is carried in procession by candlelight to the Cathedral. In Athens every parish was a stream or waterfall of candlelight, and they met in a river of candlelight as they flowed down into the centre of the city. In Pyrgos the processions of the parishes to the Cathedral meet in the crowded square where they arrive one after the other, like a long cascade of small lights. It will be seen that these ceremonies are essentially out of doors, and as secular as they are religious, with stalls in Pyrgos lining the streets, and thunder flashes like bombs going off far louder than the gunfire, which was forbidden long ago. Only the most devout get into the churches, because not everyone will fit, and it is customary for men to stand about in the Cathedral square while their women go inside, at least for the Communion service of Easter. The signal for celebration and the lighting of candles and exchange of 'Christ is risen, He is truly risen', and the breaking loose of a chaos of explosions, is the moment when the priest comes out from the church and sings the Gospel. That is when the women press inside for the last few places.

The secret of the great size and impressiveness of Western Cathedral architecture is that it was meant for special occasions like Easter or the end of a pilgrimage, and to be lit by candles from below, and the closes or large courts outside are for those vast and secular crowds who never press inside the building, but attend a ceremony whose meaning may doubtless be lost or much simplified, and whose nature has become secular: there will be a fair, there will be drinking and special cakes, or (at St Denis near Paris) it will

WHEN THOU HAST DONE, THOU HAST NOT DONE

be the only opportunity to buy parchment for the year. In England the secular and the national nature of these religious celebrations have withered away since the Civil War created nonconformity, so today if you should stray into the precincts of an old Cathedral town, 'These are the backs of the Canons' houses, These are the walks of the Canons' wives, Here the Precentor meditatively browses, God what a waste of human lives.' Orthodoxy in Greece is still a national religion. There was a feeling expressed that Giorgis and I should have gone to pay a state call on the Bishop to congratulate him on Easter, though it was not a serious obligation.

Explosions were mostly at night, increasing as we got nearer Easter like village fireworks closer to Guy Fawkes night, so the Good Friday bells the morning after the Thursday were comparatively lacklustre, though they were numerous. It was as if they were weary of excess by now, just donging vaguely for the half-remembered dead. From my balcony I could look down on hundreds of martins speeding through the electric wires over the empty street, while a few slow swifts glided in their assured circles higher in the sky. I remember that I made the mistake of reading Dante, which confused my Greek for the day. In the morning we were to sit in the main square to greet the exiles, the Pyrgos people who came home in huge numbers to parade up and down the square and to be greeted. The lights were being fixed to play in awful colour-schemes which the children adored, and even the palm trees got a haircut. A palm tree puts on a lot of dead growth of a bushy and unwanted kind, too high to clip by hand but certainly hideous, and they looked much smarter for the attentions of the fire brigade.

Gossip was about the decline of Greek watermelons, of which they have now bred a new type for some obscene commercial reason, by crossing it with kolokythia or zucchini. The result is all-victorious and entirely tasteless. I have now forgotten what the supposed advantage of it is: maybe piplessness. Outside Greece I never eat watermelon more than once a year, but the change is a pity, and I mourn for another of the minor pleasures of summer gone: as if the straw hat no longer existed, or the cuckoo no longer sang in its passion of deception, or one lived too far north to hear the nightingale, which woke me only once this year, but that once was enough, one just likes to be sure of the repertory of things. There was a fearful panic that day over traffic, generated, I think, by the television. Pyrgos is like a harbour town at such a time, in which everyone anxiously questions strangers about the state of the sea outside the bar or the creek, because age-old roots of anxiety are stirred. Traffic in fact was not bad, only the taxis were difficult as they were refusing custom and doing their own Easter shopping. I had bought a healthy armful of red and white lilies and white iris for Mitsa, but waving those was as useless as offering them to a giraffe to eat, or perhaps that elegant animal might have agreed to nibble, but the taxis were stony-eyed. Giorgis says they are most of them villains, and he may be right, but it may be a sign of age and increasing dependence on them, which we both resent. Mitsa was pleased though, when we arrived. She was like a Duchess with little inclinations of the head and a real smile. 'And expensive too,' she said.

The parade of the exiles' return that morning was a real ball. First of all it was very crowded indeed, as if it were the general resurrection of all the dead: there were many relations and at least a dozen young girl-friends of Giorgis, at whom he giggled like a happy schoolboy. Then there was a senator and former Governor of this province, since the title still exists though here its reality has less importance than it has in the forests of Evrytania. This was a savant who had taught Charis mathematics as a boy, but now Charis was at home taking an elaborate shower-bath for his fiancée's arrival. They had boldly told the older generation they were already living together, and since they would do so for the rest of their lives, they saw no point in interrupting that pleasure. The elders were bemused by this *démarche*, but it was agreed, except for some degree of tact and propriety over Easter in Pyrgos. A taxi-man from Katakolo appeared next in the parade, who used to drive Giorgis. 'I ate a lot and drank a lot and now I have no appetite for anything.' This led to a skilled discussion of triple bypasses of the heart, which would have left me boggling in any language.

An old man with his daughter appeared then who must have been the same age as this old toughy, but had a more faded look. He had served an eighteen-month sentence under the Colonels, and he was now President of the old members of the Pyrgos resistance. As a young Captain he took a hill from the Italians on his own, with a hand-held machine-gun and much slaughter. When the front broke he took to the mountains; his career in arms had started when he was sixteen. A few even older men puddled along in overcoats, though it was a blazing fine day. Giorgis and I talked of Victor Hugo and of Dickens, pooling our scraps of information and our vivid impressions like old writers anywhere. The day left me in no doubt how old we both were, not just from the hour's search for a taxi, but from the men Giorgis had been at school with, and the mangles they had all been through. His brother Paul whom I had never met was dying now in Athens, and our days were peppered with phone calls. He was a young airman who in 1967 when the Colonels came in took up his aeroplanes and went and shot at their tanks, but in the end he landed again and gave in, the squadron were never identified as rebels. Later he rose to be a high officer with NATO, and Giorgis remembered having got into a manic rage with him in 1973, still under the Colonels, over political duty. I never knew him, but he was much mourned in Pyrgos. All evening, people kept coming over to sympathise with Giorgis, as if he were already dead.

After lunch Pavlos Sinopoulos and his wife took Giorgis and Mitsa and me down to Katakolo for a coffee. There was a slight breeze which gave Pavlos a cold. We talked of a certain Vlavianos who was a mystery to me, but who had said he was my pupil, and had written about me in a literary magazine; I could not recall him then, and I do not know what I am supposed to have taught him, but my memory does blot people right out. He was a member of the Polytechnic generation of 1973, and seems to have been busy on the edges of the literary world. We talked about who he was, but none of us could add more than a question mark, though suddenly now, three months later, he has swum back into my mind and I remember him well. We talked also about rights and of how one is paid by papers or by television in different countries. This is not often spoken about in Greece, where one is usually not paid at all, but the idea of payment for copyright material is coming in, and must affect Pavlos, who inherited his brother's rights. In the last few days I have been reading his own *Night Guards*, a chronicle of the German occupation of Pyrgos. If it teaches one thing, it is the strong flavour of so small a world. It begins with childhood, when he and his friends went round singing to the mouth-organ under the balconies of girls, and someone froze them with the news of the fall of Saloniki to the Germans. They are a generation that have pulled themselves up by their bootlaces, and after an affectionate acquaintance with it of more than thirty years I feel as if I belonged to it as well.

That evening, the parade took a more formal shape. I was in the newspaper and bookshop with Giorgis; there was no question of its not being open. Years ago, we stood outside the Cathedral one Holy Saturday night, but now we intended only to watch the processions or the Litanies of the parishes, with the rest of the crowd. They were in a fantastic way similar to the old painted Litanies of Zakynthos, dramatised by darkness, and each one shorter than Visconti's masterpiece, because no more than forty or fifty at the most walked with candles in procession from each parish. This was quite different from the processions I remember from childhood, which because of English weather were always in the afternoon at the height of summer. Our school processions had a sameness and were organised like a drill display. I have always envied the boys at Downside who tried to singe the hair of the boy in front with their candles. We sang, which the Greeks do not, the most deplorable wailing hymns in droning voices, and kept time so badly that when the procession would twist back on itself from an upper to a lower road, we could hear the boys behind singing the next hymn or the last. At Beaumont they got round this problem by employing a commando of choirboys placed in groups at intervals with large field wireless sets borrowed from the Cadet Force. At Stonyhurst, the entire ceremonial was far more military, with crashing of boots and yelling of orders. In parishes those processions I saw were just a tattered and pathetic version of the same kind of parade.

The Greeks had style, they had those splendid bearded priests in finery that I think was getting its annual outing, the darkness was a dramatic factor, and they had millions of little lights fixed to the elaborate canopy they carried that lit up the priest who was splashing rose-water and other such delicious scents on everyone. The smell mounted above the smell of cigarettes and of frankincense. In the front went a tall, stark, upright cross that must have been a trial to carry. I thought how the Greeks had been at this for two thousand years, and through what a history: it had elements of Byzantine and some of Venetian or even of Roman influence, but the result was splendid, and they truly had it right, which our Anglo-Irish Catholic shambles in England really had not.

The cool wind that had been blowing from Zakynthos had fallen now, leaving the air cool and breathable but not cold. There was something real about the service, without which I assume that its dramatic nature would be empty and merely spectacular. There was a restraint about, and many signs of the cross covertly made as the processions went by. Undoubtedly the small lights give the procession a glamour, and the darkness on the edges gives one a comfort, so that I was glad that I was there and in the dark. The boys in purple robes with the candles and the man in front with the cross were familiar figures, but the carriers of the main ikon were soldiers in undress uniform like a fatigue party, and they carried on their shoulders on two poles a dome on four pillars outlined in lights, not solid but sketched, as it were, against the darkness: you could see through it and I think it held an ikon. Behind that came the priest with the scented water and the tall black cylindrical hat. The domes were extreme rococo, like ice-creams picked out with lights, but they were all different, and Giorgis recognised the parishes like a parade of racehorses. Each parish with its candles followed its own priest.

They were disordered like any crowd, but rather impressively numerous and classless like a crowd in Europe. One parish had a police band to lead them, and three candles like landing lights on the leading cross, their centre was a huge red-and-white cover under which red lights nestled. Sometimes there were eight carriers, and the older or richer parishes had those tall candles guarded with glass in brass lanterns that I think of as Venetian. All the candle-boys and the canopy-bearers seemed to strain their staves forward as if they were climbing a hill, or against the wind. I do not know why that happens, but it does explain the exactly similar stance of the leading boys in Visconti's painting, which gives them a revolutionary appearance that the aristocrats behind the priest and the women behind them have not got. Banner after banner and the silver standards all inclined forwards like accents. The Bishop himself walked in a silver glittering hat like a Byzantine beehive, and his escort and that of the military and civil dignitaries who followed him wore helmets, looking utterly out of place. Then came a detachment of Boy Scouts with enormous staves, looking shy. The dead march from Chopin played by the band added a faint touch of the Mafioso, as in a film. It was a remarkable performance.

There are no pure meanings or precise ceremonies, and come to that there are no pure religions, except for what is attained mostly by the simple and innocent. This was the whole of Pyrgos in the main square, but it was a profound acknowledgement like a deep sigh, and that is the most you will ever encounter. The fantasy at least was overwhelming, and it is not easy to forget the shining of children's eyes in the candlelight. The priests with their aspersions of scent were like the myrrh-bearers: or like those characters as the Orthodox have imagined them since the hymns of Romanos in the sixth century. They were the women who went to anoint the dead Jesus: they are important in the Gospel because they are witnesses to his death, but the Greek church has always identified with them out of a deep or popular root feeling. It is curious that in Romanos, where Mary the sister of Lazarus goes to buy the myrrh from an apothecary, a scene occurs which looks to us like pure Euripides. If that kind of source is really where it comes from, then vehement feelings about anointing go back a terribly long way.

The last poem that Nikos Gatsos wrote when he was dying of Parkinson's disease was one that he wrestled with for a number of years, but he could never finish it; this failure delayed his book of songs by three or four years, as he wanted it to be the last song in his book. He called it 'The Maniote Vespers', since it was a lament following on a murder that took place long ago. I do not know the story but the fragments of the poem are universal, it does not matter who died.

> On the rock of Monemvasía
> I went inside the church
> I sought to have some of her grace:
> Old things came into my mind
> Like a snake in an eagle's nest
> Like a candleflame in place.
>
> . . . And the Friday of Holy Week
> Will come to pass on earth,
> And someone will be crucified
> That others may be saved.
> . . . I want you to go to Vespers
> To Diroù monastery
> Where Father Resurrection sings,
> And if the Deaconess should ask
> Weep for the children and their curse
> And let her know the truth.

... From the pass of Passavá ...
... King of the world below ...

... And with a steel Damascus sword
I cut heaven into two
To have a double paradise,
One is for Costantis,
One for his brother by birth,
For little Panourías
Who was turned to dust and rust
On the solid earth.

... And for ever Good Friday
Will come to pass on earth,
And someone will be crucified
That others may be saved.

This is not a perfect or a great poem, and maybe it was unwritable because of the enormity, the weight of its theme, or because of the smoothness of his style. But it is a genuinely terrible stuttering towards a poem we can hardly imagine, and I would sooner sit puzzling over this than hear the bells ringing in some more conventional celebration. There is a frightening resemblance to the final fragmentary poems of Solomos.

For a long time in the intervals of nothing happening I sat in the newspaper shop watching some children making themselves paper lanterns, and chatting with a Pyrgos character I had never met, an elderly man with a walrus moustache who had known Giorgis's brother in the Air Force. This man had been ADC to King Paul before that good king died in 1964. He was from the village of Krestaina, an old retired officer from a happier world I suppose, like people I have met in England forty years ago who remembered Vienna in 1912. I liked him greatly, and so did Giorgis who remembered he had been a glamorous figure in his day. Now he had a cough I thought worrying and mingled indistinguishably with what must have been the thousands in the square.

I bought some currants from a stall to keep the pangs at bay; Giorgis told me they were *Sultaninas* from Corinth, but the smaller black ones were blackeyes or *mavromata* from Aigion (Vostitsa). My grandparents were called Moses and Sultana: he was from Istanbul but she was from Leghorn. I shall never know whether she was named after a sweet, plump currant as I am now inclined to think, or after a Turkish queen. Giorgis and I were both exhausted by the time we got home, and he took me off to eat at the restaurant almost next door to him, Barbasimis, which turned out extremely good. But that night I lost out of my pocket in the taxi a battered old spectacle case containing some little bottles of insulin and a syringe. It did not matter, as I had replacements, and I record it only as evidence that I was really sleepy. Still, I got to bed safely and so did Giorgis, and we both slept like people in the golden age. As for Holy Week, I felt that the worst was over: the soup was tomorrow night but I knew I was going to be let off that.

In the morning I walked to the post office for two stamps and sent off my last two postcards which I reckoned would not arrive home before I did, and then went with Giorgis to the square. There by chance we met the Mayor, yawning like a cat in the sunshine as we were. He promised us a calendar he had somewhere of photographs of old Pyrgos which I was anxious to see, because it showed the neoclassic town of before the war. I knew Giorgis had a cousin in the resistance, who was killed by a sniper in the Cathedral tower at the liberation, and I checked exactly where he fell, because I knew from translating Giorgis's first book of poems, *The Cellar*, and from stray things I had heard him say, how important and how representative this cousin had been to him. It seemed to me not peculiar or romantic, as it once had done, but just part of the history of a small country town, not unlike a county town somewhere in Ireland, where people mostly

knew one another and many of them were kinsfolk. I never asked
Giorgis about that, because he has never been to Ireland, but over
many years I felt it had become apparent. The only other poem in
that book that is about a romantic gunshot is really about Giorgis
as a little boy of about eight being handed a shotgun like a rite of
initiation and told how to shoot it at a rose bush, which he did,
but the effect on him was traumatic.

We sat at a table in the square and surveyed the world benignly.
We must, I think, have been waiting for the *Alpheios* people, who
seemed to move about in a gang. First of all some lively football
fans arrived at the next table, yelling with enthusiasm in all directions. Then much worse arrived, in the shape of a woman with
fuzzy blonde hair and blue artificial jewellery, who had once
wanted to marry Takis Sinopoulos, but was, as they say, pipped at
the post. She was now of a certain age, and formidably silly as well
as crazy with nerves. She had come from Athens, and it is likely
enough that Giorgis was the only friend or acquaintance she
spotted. A number of women attended on the Doctor all those
years ago; he was good-looking, after all, and established as a
young poet by then, and as a doctor. But the women he seemed
to favour had a glitter in the eyes; thirty years ago or more we
used to call them his Maenads, like those assertive young ladies in
animal skins who went whooping after the god Dionysos and tore
Orpheus to pieces. I had always been terrified of them. This one
was provoking in conversation too; she told us how frightened
she was about the Macedonian question. What would happen?
Nothing, we said. But what about the Serbians, suppose the
Bosnian Moslems brought in the Turks? We said it was in
the highest degree unlikely.

Giorgis said later he thought that the crazy Greek nationalists
on the border, and behind them the church, were responsible for
any tension, and that fits whatever one has heard or read about the
same church among the Serbians. No doubt it is what one must
pay for having a national church in the first place: as the British

still had in 1914. As for the Turks, Giorgis had already agreed with me that the Greek-Turkish quarrel about islands is absurd, and the more substantial quarrel about the oil under the Eastern Mediterranean should be solved by a Greek-Turkish alliance, which should carry out a joint exploitation. This was an idea I had first heard from Constantine Trypanis many years ago when he was a Minister in the Greek government: he thought Karamanlis was of the same opinion, but friendship with Turkey, which was a prerequisite, was not a vote-winning policy as things then were in Greece, and American interest was too formidable perhaps.

This chicken-brained lady lectured us about the Balkans, and went on to assure us of the support of her academic friends at a German university called Bochem. I do not know of the place, but nowadays it may easily exist. It is in Westphalia, and she recounted quite without shame as an amusing anecdote how after a dinner in the Plaka in Athens her friends from Bochem had all produced little prints of Hitler out of their pockets and drunk his toast with 'Hoch! Hoch! Hoch!' She could not understand why we should be shocked, so I said she must excuse me, but I was Jewish. She did say she was sorry, and went on to prove her goodwill and friendliness with all nations by promising us that one of her best friends in Athens was called Zizi. We saw her off without any breach of public order and she wandered away to seek out some new victim. I suppose the truth (among other truths) about the Doctor was that he had his methods with women like that. His experiments with the Maenads went on for some time before he settled on a sensible, pleasant young girl and married her. Early in our acquaintance before he realised I was celibate, he offered me a Maenad for the afternoon once; he did his best to make everyone happy and I wish he were alive now instead of the feather-witted Maenad.

It was all but a holiday, so Mitsa gave me lamb done in lemons for lunch, which was better than the best. Giorgis told me proudly how she terrorises all the butchers, who all tremble when they see her coming. She knows all about lambs and other beasts because of her father's farm, and has no compunction about demanding to see the cold store if the animals first offered fail her scrutiny. She had been out that morning to send lambs to all the family, and to the Kalamatianos family, and for her own house. In all they had cost her forty thousand drachmas, which I think is some six hundred pounds. They both thought that was a lot of money, even for the great feast of the year. Giorgis had been even more shocked by seeing a jacket for sale in Pyrgos that cost seventy thousand drachmas, about a thousand pounds.

They went to sleep in the afternoon, but I decided to walk home to the Pantheon, as I had never done it before. The traffic was infrequent at that time of day and what I mostly noticed was the wild flowers. The yellow flower they call May in Greece already predominated. It is modest and bright yellow, otherwise rather like tiny marigolds. Oranges in the gardens were in full scent and bloom and roses, particularly old-fashioned ones, dangled in the most provocative way: tea roses that melt at a touch, and in a garden otherwise full of giant cactus, what seemed to be an English wild rose of vigorous habit. A palm tree about six feet high and about three across in the trunk had developed such a mass of foliation that it obliterated the cottage behind it. I thought on this walk of a mile or two there were more old houses than I usually notice, mostly empty, sometimes boarded up, but also more stubborn, tiny, one-storey cottages, fiercely whitewashed and sometimes advertising queer trades. Since I passed close by, I inspected the old market building. It really is of awesome dignity and beauty: Athens has nothing like it. It consists of a tall archway with pillars, and five windows on each side with pavilions at the end, each of them with pilasters and columns: the whole thing is a rectangle with similar front and back. Even the buildings nearby are old and moving: yellow-painted and on their last legs like very

old men. Mr Stephanopoulos's political office, inherited from his
family, overlooks this amazing display, dead since 1945.

Why is it that so much of the Greece I know harks back to that
dead time? Perhaps it is truer of Pyrgos than of anywhere else, just
because it is so provincial, and the leaf lies where it falls; it is so
genuine and innocent also. It is also because I have come to see
things through Giorgis's own eyes, and to him and to the whole
of his generation the Forties, when Greece so splendidly fought
off the Italians and fought back against the Germans, the Forties
were a critical and exemplary time, almost like the War of Independence itself. The division in the country that followed the war
seems to me now to have been healed. The few ex-Communist
intellectuals spin their Marxist analyses outside the cafés, but they
spin them with too fine a thread, and political conversations are
boring nowadays, as Giorgis said to me. One must look into the
poetry of one's friend to see what truly concerns him, but with
Giorgis now it is dreams, as it is with so many old poets. Still the
dreams go back to old days. He is a young lift boy in love with a
girl from the top floor, or a prisoner or a gaoler in winter in
a ruined fortress in the snow in Russia or in Germany, or he
grieves over the time lost from love. These new poems are personal and some are about the poet and his poem; they are scarcely
about the Forties.

> Silence is an unfamiliar woman
> who comes in the night.
> She comes up the stairs
> without the sound of footsteps
> she comes into the room
> and sits down on my bed.
> Brings me her ring
> kisses me on the mouth.
> I strip her.
> Then she gives me the needles
> and the three colours

the crimson and the yellow and the black.
And I begin pricking
upon her skin
all the things that I did not say to you
and that I never more shall say to you.

When a poet dies there is for most of us nothing left but the poems, and they begin to speak to us in a different way. In the poems, or rather the songs, that Nikos Gatsos chose to be remembered by, the same theme of Good Friday is sounded again and again. I was surprised to notice it but it is so: many of them are about deep suffering. It is always old suffering, maybe age-old.

Bow your head woman
because Lent is coming
they will crucify the angel
and the thief again.

They say they came on Tuesday
and took Iakoumi away,
out of his own house,
as he ate there at midday.

Shut the window woman,
it's nearly ten past twelve,
I have told you so many times
these are evil days.

Friends are lost woman,
a brother is a snake
trim the flame in the candle
and let's have a little light.

Tell me great-grandfather's oath,
if I don't come home one night
remember me somewhere or other,
and see the children right.

> Shut the window woman,
> it's nearly ten past twelve,
> I have told you so many times
> these are evil days.

In that poem, written long ago, Nikos had sketched out the territory of his last poems. His generation is a little older than mine and so much the harder for me to understand, but there is surely a fearful intelligibility and directness about his poetry. It rhymes of course, but I am unable to capture the rhymes without losing the clear meaning.

Holy Week was not quite over, because on the Saturday night another night festival follows, but one which is wholly unlike the one with the procession on Friday. For one thing, this was very much a family affair, and for another it was much interrupted and enlivened by thunder-flashes, an enormous number of which had got into the hands of boys and young men. Even the sacred chanting of the Gospel could hardly be heard, and quite a nasty fight developed between two young men, one of whom had bombarded the other in the balls, but that was squashed as swiftly as it erupted. We had been hearing the bangs and crashes and echoes more often as the big night approached, but the crescendo was to come. Later, people spoke about the police intervening in future, because the little bombs have been getting worse for years. I expect therefore that I heard it at its worst: it was only fun of a kind, as a traveller I once read said of the gunfire in the city of Naples, '*parce que le coup du fusil leur flatte l'oreille*': 'gunfire has a special charm to Neapolitan ears'.

Off we went in the evening to the Kalamatianos house, which was buzzing with preparations, and smelling of herbs and soup. Everyone was brushed and polished and made ready, and as we were seated in the rather grand drawing-room, people kept arriving. It was all candles, scent, introductions and greetings. The lambs, of which there were a number ready to act their role, poor things, were peeped at and commented on. An atmosphere of hearty Pickwickian goodwill prevailed, and of bustle and rush and last-minute excitement that were Dickensian, which I have not seen in connection with going to church since I was a boy of fifteen in 1946. Papa Kalamatianos in his grandeur, and the males with washed, shaven, shining faces, uncles and cousins, ties, linen jackets, aftershave, the tall boys and the hundreds of women, we set off on the short walk to church, which was St Spyridon, tucked away below the square towards the sea, the focus of sincere affection and pride, the centre of life once a year. I remember it as yellow and as white as a narcissus, but that may be a trick of the memory of light. David Jones says somewhere that candlelight and whitewash are the finest sight in the world.

I took my stand in a corner of the large, irregular church courtyard, behind the door and I hoped unobtrusive, as the crowd swelled and the kinsfolk blossomed around Christos and Giorgis. Mitsa suddenly appeared and gave me a candle to hold, which she had bought days in advance, and someone told me that the parish had got the holy flame from someone who had been to the Cave, that is, the tomb of Christ, at Jerusalem where it was kindled. How he carried it on the aeroplane and on what occasion it was kindled are mysterious, but I duly packed away my candle when it was all over, and gave it for a baptism in Worcestershire, the same candle if not the same flame. I felt like the character in Samuel Butler who procures a little bottle of Jordan water for a baptism, then loses his temper over the difference between a cock and a hen lobster: 'What is the point of my getting Jordan water for a child whose father does not know the difference between a cock and a hen?' Armed with my fine brown beeswax candle, I stood and watched the crowd swelling and swaying. From time to time a lady would come out of church to tell us the other ladies were all right, but the congregation was crammed and stifling. Then with a swift and businesslike air, the priest swirled out to the lectern, there was a lighting and a reverberation like machine-gun

206

fire from every direction as he began to chant. It was like being in the middle of a battle, at the end of a cowboy film: once could not take in more than the general effect.

This underlined the strong impression I got that the big moment was an affirmation of family solidarity and unity. 'Christ is risen,' they said to one another with passion, with bright, serious eyes and expressions of sincerity: it was an exchange of vows, an identification, and as the little groups and the big groups into which the huge throng had disintegrated exchanged compliments more coolly and formally with other groups, the message of the season went right round the parish. It went to old ladies on their balconies on the way home. It was an affair of the family group, not of the individual. Mitsa and one or two other women stayed on to take Communion, but they had all come outside first to share the Christos Anesti. The bombardment did not stop all the same, it maintained its incredible level after we had all gone home along the lane past the Kalamatianos fields and the farmhouse where the brother lived, with its truly gigantic wine-barrels called Mississippi and Orinoco and Thames standing outside like elephants grazing in the cool grass.

Charis took me back to the Pantheon, and I do not think the night soup eaters sat long, because the climax of the festival had really been Christ is Risen, the moment of genuine and shared belief, like that moment as a child when we got home from the midnight Mass of Christmas, and everyone said Happy Christmas. What we had in common as a family unit I suppose, and shared with other families, was a devotion to innocent happiness, but it was not, now that I look back on it, quite as impressive as the Easter of the Kalamatianos family. I am not suggesting any lack of faith among the English suburbs, but a difference of emphasis which had entered deeply into the national culture soon after the end of the war. Charis and I rushed home through long film-shots of dark and sub-ochre lanes and streets. We passed a butcher's shop as silent as the grave, called Meat Boutique. Charis probably went to bed as soon as I did, because he was appointed as volunteer to the honourable task of assistant lamb-roaster, that is, full-time spit-turner and slow charcoal fire-tender, and his duties began before six in the morning if the lamb was to be ready by two in the afternoon.

I slept to the noise of a last few explosions, but woke to the sound of a fusillade from a new direction, from what were usually quiet residential streets. My diary reads, 'Easter Sunday: this morning they are happy with the new game of putting bombs under cars to tease the car alarms, so that after every bang you get the ringing. Last night there were two and a half thousand thunder-flashes let off in one village alone, near Pyrgos.' The day began in a sea of ground-mist which magnified these noises, but I was first woken by a loud, wailing train-hoot.

8 : The Arcadian Mood

EASTER and the feast of St George on the twenty-third of April are often close together and they may coincide, but the day of St George was traditionally the day that the flocks arrived in the high grazing grounds in the mountains, the *voskotopia*, where they spent the summer. This has nothing to do with lambing, because lambing was not as predictable in the past as it is now. It might happen at any time and in any inconvenient place, as Virgil makes plain in his *Eclogues*. So the availability of young lambs for Easter must in the past have been an uncertain matter. On the other hand the way they are always traditionally cooked in the open air is so universal among the Greeks that it seems like a relic of an older way of life.

It is a question of how far the flocks go, I suppose, or how far they went. In Spain there is now an idealistic organisation which is applauded by the old shepherds who survive, and greeted with cheering in the high villages, that intends to restore the old routes of transhumant sheep, right through modern cities, up into the mountains, and the map they follow has charted lines like those on the palm of a hand from one end of Spain to the other, from Portugal to Granada. In 1996 they will go through Madrid. Certainly the Afghan Cuchi or 'travellers' even within my memory used to go up every year from the tribal territories of Pakistan right across Afghanistan and into Russia across the Oxus. But Greece is another matter. In Eleia the simple way up into the nearest mountains appears to prevail, but the high grazing grounds everywhere are mostly occupied from some given direction: it is a difficult question how far the flocks go. The oracle of Zeus at Dodona is quite high, between Mikra Choria and the sea, but the ancient pottery found there seems to be made almost entirely in the north Balkans. There was a tannery in ancient Athens that specialised in hides that had come from Kythera. The fate of Oedipus depends on two shepherds who happened to meet feeding their flocks on Kithairon, one from Thebes and the other from Corinth. In modern times the furthest I have known any transhumant sheep to move was from Ano and Kato Doliana in eastern Arcadia, where they used to cross over into mainland Greece and graze on hills towards Kithairon in summer.

Philip Sherrard had a story of Taygetos, that great central bone of mountain we think of as Spartan. He had spent the night in a village south of Sparta, where he had been assured there was an easy track up the mountain, but when the morning came his hosts were reluctant to let him go up such a dangerous wall of rock, and only in the end agreed provided that they came some of the way to keep him company. They evidently hoped that when he saw it he would turn back. Still, he persevered, it seemed a harmless, pleasant path, and after dramatic farewells at the foot they let him take it. When he came to the top at about lunch-time, he found a quite isolated pastoral scene, whose only inhabitants were a flock of goats and a goatherd eating olives and cheese. He invited Philip to join him, which he was pleased to do, so Philip asked where he had come from. Where had he been last week? The answer was Chicago, where he had worked in a restaurant for twenty years. He had brought up his flock to this flattish pasture on the mountain-top for the summer; they had come up from the Arcadian side of the mountain.

This kind of journey has entered deeply into the imagination of the Greeks. The songs called 'klephtic' ballads are about outlaws who lived in the mountains and defied the Turks. The novelist Papadiamantis makes the point that there was only a short period of about half one generation, after the outlaws stopped preying on the peasants and before the tax collectors of the new state took over. It is unfortunately true that these outlaws survived in business to the Dilessi murders, that is, long enough to start kidnapping and murdering tourists and have their misdeeds reported in the *Illustrated London News*: and modern publicity has tarnished their old image. St George's day was their festival too in their hide-outs, and their way of life overlapped with that of the herdsman. And who sang the outlaw songs? Who made them up but villagers? They were remembered of course and handed on by oral tradition, in villages which were sometimes as isolated as any wilderness, and a great mass of most interesting material was transmitted with them. At some point in the tradition which has not been fully explored, the Serbian songs and the Greek songs were entangled and cross-bred, though whether that happened between herdsmen under the Turks, or during the Slavonic period in Greece before the Turks came, or more recently in North Greece, I am unable to say. I made an attempt once on this territory in *Marko the Prince, Serbo-Croat Heroic Songs*, with the help of Professor Sveto Koljevic and Professor Ann Pennington. In the early nineteenth century, even the collectors of Serbian and Greek traditional poetry began neck and neck, yet the *Canti Populari* of Nikos Tommaseo, printed in Venice in 1842 in four volumes, is still the only publication ever declared to contain translations of Serbian poetry into Greek.

I apologise for airing this obscure problem. All I deduce from it is a lost world that was once in common, a world that becomes visible for a moment in the celebration of Easter in Greece. St George's day has shrunk to become only the personal feast day of all persons called George. The handful of poems that remain from the eighteenth century and earlier convey strongly a sense of freedom, and that is implicit, I think, in the meal of Easter Sunday, which is in a way a reversion: it is eaten out of doors wherever possible, and old songs are certainly sung, and traditional dances are danced. The hero of such occasions is from an older generation, and there is a libertarian, generous spirit about him. The outlaw songs include numerous unhappy endings, but sometimes they are lighter.

> Mount Olympos quarrelled with Mount Kissavos, and said,
> 'Turk-trodden Kissavos why growl at me?
> I am Olympos, famous in this world:
> I have six times ten peaks, forty-five springs,
> at every spring a leafy bough, on every bough an outlaw:
> and at my root runs a river of basil.'

Giorgis and I saw a television film in which he appeared and was astonishing, saying things that once he had muttered or said by chance as if they came out of his dreams, but now he spoke them crisply and powerfully. The film was about our friend the Doctor, Takis Sinopoulos. It was better made than such things usually are in England, but whatever was most moving in it was swallowed up in Takis's great poem 'Nekrodeipnos' ('Dead Men's Dinner'), a lament for all the dead of the Civil War in which, as I have said, he served as an Army doctor. It is a deeply humane poem and one that no one else was in a position to write; what it expresses is the grief of a lifetime. That war had a more terrible effect on him than on anyone else I knew. It burst out of him in sudden floods of tears, and it is the reason why he was so determined to live fully, which is also why he died young. The tragedy of his widow, who died in the end of an overdose, is a remoter effect of that same condition in him. Now it is as if he has taken his place with the others in his own poem, 'Nekrodeipnos'.

Mitsa's gaiety had returned with the festival and the season: in the car she was clicking her ecstatic fingers to the ancient pop song, 'Tonight you make a BAM! They see you and put on the brakes, and slow down every tram, tonight you make a BAM!' She was particularly keen on gathering wild greens on this day and stopped the car to do so. We called on our old friend Barouxis, a local journalist even older than us and yellow with fever, and while he swayed in the road and we greeted him, Mitsa dived into his garden where greens had all but swallowed up the house. We got to the Kalamatianos assembly in cheerful spirits, past the exhausted church and the expended whizzbangs, past his father's farmhouse where his brother still lived as herdsman of the elephantine barrels. By the light of day they were more tremendous than ever, whale-like in a meadow of fresh grass. If they were full they would have taken a dozen cart-horses each to pull and each would have occupied its own goods wagon on a train.

Things began gently. Someone got me a chair where I wanted to be, near the fires to watch the cooking. Above us towered the block of flats which Christos had built and in which he lived, really in a corner of the field near the barrels. The one I fancied most was Orinoco. On two shallow pits the two spitted lambs revolved. One of Christos's brothers, who I think was a ship's engineer, was in charge of the roasting and Charis was trying to learn all his secrets. He informed me with some glee that the way you tell when the animal is ready to eat is by poking your finger into its bottom, and as soon as it does not burn you, that is the moment. Little bits of kokoretsi, which is entrails cooked separately, began to come round on plates, and glasses of the most delicious wine, and then Christos's brother Giorgis decided it was hot, and brought out three magnificent straw hats, one of which he wore, one I wore, and the third went to the poet, who looked embarrassed by his and grinned like a child. Luckily for me, Giorgis Kalamatianos decided that I did not mind looking ridiculous and was a good sort, so we soon became best friends. Another brother, Loukas, took the head of the table; he looked like a Gatsos cousin and wore a suit and a shy smile, but I observed in him a deep supply of good nature, I suspect Orinoco and Mississippi must have run in his veins.

The lamb tasted better than any other I have ever eaten. I have in the past been at Greek Easters in the country where the lamb is spitted and cooked by boys in the same way, but it was never as good as this. The British School of Archaeology at Athens used to celebrate Easter in a body, at some favoured and carefully organised country spot, I have forgotten where. It was near a tavern probably, and I am sure there was dancing, because I can remember a now distinguished professor performing amazing capers of his own invention, like a puppet trying to dance away his strings. It is not surprising that he was a bit drunk, but can we ever have been so young, all of us? There is a tendency to equate the Easter lamb with the sacrifice of the Lamb in Revelation, but I do not feel happy about the connection. I do not think it is ritually continuous with the Jewish habit of eating a lamb at Passover either, though we may be certain that the Lamb in Revelation is the lamb of the Passover, and that the ritual carried out then and the words said at that supper go a long way to explain the Gospel account of the last supper, and the Christian liturgy that commemorates that. But the lamb you get for lunch at Easter in Greece is a symbol of mountain liberty, if it is a symbol of anything at all.

We had cooked two lambs out of doors on charcoal and two more indoors in the oven. One I think was given away to neighbours or the old or the poor, but we got through three of them, because we were a huge party at both sides of a table stretching the length of the house. People arrived later or just dropped in to share in the rejoicings. I remembered what Giorgis had told me about his own great-uncle, the one with the flocks and the pair of gold-mounted pistols who used to set up his tents in the great square at Pyrgos once a year to feast the mayor and the council and the Governor when Pyrgos was a small town. The *graviera* cheese, the wine and the lamb could not have been any better in those days. We are to think of the early nineteenth century and the first years of Greek freedom: before that such a feast would have to be in the mountains or at night.

There came a Pasha, from Nevropolis
he came to herd the men at arms, to hunt the outlaws down:
and looking for the priest, and for the learned man:
Now where are you my priest, my outlaw, learned man?
Come and bow down to me, and let your brothers come,
and bring your cousins with you, and bring all your kin.
The pathways weep for you that you have walked,
the cold springs weep for you, they weep cold water down.

It is small wonder that the pictures we have of the outlaws of those days make them look like leopards, like wild animals. There is a stone relief of one at Our Lady of Lampedon on Mount Pelion, done in 1796 to commemorate a Captain Basdekis.

> Easter today Demos, today the feast:
> the young men rejoice, they shoot at the mark . . .

The young men have no English equivalent, the word for them, *pallikaria*, means 'braves', for better and for worse. Once it had only a good sense, though today its bad sense has taken over in prose, though not in verse, because society has altered, but verse has not. Yet without reference to that antique world and its values, it is not easy to discuss the resonance of Easter rejoicings. Mitsa danced a traditional dance, the brother Giorgis, custodian of the wine-barrels, danced and sang, so did Christos. Louis, who was elderly, spilt wine down his waistcoat and did not care. The young cavorted. The eldest boy leaped over the shoulders of his young brother, who was six foot high. A lady not so very young sang and danced brilliantly. Mitsa dived away into the meadow to gather more greens. Giorgis of the barrels sang folksongs new and old: one, he said, was Kephalonian about what 'the priest told me', how there are thirteen Gospels and not twelve; some of his songs were old and moving. It was demanded that I sing, so as it was clear that nothing mattered but showing your back teeth I briefly showed mine with the only four lines of 'Barbara Allen' I know.

It was a remarkable afternoon, essentially a family celebration of the Kalamatianos family at full strength, and long may it last. The land, mostly a single meadow, stretched from the old family house next to Saint Spyridon to the chapel of St George in the Second Cemetery: some goats and rabbits and so on lived at the far end, but really it was like a large park. I knew by then that the family had some Zakynthian blood but I had wondered about the name, because such a local name after a large town like Kalamata often implies refugee status and a change of name after a vendetta or feud to the death: and that turned out to have been what happened, several generations ago. The murder, or whatever it was, had happened in the Mani, and when the ancestor who was being hunted escaped he used to give his name as 'from Kalamata', Kalamatianos. Sometimes a Greek in that position wanders a great distance away, to Athens or New York, and at times they go home after twenty years or so, but in this case whoever it was had married and settled down, and when the time came that no one had the obligation to continue the quarrel, he had his own life in Pyrgos or on Zakynthos. The Mani after all had been a poor place: in the nineteenth century, I think about 1840, the wandering Earl of Carnarvon records that they raided Kalamata and looted it for every nail and every window frame they could find.

We dispersed with a pleasing sense of well-being, undoubtedly well oiled but the fresh air and the high spirits had kept us sober enough. All the same, Giorgis and I agreed that the rest of the day was for repose. Still, the condition of diabetes meant that I had to take an injection in the evening at about nine, and after that I had better eat. So I wandered out to see if anywhere was open and went in the end to the restaurant by the Cathedral. There I ate some more lamb to see how different it was, and found it like good English lamb, utterly inferior to that magical midday feast. It must have been about ten when I was sauntering home, just crossing the road above the hotel, when someone shouted from a car. I waved in reply, assuming this was just a bit of jollity, but it was Giorgis and his friend the village schoolmaster in his Deux Chevaux. He reprimanded me for desertion and they carried me off to a bar, belonging to a brother, which at night and indoors was of a shattering noisiness. Later I discovered our conversation had been taped, though I did not think that could possibly have worked. We had talked about journeys and I think about water buffaloes. I do not recall whether there were ever any in Greece, though there were at Paestum in the eighteenth century, and camels at Livorno in the nineteenth. I did once see a water buffalo in what was then Yugoslavia but I sadly wonder if it has survived.

Next morning being the twenty-third, although Giorgis had put an advertisement in the paper that he was not celebrating, was all telephone calls, and visitors to the house who had to be entertained, all bringing presents. I managed to find him a bottle of Glenfiddich, whisky being popular in Greece but the colour of labels and the quality of different kinds, particularly malts and single malts, the darkest of mysteries, as, come to think of it, most whisky is to me. I like what I believe I should like, what the expert tells me. This was also the day when I must be interviewed for *Alpheios*, the literary magazine. There had been a lot of prep-aration for the big moment, they had held an editorial committee about what questions I should be asked, which like most products of committees where somewhat banal, I thought. The young man who was to ask me the questions would have done it better on his own, but he was shy and diffident, as well as sweet-natured, and the most charming new friend I had made in years. He was named Iannis Siderokastritis. Even now things were not to be perfectly simple.

We met a little late for a coffee in the square and took off for Katakolo. There was the tiny, empty train called the Arse-dragger starting its summer season. There in the harbour was the season's first Adriatic Line steamer, off to Venice next day by way of Zakynthos, I think; she was named after a port to the north of Germany, the *Arkona*, and must have started life on the frozen side of Europe, which might as well have been on the other side of the moon. Was the old Arse-dragger hoping to pick up passengers for Olympia? As for us the tapes were not working, but Iannis borrowed some out of a child's recording machine belonging to his son. We went to his house and had lunch with his wife and her mother, the little boy and a silent Romanian girl who I thought was a sister-in-law. That was not quite right and there was going to be a drama about her. She was engaged to Iannis's brother who ran the new bar in Pyrgos, but her residence permit for Greece was running out and only marriage at once could rescue her from the threat of expulsion. She did not want to go back, everyone liked her and the brother wanted to marry her, but the plans for marriage in church were disrupted by Easter and as for the plans for a secular wedding, they were rickety. We did not know this at the time, and on the twenty-third of April we were all moving about quite tranquilly. Iannis's mother was a beautiful lady with a lovely garden; she came from Constantinople like my grandmother.

The little boy was quieted, the interview took place and I went home to sleep for an hour. Then we were summoned to the celebrations of the name-day of Giorgis of the wine-barrels, which took the form of a huge family dinner in a restaurant. Meanwhile the constant visitors and the stream of phone calls at the poet's house did not cease. When I asked him how many there had been he grinned a lot, and said, 'And there'll be others.' The presents seemed mostly to be cloudy Mandarini and Benedictine and Mastich: sweet liqueurs. When I told him the highest consumption of brandy and Benedictine per capita in England was at Clitheroe he wanted to go there. We drove to a country restaurant for the feast, to find a row of cousins, from very young girls to very old ladies, and I found myself opposite the grandmother of the whole tribe. Giorgis Kalamatianos behaved impeccably and conventionally in a fine silk tie. Whatever I said was always translated or repeated for the benefit of the old ladies, who crowed when etiquette demanded it. Giorgis Pavlopoulos was talking about Spanish literature, and among his phrases built a niche for Gustavo Duran, which I thought moving and appropriate. A little girl of twelve called Maria announced there were twenty-three of us at table, I made it twenty-five, but she refused to crawl along under the table and count legs. We discussed phantom horses and whether Giorgis had only one leg and why it was a mistake for her sister to study psychology. It was a very different kind of party; a number of these feasts were in progress in the same restaurant, and a hundred yards up the road there was a wedding party.

By this time I felt I had fallen into a network of extended families. I could not have gone on much longer without a disaster, because I had little idea what anyone's name was. It was like one of those parties during the war that took place in the Cretan mountains with a boy on look-out duty and some eagles hovering over the dust track that did duty for a road, when more and more figures in sheepskins came stamping in from the cold, and the drink circulated, toasts were drunk, dances were danced and lambs consumed, but no one had any idea what anyone's name was, or even understood their language. I was told of such a feast in Crete when a German patrol suddenly arrived and all the guests, who were English from under rocks, had to be hidden in a cellar under a barrel. The Germans thought the feast was prepared for them, and trotted off late in the afternoon shouting about good friends; then that night the Cretans crept up on the place where they were encamped in the valley below the village, and killed the lot of them: indeed they did not dare to leave a man alive.

Now I had only a very few days left, but I was determined to make one last try at the Falls of the Styx. I knew by now that the maps we had were as unreliable as the guidebooks, and I had attained complete peace of mind as to whether we found the place or not, but I did want to explore that part of the Peloponnese, the north-western corner, and I wanted a last day out with Giorgis and Iannis, and I knew that whatever happened we would see things that were worth seeing. There were ancient sites I had not visited in many years, or possibly never visited, I was no longer sure. I had better admit here that going back was no use; I went to places I had certainly been before, but I did not remember them: what I had seen or not seen was all covered over in the same mist. Even now, little more than two months afterwards, I can hardly retrace the route we took. That of course may as easily be due to the inadequacy of maps as to the oddity of any roads we followed.

Memory is a strange matter. I remember more about Kythera where I have never been than I do about these sunlit villages where I was such a short time ago. Yet I would have said that one of my firmest fixed memories about Kythera was the postcard a schoolfriend sent me as a boy of Watteau's *Embarquement pour Cythère*, with the silks billowing like sunsets, or else Baudelaire's marvellous poem. So the other evening I sat down to reread that, in case it should be useful for this book. The whole long middle of it is so disgusting it is unquotable: it is about a corpse 'just nicely ripened' on the gallows being torn to pieces by a vulture, and it goes into endless detail about this filthy process. I had completely forgotten that part of the poem, as if I had never read it. Now that I have it freshly in mind I do find it a wonderful and extraordinary poem, but the cost is somehow disproportionate.

> My heart soared and then glided joyfully
> around the rigging as the free birds fly,
> where like an angel drunk with the bright sun
> the ship rolls swimming in a cloudless sky.
>
> What is that sad dark island? Cythera
> the land famous in song the sailors call
> banal Eldorado of the old lads:
> look there – it's a poor country after all.

By the end of the next verse the sexual scent of tuberoses has become overwhelming and one can foresee that things will not end well for Eros. What an extremely unGreek poem it is. No doubt the Greeks feel as much shame and guilt as anyone else all the same. If there ever was a society that operated by honour and shame and never felt guilt at all, that is not Greece: it is not even the pure and passionate *Iliad*, or the boyish honour competitions of the upper grazing grounds. And yet although the ship swimming like an angel drunk with the bright sun has a tincture of Solomos about it, the poem of Baudelaire that more closely touches the Greeks or the Greek soul, if I may use such an expression, is 'The Voyage', in its last two stanzas; probably it concerns all modern souls.

> Old captain death, up anchor, it is time:
> this country tires us out and the sail clings,
> and if the heavens and seas are black as ink
> you know our hearts are full of glimmerings.
>
> Pour us your poison, it will do us good.
> This fire so burns our brain, this is our cue:
> dive in the gulf, then heaven or hell, who cares?
> At the bottom of the unknown, to find the new.

I have spent a page dwelling on Baudelaire because out of the mists that cover my memory, he is something I can recover, and because I know that Giorgis adores him as much as I do, and it is Baudelaire we must talk about when we meet again.

Still, it was not Kythera I was longing for now, it was the Styx. I wanted to make some attempt to find it. It sounded like a great natural wonder, a toppling high mountain where the snow came drenching down as water, falling so far that it evaporated in mist before it touched the earth, and leaving the rock streaked with strange colours. I must make it plain to the reader what was knowable about this phenomenon, and how we know it, by guiding whoever is interested through a chapter devoted to my ramshackle researches.

9 : *Unexpected Melody*

IT was Pascal who remarked that in writing a book the very last thing one discovers is what should go first: and it occurs to me only now that I must explain something about the ancient River Styx. It is a serious and solemn name and the gods swore by it. It dripped, as it were, from the beard of Zeus. Whether it was on earth or in the other world poses a curious problem. In the *Odyssey*, the hero Odysseus goes to the end of the known world, to a region of mist and darkness, to hold communication with the dead. This he does by slaughtering a black ram over a pit, and the ghosts of the dead come fluttering out of the pit, but when they drink the ram's blood they can speak.

Scholars usually put that oracle of the dead beyond a region of lagoons and marshes in the west of mainland Greece and north of the Peloponnese: no doubt to many Greeks, particularly to those who lived in Turkey and the Aegean islands, that unpleasant area must have been the far end of the west: it was a region where you could walk all day through waist-deep water between reeds and meet nothing but a snake swimming. It was the feverish, poisonous country where Byron died and so many Greeks a little later, in the small town of Missolonghi. There are a number of place names, including the important name of the great River Acheron which creates the mud-flats and the islands and lagoons, that are in common between the real world and the underworld. Twenty or thirty years ago, close to a great waterfall of the Acheron, the archaeologists found that there had really been an oracle of the dead in ancient times, though I do not remember how it worked. Plutarch speaks of a Lethe somewhere in Portugal, and there was another Acheron in Calabria.

But these queer and mystical regions will not do for anyone who uses a map: and the *Odyssey* does seem to have a vague idea of where places are: it knows where Crete lies and where Sounion lies, near Athens, it has some idea of Nestor and of sandy Pylos, though I doubt whether the palace of Nestor and his famous bath were known to Homer: they were in the wrong place, and deeply buried centuries before the poem was written. The whereabouts of the Cyclops and other peculiar inventions or mythical places can be fixed further west by the archaeological discovery of a cult of Aeolus north-east of Sicily, in the Aeolian islands, just where it ought to be. The home island Ithaca, or Ithaki, has not altered its name, though scholars have been found to push it a few miles north: but it is even further west, being an island out at sea, than the region of perpetual mist and darkness at the end of the world, where Homer puts the oracle of the dead: so maybe the semi-underworld idea is older than the *Odyssey*, where Odysseus is King of Ithaca, has cattle on the coast and may, as it were, have sailed a toy yacht on the Acheron lagoons as a child.

Most of us have our idea of the Styx from the dramatic oaths of the gods in Homer or from the underworld, and in particular from Virgil. There is no doubt that Virgil has a more developed idea than Homer of the underworld. One of the links between them is an amazing painting of the early classical period that once existed at Delphi, depicting a version of the underworld of the *Odyssey*, with remarkable variations, which survived long enough to be very fully described by Pausanias, although now not a crumb or a fragment of it remains. It may be said in general all the same that people are extremely conservative about the next world or the underworld, and the images can be traced both in Italy and in Greece. In Italy, it is highly likely that the paintings in the cave of Orcus, a name equivalent to death, give a respectably pre-Christian and Etruscan or preclassical date to beliefs about purgatory that resurface in the middle ages, and still survive in phantom form in Catholic countries. 'This ae nighte, this ae nighte, Every nighte and alle, Fire and fleet and candle-lighte, and Christ receive thy saule.'

There was a queer and diabolical sort of creature in the picture at Delphi coloured like a bluebottle or a meat-fly, whose function apparently was to strip the skeletons of the dead by eating them and leave the bones pure white. Pausanias is rather frightened of him and indeed the repellent creature is not likeable, and does not fit into normal mythology: it occurs in a region of the painting full of magical and traditional figures that are not Homeric, the punishment of patricide and of sacrilege for example. 'Above all this is Eurynomos: the officials at Delphi say Eurynomos is a daemonic spirit in Hades, who eats away the flesh of the dead, and leaves them only their bones. But Homer's *Odyssey* and the *Minyad* and the *Homecomings*, all of which mention Hades and its horrors, know nothing about any daemonic Eurynomos . . . he shows his teeth, and the hide of a vulture has been spread for him to sit on . . .' Next to him are two Arcadians. It is, to say the least, a curious coincidence that we do know a lady called Eurynome, at Phigaleia, where her sanctuary was 'inaccessibly situated in broken country' in the gorge of the Neda, a mile or two upstream.

Her sanctuary was in a dense cypress wood, near some natural hot-water baths: Pausanias has never been there, and no one since has found the place with any certainty; Pausanias has only looked her up in a reference book. The local people said she was only Artemis, but Homer in the *Iliad* gives the same name (18, 398) to a daughter of Ocean, and associates her with the very ancient goddess Thetis. Her statue was that of a woman 'tied with golden chains', and fish-tailed below the waist. The Phigalians had another sanctuary four miles away to Black Demeter, who was raped by Poseidon and gave birth not to a magic horse as she did in other versions of the story, but to the Mistress, and elsewhere in Arcadia Demeter is a Fury. Pausanias interprets that to mean that she disguised herself as a mare but Poseidon turned into a stallion and raped her, which made her furious. That is obvious rubbish, she was an Erinys, one of the classical Furies, in Arcadia. This most sinister side of her would be unpopular in the wider Greek world, which had accepted the tamer version of Demeter offered in the Eleusynian mysteries, in which even Roman emperors were initiated.

There is certainly a tangle of religious cults to do with madness and pollution and its cleansing, and to do with the underworld, that flourished in the Arcadian mountains. Among them is an extremely queer localisation of Homer's Styx, which Pausanias believed some strange stories about, though he had never seen it. Virgil appears at first to have left us almost a map of the underworld and its rivers, Lethe for forgetfulness, Acheron meaning death, Cocytus the river of wailing and Phlegethon the river of fire, and Styx 'nine times interfused'. But the question into what sea these rivers flow remains without an answer, and any question of their whereabouts is still more difficult, because although Virgil paints his fullest picture of the underworld in book six of the *Aeneid*, he is elsewhere reluctant to banish these rivers from the face of the actual earth.

In the first *Georgic* he has hardly begun his advice to farmers when he diverges into the course of the seasons. In order to explain this (231) he gives the belief in the shape of the earth and its zones that was conventional in his time, a hundred and fifty years before Pausanias wrote. He knew the earth was a round thing; that had been accepted Greek science for some three hundred years: the days when the earth was shaped like the drum of a column or like a leaf floating in a dust of stars were alas over; it was an apple-shaped thing like the other heavenly bodies. Still, it was possible to believe that, and still have only the vaguest idea about its other side, and if Africa had really been circumnavigated, the implication that one could pass the tropics had not been grasped by most people, so that the idea lingered into the middle ages that somewhere on earth there were dog-faced people, and people who lay in the giant shadow of their own large feet, which they held above their heads like umbrellas, and the amazing antipodeans. The theory of the force of gravity that applies equally all over the earth as if the whole thing were one magnet was slow to develop. So although Virgil pays at least lip-service to the truth it lands him in an area of speculation he does not hope to master.

> The golden sun by twelve stars rules
> heaven's sphere set out in its exact parts.
> Five belts hold heaven . . .
>   (*Geo.* 1, 231–3)

He speaks of the heavens in terms of what lies below them on earth. The belts are the zones, one torrid and two polar with black rain and solid ice. Between them, two zones are permitted to poor mortals, and over them obliquely passes the road of the twelve constellations, that is the twelve months, I think. The world slopes up to Scythia and down to the Libyan desert. 'This top is for us for ever high, but the other the dark Styx and the deep Ghosts see underfoot' (242–3). It would be useful to enquire, 'Under whose feet?' Certainly ours: I am sure it is no help to observe that near the end of the second *Georgic*, where Virgil glorifies science, he says, 'Happy is the man who knows the causes of things and has all fears and inexorable fate and the rumbling of hungry Acheron underfoot.' The noisy river means death, and in Lucretius (1, 78), whom Virgil remembers, it is religion that is trampled underfoot. In the *Georgic*, though, underfoot is the opposite of high and has a topographic meaning. Mynors comments in his edition of the *Georgics* that the idea of the underworld being in the southern hemisphere 'was bound to arise during the development of Greek scientific thought'. This seems to me extremely queer, but it appears to be what Virgil meant.

He thinks Virgil picked up this notion from some Greek theorist unknown to us, and comforts himself with a gesture towards a work of Cumont, published in Paris in 1942, on Roman graves and their symbolism, which (so far as I remember it) does not really help. Mynors goes on to say, 'If we believe [as Virgil tells us] that the southern temperate zone is inhabited by mortals, the Ghosts will be confined to the Antarctic, which with its intemperate climate and dubious illumination is not unsuitable.' This preposterous idea is the equivalent of saying that the ghost of my grandfather inhabits the body of an Emperor Penguin. Why, after all, the Antarctic and not the Arctic? Cumont, a scholar of the winged-collar generation but no worse for that, though more useful as an archaeologist than as a student of literature, says this business of souls is for Virgil a kind of mythology he uses for a literary purpose: 'with an imprecision he judges poetic'. This is on the whole wildly untrue of Virgil, and it should not put us off the scent of the Styx and of where Virgil had heard that it was. In the sixth book of the *Aeneid* he is elaborately detailed about it in a region that is underground.

In the last *Georgic* the Styx appears in a context of great beauty which prefigures its use in the *Aeneid*, here in the underworld explored by Orpheus (4, 480 and 506).

> . . . whom now the black mud and the shapeless reed
> Cocytus that slow marsh that unloved water
> hems in, and Styx nine times interfusing . . .
> . . . she floated freezing in the Stygian skiff . . .

Elsewhere (3, 551) Virgil confirms that the Styx is dead water, cold and dark, since he speaks of hell's 'Stygian darkness'. It is only in this queer passage in the first *Georgic* that it seems to be at the south pole. Or may that mean that the south pole is lower down than the underworld, and the Styx and the kingdom of ghosts look down on it from their region in the underworld? It is a Roman convention and one that Virgil is using in this passage, that, sphere or not, the world slopes downwards: up to Scythia and down to the Libyan desert. Maybe he intends to give us an alarming touch of vertigo by the word underfoot, and maybe the phrase of Lucretius was in his mind when he came to give his firmly Greek account of the shape of the earth.

It is important to rescue Virgil as a poet, and I hope I may be permitted to illustrate with a less perplexing example how he works, improving his phrases until they reach a kind of perfection. If they are repeated after that it is rarely or for a special purpose; for instance, the battle of two bulls in the wilderness of Calabria is referred to towards the end of the *Aeneid*, and it is intended that we should recall the *Georgics*. But in his working towards an effect he is a subtle, very tentative writer. In an *Eclogue* 'among the untamed bushes gleams the grape'. It happens when 'the soft barley paints the field yellow', so we can see that the colour contrast and the other sensual contrasts are important, the wild or untamed and the soft for example. In the second *Georgic* we get

> Apples when they feel the strong treetrunk
> and their green virtue climb up to the stars
> by their own force and in no need of ours,
> then all the woods are heavy with increase,
> wild bird-houses gleam among bloody fruit

For Virgil, poetry is in no way imprecise, and his best effects are those of precision. But we shall not find the Arcadian Styx in his verses, his Styx is a slow-moving river in the dark and it flows into and out of itself like the most bewildering of knots. The river we are looking for has some importance and great dignity. The earliest description of it is by Hesiod in his *Theogony* (785 and 805) which may well be pre-Homeric. It is cold water dripping from a high crag on to rugged ground. Herodotos may not have been there but he is perfectly matter of fact about it and about the city called Nonakris where he says it came out of the rock, and he tells us, writing in the fifth century BC, that the Arcadians used to swear by it. There is no reason not to believe him, and the fact that the Styx had a grip on the imagination of poets as early as

Hesiod and Homer does not mean that the Arcadian Styx got its name from Homer. That is always possible with any question of Homeric geography, particularly with the identification of tombs, but the coincidence of swearing is harder to explain away, and Hesiod already knew exactly what it was like.

Herodotos (6, 74) is discussing a quarrel between Spartans, one of whom caused trouble in Arcadia. He wanted the Arcadians joining his conspiracy to swear by the water of Styx at Nonakris. 'The Arcadians say that the water of Styx is in this city, and indeed there is something of the kind. A little water comes out of a rock and dribbles down into a hollow, and a circle of dry-stone wall runs round the hollow.' The word for hollow might mean a glen, but Herodotos cannot personally believe this is where the gods swore. Has the Spartan got the idea out of Homer, as this is the first human oath we hear about by Styx? 'Nonakris, where this spring happens to be, is a city in Arcadia towards Pheneos.' Kleomenes, whose conspiracy this had been, was arrested by the Spartans and promptly went mad, a hazard of the Arcadian mountains, and murdered himself by degutting. Most Greeks said it was the vengeance of Delphi, but the Athenians said it was for attacking Eleusis, and the Argives said it was for crimes done in Argos. No one says it was for what happened at Nonakris, unless Herodotos may be thought to have implied that.

It is in the nature of things that for Homer the Styx is not in a particular place and equally natural that Herodotos pretends to know all about it; there is no inscription near the waterfall to his knowledge, but he knows about the dry-stone wall in a circle that renders the place holy, or taboo. It was what the Greeks called an *abaton*, a place not to be trodden, like the meadow memorably described by Euripides near the beginning of his *Hippolytos*. Hesiod describes somewhere definite but without locality, although Iris flies off with a golden water-pot to fetch water from the Styx for an oath-taking among the gods, so that we know he does envisage an earthly postal address so to speak. The nearest we have to a precise address in Homer is in the *Iliad* (2, 748) where 'a branch of the Styx' flows into the Peneios somewhere near Dodona, 'but floats on top of its current like olive oil, because this is a branch of the water of Styx, the oath of fearful power'. The waterfall seems to be known to Homer also, but only in the underworld (8, 369). To know more we must look for Nonakris. At some point after the death of Alexander, the poets began the typically teasing or riddling custom of saying Nonakrians when they meant Arcadians, and the tease probably had an origin in epic poetry: it may be that loose confederations of Arcadian hill-towns would meet and swear oaths of loyalty by the Styx in the archaic age or the pre-Homeric age: we have no way of knowing. When the great city Megalopolis was founded, any reference to the primacy of Nonakris would have been wiped out. Indeed Nonakris itself was all but obliterated and no one has ever localised it convincingly. That is why there has been all this difficulty about the Styx, with which a most impressive mountain waterfall has been identified for nearly two hundred years, on grounds of general probability. Styx has two sisters who are worth mention-ing, because Hesiod makes her a daughter of Ocean, and therefore sister to Thetis and to Eurynome. She married Pallas, who may well have been the Moon's father, but their named children were only Victory and Strength.

Those scholars who write clear, encyclopaedic works give clear references to the whereabouts of Nonakris, but it is reasonable to ignore them; in modern times they mostly depend on Philippson's nineteenth-century German work and an article of his in an Alpinists' magazine. W. M. Leake wandered about looking for the waterfall in the 1800s and offered a guess, but that has never been confirmed. Everyone is forced back on Pausanias, who did tour Arcadia just as Leake did: Leake with a full-blooded efficiency as became an officer of the Waterloo generation, surveying the defences of Greece as a Turkish province with a cavalry escort and an eye to the possible entry of Turkey into the war with Napoleon, but also with serious scholarly acumen. What Pausanias says (8, 17, 6) is 'As you travel west from Pheneos into the setting sun the left-hand road leads to the city of Kleitor, and the right-hand road takes you to Nonakris and the streams of the Styx. In the old days Nonakris was an Arcadian town named after Lykaon's wife, but in our own times it lies in ruins, and there is not a lot you can make even of the ruins. Not far from these ruins is a high crag: I have never seen a rock face so high; the water falls sheer down it, and this is the stream that the Greeks call Styx.'

The melancholy truth is that he not only offers little clue as to where the falls may be: that information can be supplied. But he offers even less help about Nonakris, and holds out small hope for the investigation of its ruins. He saw only the ruins perhaps and the mountain. Snow and landslide and probably earthquake have done their work since, and we must assume that Nonakris has now been wholly obliterated. The only clue we have is that a road led there from the east, from Pheneos and Mount Kyllene. After dealing with the bizarre miracles that can be worked with the water, Pausanias says that Lousoi 'was once a city', but it is inside the territory of Kleitor. He has discussed the mad daughters of Proitos who were taking refuge at a cave in the mountains now called Chelmos, until they were brought down by a wizard who cured them at Lousoi. The place used to hold games, and the only other thing we know about it is that Aristotle says the local mice (voles?) could swim. So can the chickens in Hook Norton. 'Above Nonakris stands [Chelmos]', which he calls the Aroanian mountains. There are a few other possible inferences: if Kleitor owned the territory of Lousoi then Nonakris cannot have been there, and if there were a route from ancient Pheneos to a place like Planitero that avoided Kleitor it would still not do, because it would not be near the falls. I advance this last view with uncertainty, because there is now a trout farm at Planitero where fast-running water turns to lakes with the fish, and swans and ducks; you see Chelmos nodding above your head with his tall, snowy cap, while you have lunch, but I did not adventure beyond the road that ends there. It is highly probable that the road to take from Pheneos is the one northwards to Zarouchla and Solos, which is the traditional route, and brings you to a famous and likely waterfall. Pausanias takes Nonakris and the Styx first, then the mountain itself with the daughters of Proitos, then Lousoi which no longer existed, or which he did not find, and then what we call Kalavryta, so he has crossed over the north side of Chelmos, and not by Planitero which is the south side and would lead him straight to Lousoi.

What later writers have to tell us gets swallowed up into mist and romance. Apuleius pictures a dragon-guarded mountain cliff with a black waterfall that waters the Stygian fens: the falls were associated with dragons as late as 1805, when Leake found them; they were still called Mavroneri in the Thirties of this century, that is Black Water, from a black stain on the rock. A late antique writer on mythology says the water itself was black because Demeter saw herself furious (with Poseidon of course) in the mirror of the pool and blackened it for ever in a fit of rage. Or might she not have been furious when she was reflected as a horse? Pausanias tells us the water was fatal if you drank it or if a beast drank it. 'Once upon a time it brought death to the goats that first tasted its water.' This deadliness is recorded by Theophrastos, Aristotle's pupil, by Pliny and by Seneca. Since it is presumably not true, we would do better to consider the goats. Someone has found a dead goat up there, surely. The water 'dissolves glass, crystal, agate and pottery' and corrupts all metals, but a horse's hoof survives. This must mean that some old shepherd found a hoof in the water, undissolved, that is all. The belief in its acid quality was one that takes us far afield all the same.

Frazer, who gathers most of the material in his commentary, was excited by comparative mythology. To show that the oath taken on Styx water was not unique, which of course it was, he adduces a native Sicilian tribe from Macrobius (Sat. 5, 19, 28), who venerated subterranean springs, and Damascius in his life of Isidore, who discusses an Arabian pool. Frazer goes on to tell us about water dipped with the King's weapons in Cambodia and Siam, the disgusting alliance rituals of the Karens of Burma, Buru in the East Indies and the Selebes in Papua. It used to be remembered in Trinity, Cambridge, that Frazer was or became a sucker for these stories, and young members visiting their old place of education from outposts of empire were regularly put next to him at dinner to entertain him with bizarre inventions later to be discovered in his works. Still, in 1898 he quoted chapter and verse, and at such length that I doubt his mastery of quite all the sources he notices: I wonder how good he was in Dutch for example. The truth about the water oath can be discovered by a glance at Homer: it is an oath by earth and water, or by land and water and all they feed, or earth and water and the sun. The only queer thing is how the Styx got mixed up in it, and the only analogy I can think of is the word *Iordas*, the Jordan, which becomes in Mandaean (in Iraq) the ordinary word for water, and in the catacombs a word for water that runs in paradise.

As for what would survive the Styx, Justin, like Pausanias, maintains it is a horse's hoof. Vitruvius, Pliny and Arrian insist on a mule's hoof. Plutarch says twice it was a donkey's hoof, but a large number of writers from Kallimachos onward, almost all of them of deep obscurity and all of them professional scholars, who got their information directly or indirectly from that great poet and informer Kallimachos, maintained that any vessel made of horn would do to carry the poisonous water. Aelian on the nature of animals said it had to be made of the horn of a Scythian ass, 'which Leake drily observes must have been exceedingly difficult to obtain'. Theophrastos suggests cheating by tying a sponge on to a stick and just dipping it in the water, but I know that Pausanias was interested in horn, since in discussing something else of no great relevance he suddenly remarks, 'By the way, the tusk of an elephant is not a tusk but a tooth.' He is talking, if I remember

rightly, about the mammoth horns that in his day were on exhibition as the tusks of the Calydonian boar in Caesar's gardens
beyond the Tiber; Suetonius in his *Lives of the Caesars* says that
Augustus had a mania for bones and relics of that kind. As for the
queer horn of the Scythian ass, Frazer offers us the pleasing
consolation that Hyllos son of Herakles had one small horn on
the left side of his head, but Epopeus of Sikyon killed him, took
his horn and carried Styx water in it, and so became king.

Once in this mood there is no holding Pausanias. The gods give
the poorest things power over the strongest, he said, pearls dissolve
in vinegar and diamonds dissolve in the blood of a billy-goat. The
medical writer who is the only other authority to comment on
the billy-goat and the diamond adds that you have to feed your
goat with bay leaves alone, give him nothing to drink, do it in
August, burn his blood in a pot and then roast it in an oven, grind
up the resulting powder with white pepper on a Sunday or a
Thursday, and then it will cure the stone. This is of little relevance
to the queer belief about diamonds, let alone about pearls, but
Frazer thinks (in my case quite correctly) that we will like to be
told it. It must have something to do with the hottest things and
the most Apolline, treated in the hottest way. In the same sort of
way Theophrastos believed you could get precious stones from
the concretised piss of a lynx. In fact Theophrastos on stones, of
which there is an excellent modern edition, is the best place to
enquire if you should be seriously puzzled about this sentence. It
is only leading up to the climactic sentence about Styx. 'I have
no actual knowledge that this water was the poison that killed
Alexander son of Philip, but I have certainly heard it said.'

Frazer is utterly dismissive of this report, although it is in
Arrian, in Plutarch, in Vitruvius and Pliny, among others. The
story was that Aristotle put Antipater up to sending Alexander
some Styx water in a horse's hoof. This means that we can date
the popular belief that some knowing old man might know about
this poison: that is, this bit of folklore. At the time of Alexander's

death the vast fertility of romantic and magical and wild or bizarre tales, and more important still the willingness of people to believe them, were an unforeseen force, but that powerful force swiftly showed what it could do in the popular life of Alexander that was written at once, and the prolific, swiftly growing Alexander romance which grew from it. This new attitude meant the end of the classical age and human history took a catastrophic dive. For a few years there were survivals like the poet Horace, but already in Theokritos the willingness to be delighted with nonsense in a new and decadent way does alas begin to become visible. By the time we get to Ovid (*Met.* 15, 332) the water of the Styx is deadly by day but harmless by night, and he believes the deadly water emptied into the lake of Pheneus, the Stymphalian Lake. Magic has faded to mere romance, and the combination of romance and rhetoric ruined poetry.

We are left with some ruins 'near' the waterfall, always assuming that we have the right waterfall: one would guarantee the other, and we may disregard all the magic and all the folklore. Frazer is the best guide; he was there in October 1895 and had a wonderful time in the way the Victorians enjoyed, though he ought perhaps to have taken more notice of the different kind of high spirits Pausanias was in. No doubt he was using reference books: on Mount Kyllene he tells you about snakes above the snowline and albino blackbirds, and famous tombs elsewhere, and the wood used for sculpture, and the mountain where Hermes discovered the tortoise; on Mount Chelmos he tells you about the Styx and the caves, and at Lousoi about old athletic games; at Kalavryta he tells you about a spring that cures rabies. These chapters are all of a piece, and when he comes to Kleitor you get the famous singing trout whistling like thrushes. As to why Pausanias should be in such a good mood, I think he loved the landscape and was amused by the trout and the blackbirds, and who would not be happy in such a place? '. . . white wild boars and white Thracian bears, and the Libyan breed of hares is white, and I have seen

snow-white deer at Rome, and was astounded by them.' He liked
natural wonders, and who does not?

The Victorians are too solemn about Greek landscape; I had
always wondered what heavy influence hung over Matthew
Arnold, whose verse play *Merope* has long heavy passages of
description that are like long avenues of gloomy trees, and really
scarcely digestible.

> We bounded down the swarded slope, we plunged
> Through the dense ilex-thickets to the dogs.
> Far in the woods ahead their music rang;
> And many times that morn we coursed in ring
> The forests round that belt Kyllene's side . . .
> . . . his new city, which he now
> Near Lycosura builds, Lycaon's town,
> First city founded on the earth by men . . .

This is the hunt in *Merope*, where stag and hounds and huntsman
all get washed down a cavern from the Stymphalian Lake. Maybe
it is the tendency of English poetry to revert to Scott and the
Trossachs that has gone wrong? Arnold after all is famous for his
finely tuned ear. Here he is in a lighter passage, though it will end
in Arcas murdering his mother whom he meets on Chelmos in
the form of a bear.

> But the sweet-smelling myrtle,
> And the pink-flow'rd oleander,
> And the green agnus-castus,
> To the west wind's murmur,
> Rustled round his cradle,
> And Maia rear'd him.
> Then, a boy, he startled,
> In the snow-fill'd hollows
> Of high Cyllene,
> The white mountain-birds;
> Or surprised, in the glens,

> The basking tortoises,
> Whose striped shell founded
> In the hand of Hermes
> The glory of the lyre.

One can see that the white bird comes from Pausanias but he has forgotten that the disgusting tale of Hermes and his blood-sports with the tortoise belongs to a different mountain. The flora is reminiscent not of a Greek mountain (no sage, no cistus) but rather of Torquay.

> But his mother Callisto,
> In her hiding-place of the thickets
> Of the lentisk and ilex,
> In her rough form, fearing
> The hunter on the outlook,
> Poor changeling! trembled.
> Or the children, plucking
> In the thorn-choked gullies
> Wild gooseberries, scared her,
> The shy mountain-bear!
> Or the shepherds, on slopes
> With pale-spiked lavender
> And crisp thyme tufted,
> Came upon her, stealing
> At day-break through the dew.
>
> Once, 'mid those gorges,
> Spray-drizzled, lonely,
> Unclimb'd of man –
> O'er whose cliffs the townsmen
> Of crag-perch'd Nonacris
> Behold in summer
> The slender torrent
> Of Styx come dancing,
> A wind-blown thread – . . .

Even though this is lighter and better, it still will not do. The best scene is that of Nonakris perching on its Germanic crag, and that is quite imaginary. The wild gooseberries are surely English or French, as the lavender and thyme might be; he does not mention any of the riotous Greek flowers because he has never been there. But the lentisk and ilex give him away, and the belts of forest round Kyllene (where Ovid put one huge forest of cypresses). What has happened is that Arnold is mad keen on going to Greece, he is about to go, and he writes to Colonel Leake in London to thank him for the many lines of local colour he has borrowed from Leake's Peloponnesian travels for the play he has just finished, which is *Merope*. Leake is an accurate, useful writer and the best topographer ever to have worked in Greece, but reset as poetry his landscape passages hang heavy.

The exhilaration of Leake's Greek journeys is still to be felt; here it is lacking. In Arnold's poetry it is closer in 'The Scholar Gypsy', of which the key is 'near me on the grass lies Glanvil's book . . .', a work that touches on gypsy magic, which Arnold linked to Clough's experiments with mesmerism: how one might by sheer imaginative power bend the minds of men and alter those mental currents that determine human history. It is a very bookish, dotty idea, adopted gratefully by Yeats in his essay on Magic, but then Arnold was a very bookish poet and he never came to Nonakris, so Greece in his poetry remained a pure Victorian ikon. Tennyson fortunately worked from the paintings of Edward Lear, although there is, come to think of it, a creeping gloom in the edges of his oil painting of Bassai at Cambridge, probably because the landscape was filled in from some rocks in Leicestershire, where Bassai really has mountain grass, not rocks, and the tortoise was copied from an old drawing he had of one in the London Zoo. Arnold's Greek landscape in *Merope* is worse: it is as I have just said a pure Victorian ikon, a fake.

Yet Frazer, whose journeys are quite real, does convey in his search for the Styx at least a mountaineer's or an explorer's passion. A few miles downstream and a few days later, on a day when he was so happy that he fell to dreaming of 'sandy Ladon's lilied banks', he got totally lost and disoriented where the Ladon, the Erymanthos and the Alpheios meet not far from Aspra Spitia, but on the day he set out for the Styx he was in full control (Vol. 4, p. 248). His track from Pheneus to Zarouchla is one of the most beautiful in all Greece. 'The grandeur of the mountains, the richness of the vegetation, the fragrance and charm of the pine-forests' and the distant views of blue water make it the most agreeable of Greek memories. You climb through 'the luxuriant gardens and lanes' of Phonia to a ridge that reveals the magnificence of Chelmos, 'its bare summit and pine-clad lower slopes'. You see a monastery high up, which you must pass, on a path that leads by white poplars, cypresses and ferns down to groves of plane trees, then up again through oak woods, and beyond the monastery and still climbing, 'a maze of beautiful woods and dense, tangled thickets, threaded by rills of sparkling water', some bare slopes and then 'the pine forest for several hours'.

Frazer is riding, though no doubt it would be quicker to walk, but dignity and luggage called for mules (he says horses) and guides. Without a guide the paths are not quite as easy to find. Also the language in which he tells his tale 'between verdant glades and sombre pine-forests' is heavy in the overloaded Victorian manner. He notices 'the delicious odour of the pines and the freshness and exhilaration of the air at a height of about 6,000 feet', and he is excited by the descent of the north slope towards Zarouchla, where the view is mountainous, but the spell of 'plants of which I did not know the names' and 'romantic' rivers and 'blue and purple mountains' is not broken, and will not be until the 1920s. He goes down the Crathis (Akrata) where it is a 'clear, rushing stream' and easily fordable. The path climbs a little on the far side but still follows the valley downstream, until it meets 'the glen of the Styx' itself. You ascend that: it is 'deep, narrow and almost oppressively grand', more like a canyon or a defile than a glen. The mountains are terraced 'and on the terraces are several very picturesque villages'. At the head of the glen soars the mighty cone of Chelmos. There are fine horse-chestnut trees, and night-ingales sing from February to June. Solos is on the eastern terrace with Gounarianika, Mesorougi and Peristera on the western side. They are collectively called Kloukinaes, and Frazer reckons one or other of them must be Nonakris. This can only be called a valiant guess, but the journey took him five and a half hours, so he has a right to guess.

'The walk from Solos to the fall and back is exceedingly fatiguing and very few travellers accomplish it; most of them are content to view the fall from a convenient distance through a telescope.' You can ride two miles of the five, but you need guides (one to hold the horses). The path wanders, but in twenty minutes you see the falls, and in another five minutes you cross over to the left bank: you have climbed high on the right bank of the Styx, and the rock is slaty light green or grey. The entire north face of Chelmos is a line of terrific precipices, in many places overhang-ing. The cliff where the water falls is the eastern and lower end of these precipices. From a distance the black (and red) streaks on the rocks are visible, but the water, which tumbles some six hundred feet from the snowfield at the top, disappears in mid-air, turns to vapour, and does not seem to reach the ground at all, though a pool of clear water forms below it and from that the river runs down. This phenomenon is well enough attested elsewhere in extremely high waterfalls, and I have myself seen it, much to my surprise, in Nuristan. Frazer says the water was 'not excessively cold', but in October he thinks it did not come from snow. The Admiralty guide to Greek footpaths and mule tracks (1916) differs a little from this account of the falls in its hardbitten way, but I am in no position to arbitrate. Poor old Frazer heard some dogs barking and the echo 'had a weird impressive sound that suited well with the scene, as if the hell-hounds were baying at the strangers who dared to approach the infernal waters', but the guides kept them off by throwing stones at them, a simple signal well understood by Greek dogs.

It was a scene of 'sublime but wild and desolate grandeur', and it is surely one of few scenes in Greece where nature on her own can rival the antiquities of the fifth century, and the impressiveness of literature, let alone the formidable horrors of myth and religion. The ridge, which is usually snow-covered and from which the water falls, is nowadays called the Nereid's ridge, Neraidorachi. On the cliff, various cretins who have climbed up to it in modern times have carved their names or initials, and the date of their visit: including the booby King Otto, 1847. No doubt, as Virgil puts it, the Nymphs howled from the crest. When Leake discovered this wonder of nature in 1806, the Greeks he met had never heard that it had an ancient name, and it remains possible that it never did. The trees are still remarkable as you would expect, in the valley of the Krathis: but today the approach is from Kalavryta, about ten miles by car to a mountain car-park and about another five on foot, though neither by that route nor by the Solos route has anyone ever found Nonakris. The question therefore remains open, and without archaeological evidence it cannot be solved, where is Nonakris?

Long ago I read a travel book by a Cambridge classicist called, I think, Lucas. It was a charming, unpretentious and to me most interesting work, written in the Twenties or Thirties, and it was the first to interest me in the Falls of the Styx. In the casual manner of an experienced Alpinist he made the expedition seem an easy one, which he and his wife had accomplished with their walking-sticks and no guides. I wanted to repeat their journey thirty years ago, but by then I had lost or given away his book and forgotten its title. 'From Olympos to the Styx', can it have been? I remember staring with awe at Diakofto, the cleft in the mountains between where the train takes you up to Kalavryta, from the steamer that first got me to Greece, but I have never taken that train.

10 : Virtue Is Beauty

IN order to set out to discover America, you need to have information that it exists. So we had of the Styx and its magical waterfall, but how to get there was most uncertain. We set out therefore to see as much as we could on the way, and perhaps, who knows, we might get to Kalavryta in the end, a place attainable by the railway, though I had never been there and Giorgis I think only once. The whole point of our expedition was going to be the route, and that was a success, chiefly because of luck and because at critical points we conjured roads into existence by willing them to exist. The maps we used were so bad that even by using them I have failed to retrace our steps. Half the time I think we were in wonderland: certainly we were in a much older Greece than I had ever hoped to see again. It was a reward for ignoring the east of Arcadia, Mantinea and Tegea where the stone came from Doliana, and Nestani that I used to love so much, and rich seaside Astros and Leonidion with its queer-coloured cliffs and tall trees, and Stymphalos where Herakles beat up the birds, and the excellent wine if you turn west from the Gothic ruins of the Cistercian monastery, which are just like English monastic ruins really, except that they were built with reused ancient stones. '*Corage nos fait antiquitas, que tout ne sie vanitas,*' as someone said at the time.

Iannis arrived at nine in his very brave little dusty car, and we all clucked over the maps, except for Mitsa who left us to it. We were off by ten I am sure, and out of high spirits we took the old road to Olympia, and marvelled at its ups and downs and twists and turns, because Iannis still travels it to school, and I used to walk it once a week about twenty years ago. It lay there not even dusty but gently glowing with a counterpane of wild flowers up to its chin. We had to shut our eyes as we passed the indescribable horrors of modern Olympia, to which this good old road faithfully led us, but we turned off as soon as possible, uphill among the flowering bushes and the dense plantations of pine to Lala and the wind. It is only as you pass Lala into the flat open plateau that lies north of it that you see the point of the large army that the Aga kept up there. It is a splendid ground for exercising cavalry, indeed it is excellent for playing soldiers of any eighteenth-century kind. He had many, and like a good Turk he kept them in tents. There is even a tent in my old print of Olympia before it was excavated: I would call it small but grand, not so mobile as a turban or a parasol, but easily moved for the convenience of a high officer. One would take a nap in it but not spend the night: the Aga's palace was a substantial one in Lala.

But here at Pousi, very tiny and very quiet, was the site of the first battle of the Civil War. Kolokotronis and his friends had determined to attack the Aga in his lair with their very few imported guns, their muskets and their yataghans. One would have said this was a hopeless idea, and of course Turkish reinforcements came racing from Patras. They were mostly 'Albanians' because Albania was the local supplier of 'native infantry' or mercenary soldiers to this part of the Turkish empire. But since the population then grouped as Albanians was so very mixed, and since Greeks among others served as conscripts under the Turks, it is as ludicrous to be racist about this war as about any other. One can only say from the names of the Greek dead on the war memorial that they are the names of villagers, and they are all Christian, and Giorgis remembers and still knows a number of their families. This battle near Lala, at what is called Pousi, was an overwhelming victory for the Greeks.

They started on the defensive, with their backs to the forest, but they had chosen their ground and stood their ground, and against the odds they won. They burnt Lala, I suppose. Now it is a very quiet place, a perfectly quiet sanctuary on a hilltop among a hundred hilltops. To the north it looks at Chelmos and to the east at the central mountains of Arcadia, to the south far beyond the Alpheios and to the west the sea. The memorial is a stone cross you might see in any English village, standing in an enclosed rectangle of ground, fenced off from flocks and from agriculture; a small chapel stands there which is shut. There were a lot of purple anemones in the grass, small ones as befitting a hilltop, and late in the year but still numerous. Anemones are on sale in the streets soon after Christmas in Athens and by the end of April they are finished almost everywhere; I was pleased to see them again in their natural profusion, growing wild among fresh ferns just uncurling. The place is a miracle of quietness.

Before we left Pousi another and a very different surprise awaited us. On the west side of the road, just a few yards further on, stands a modern stone memorial to the members of the Greek resistance who fell here in a battle with the Germans. I had often heard about this battle but never read about it. I knew only that the resistance had ambushed a German convoy here, on the edge of the forest, as it travelled from Kalavryta. It must have been heading for Pyrgos or to embark at Katakolo for North Africa; no one seemed to know. It was virtually annihilated, and no one got through the ambush, though the tail of the convoy fled back through the forest as far as Kalavryta. That was the occasion when the village at Olympia came close to perishing: the first they knew of the battle, which thirty years later those who remembered anything said was 'in a pass through the mountains high up beyond Lala', was the arrival of a heavily armed German force from Pyrgos, and the whole village being lined up.

I remembered this, and had always wanted to see the place, if only because it seemed to offer a clue to the rough road from Elis to

Olympia, the short cut across the mountains that Pausanias described. It offered little help really with that problem, though it was an ancient route to the upper Erymanthos and the upper Ladon, meeting-places of the flocks, and to the rich cities of Psophis, and Lousoi which had games of its own, and Kleitor with its huge territory. An inscription was found at Arcadian Orchomenos which recorded in the fourth century BC the boundaries of the Arcadian cities at a time when the Arcadians were just coming into being as a state, but the lands of Kleitor had spread by the age of Pausanias. There were more names on the resistance memorial than there were on that of the War of Independence, and the place is a wild one. Some men from Pyrgos certainly fought there, and one or two from Olympia, but the armed resistance drew men from far afield, and the conditions that followed the war have not favoured the writing of a full history. Even in the Seventies people did not like it to be known that they had ever taken up arms in the Greek countryside, nor did they trust all those who had once been their allies, nor do I blame them.

The forest into which we now drove was a place of heavenly beauty, though more like a park now than a forest. It used to be denser, and it was one of the great forests of Greece. I think Giorgis called it the Forest of Kapsalis, but so far as one could see from the road it was bare bones, a few mighty trees and the sun just fingering the ploughed land between them. We passed some farms too, but as we progressed they became fewer. We were now following the valley of a river which spilt across the road at a village high up the hillside called Lampeia. The water-springs there are the making of the great river Erymanthos, though the stream has run down before that from Basilaki, which is on the road across the Peloponnese through Langadia and over Mainalon from the Stymphalian Lake, which the Germans constructed during their occupation of Greece: it is the road that passes through Olympia itself.

As for Lampeia, it is an ancient name reused for the wrong place, I believe. Near there in the most modest of cottages, Papandreou the historian of Eleia and headmaster of a grammar school was born, almost on the borders of ancient Arcadia. It is a beautiful village, like Portaria on Mount Pelion with its fine merchants' houses, and I greatly envied an old man I saw skipping downhill from stone to stone after his sheep. Old Mr Papandreou (1859–1940) wore a wing collar, trim beard and full moustache and the expression of a bulldog. His first work was about the antiquities of Kalavryta (1886), and apart from a slighter memoir about the War of Independence, so was his last (1928); even his great history of Eleia was written there, though it was printed in Pyrgos by the Eleian community of Athens and the Piraeus. The truth is that he was at heart an Arcadian: Achaia and Eleia are scarcely places at all, they are simply communities of coastal people, but strike inland and you are in ancient Arcadia at once. We had already passed close to the village of Simopoulos, and at the next village, where we stopped in some confusion about the route, we would be at Tripotamia, which is Arcadian.

There Giorgis suddenly announced he had an aunt. An old lady came bustling out of a tiny dark uninviting doorway that seemed to be a small café, and they recognised each other and fell around each other's necks. She was the mother of that slightly older cousin of his who had been a resistance captain and was killed at the liberation of Pyrgos. She seemed a dear and unadventurous old lady. It was only when I was introduced and made to sit down (I had been exploring the village and stretching my legs) that Giorgis pointed to the café's one outdoor table: it was the top drum of a fluted column of grey stone, with its Doric capital on the flat top of which some ancient temple roof had once rested, but now nothing rested there except a coffee and two glasses of lemonade. We sat on other bits of ancient building or on plastic chairs, whichever was nearest. An elderly shepherd who had come down from the hill joined us, crook in hand. He seemed not to want much except to satisfy the vast, unfillable receptacle of curiosity that every Greek carries with him as a birthright. When we separated he asked Iannis for a cigarette and took a handful; he went off again to his flock very happily. We never found out where he came from or where he went. Giorgis met another cousin he had never seen before, on holiday from Athens, and there was much handshaking and happiness and exchanging of family news. The aunt was enormously pleased to hear Charis was marrying: she looked well old enough to be a grandmother and a great-aunt several times over.

Just round the corner as we turned off the main road lay one of those hillsides thickly seeded with ruins which mean a classical site. When I was working on a brief commentary on Pausanias in the 1960s, I cannot have known this area well enough, and I now observe a number of stern refusals to identify this and that. In Frazer I note a similar confusion, but I think the truth is that this whole meeting-place of roads, of valleys and of rivers must have been God-given as a meeting of flocks, and was therefore rich and well-populated in ancient times, so that there are now too many ancient sites, rather than too few. The twenty-third chapter of Pausanias on Arcadia ends with an amazing list of village names – Argeathai, Lykountes, Skotane, the oak forest of Soron, Psophis itself, Paos and Seirai – and we know that Psophis was once called Erymanthos like the river, then Phegia, finally Psophis. Pausanias in dealing with Psophis is much bemused by the quirks of Arcadian genealogy and mythology, but Psophis is clearly Tripotamia where the Erymanthos meets Aroanios and another river. It used to have many more antiquities visible than it has now, but the ruins of its little theatre are clear enough, and I suppose the column that was the café table stood in the small temple of Erymanthos. Frazer does indicate where things were a hundred years ago, but he tamely follows Leake in disliking the situation of this beautiful place because it had no open views. I would like to spend weeks exploring it.

Pausanias climbs a hill to the south of Tripotamia, heading for Thelpousa and the valley of the Ladon, which Frazer who followed said took about six hours, but we turned left away from the main road and the river, through an enchanted landscape of grazing-grounds, wild flowers and willow trees until we came in a few miles to a place Giorgis and Iannis were anxious to show me, where behind some houses an ancient vine grows in some plane trees. It covers at least sixty feet by sixty feet of hillside, a small chapel has been built in its shade, it was just fainting into leaf, trembling into leaf, though I do not know if it still gives fruit. I was assured that Pausanias mentioned it, but one is told that all over Greece about any very ancient tree, and I can find no trace of it in his text at the moment. He is very keen on sacred trees, like the Syrian bay tree into which Daphne turned, Athene's olive on the akropolis of Athens 'miracle-born out of the living rock', and the palm tree where Apollo and Artemis were born, and he does not despise the vine, but I think he missed this one or no myth attached to it. It is certainly of the most incredible antiquity: I have never seen vine-branches like it, so huge, so sclerotic, so fossilised. Its vast split trunk recalled the most ancient olive trees of Zakynthos. It must certainly be some thousands of years old.

Although I had explored this country in the past I found my memory of it all had quite gone: the only way to know such a place is through the soles of your feet, and even Frazer travelled too fast. It did not take us long to get to Kleitor, where we did not spend long looking at the antiquities, of which I had some dim recollection, but we were thinking about lunch and put ourselves in Giorgis's hands. He was going to deal us another surprise card, and after some hesitation over roads he produced the ace of trumps, at Planitero, which lies well to the north, and nearer than any other human inhabitation to the tall and graceful peak of Chelmos, an almost sheer conical cap of snow towering thousands of feet above us into the sky. The snow sparkled in sunlight and beside the road a torrent of snow-water glittered and rattled and washed almost underfoot. There began to be rock on one side of us with trees bursting out of it, and suddenly we were in an entire wood of mature and beautiful plane trees.

This went on for about a mile, and one could see that the

municipal engineers of Kleitor had been at work for a hundred or more years to tame the power of the torrent, which ran swirling over the roots of the enormous trees. It was as if one could wander between the feet of elephants as they gazed and drank. I do not know which was the greatest natural wonder, the trees or the water or the towering peak of Chelmos. Under the trees we found a hut, a series of lakes and some gravel to park the car. The water was fast-flowing and clear and there were some wary-looking fish swimming in it, a few ducks, and of all things a pair of swans. The fish were trout, but there were also salmon, whether planted by nature or the hand of man: the place was a fish-farm. You could eat where you liked on a series of islands joined by wooden bridges. You ordered in the central restaurant and they brought your food out to you. It was all on the level of a public park on a bank holiday, with plastic chairs, ghastly bad taste everywhere and oilcloth on the tables, but the surroundings were incredible: they made you gasp. We ate trout, which was neither brown trout nor any other kind I have seen or eaten before, but fresh and delicious. They had rather coarse and black skins.

Alas, they were not the famous singing trout of the Aroanios that Pausanias mentions (8, 21, 2). Frazer says those had no doubt been trout, caught in nets or shot with 'dynamite bullets'. He was told they chirped like birds when they were netted and that an assembly of them would give out a low musical hum. Pausanias says they are 'supposed to sing like thrushes. I have seen them caught, but I never heard them singing although I stayed beside the river until sunset which is supposed to be their favourite time to sing.' There certainly do exist fish that make a chirping noise, but these thrilling trout must have been wiped out in the end by the dynamite bullets. At least, they are not to be heard today, and no one is alive who pretends to have heard them. Ancient authorities agreed about them, although they were not all quite sure where the river was, and modern reports confirm the strange fact, so Frazer's scorn is quite out of place. D'Arcy Thompson permits them entry under their local ancient name *poikiliai* into his splendid *Glossary of Greek Fishes* (1947), but I do not think he really believes in them as I do.

We left that place after a short walk with the roar of water in our ears, very reluctantly. This time we turned right from our side-road, and headed as we hoped for Kalavryta, and maybe for the Falls of the Styx. We climbed up past the caves and the underground lake, and our road followed the glen uphill past Lousoi where an ancient town was, and where the dirty mess was disposed of after the legendary daughters of Proitos had been cured of moping madness. What dirty mess? you may well ask. They were cured with black hellebore, which is a purge and usually lethal, or by waving a pig over them, later slaughtered, so you may take your pick. The stream looks innocent enough on a spring afternoon. Dionysos certainly had a quarrel with these girls, according to the most venerable of authorities, Hesiod himself. As for the name Lousoi, there are several places with names like that, each with its own legend of mythical ladies' ablutions, more than one of them in Arcadia. Games were held up here, about which one would like to know a great deal more.

The glen opened out to fir forest and snow-smeared mountain ridges, but after a little uncertainty the car overcame the steepness of the road, which was excellent tarmac at this point, and careered down the far side to Kalavryta. Here a memorial informed us the Germans had killed fifteen hundred men, women and children, the whole population as far as they could catch it, and they did catch most people, as they arrived in the afternoon. The clock on the Cathedral tower has been kept stopped at that hour ever since. They burnt down the whole town. I do not know who was in charge, and I am sure he is dead long ago. They took the people of Kalavryta out on to the mountainside above the town and there they machine-gunned them; it was vengeance for the attack on their convoy, but whether it was done by those who got away (as I suspect) or by some special execution squad, I have no way of discovering. Now the town is rebuilt, it looks innocent enough, even flourishing, and if you cannot read the memorial or what is written on the Cathedral, it looks like a place with a happy history. It even has a railway station.

Its ancient name was Kynaitha. In the middle ages it belonged for a time to the French family of Humbert Tremouille, who built themselves a fine castle possibly on the ruins of the ancient akropolis of Kynaitha: the first feudal lord of the barony was Otto de Tournay, and the *Chronicle of the Morea* lists him as a large landowner. In 1990, the place was full of water-springs, which occasionally flooded the bazaar, and plane trees grew in the streets. The castle, which is a ruin, was called Tremola, it lies east of the town; Frazer can see no way of deciding between Tremola and Salmena, where some graves have been found, but it appears to me that the water and the position at the head of the glen favour the castle for a strong-point, and the modern town for the site of the ancient one. Pausanias speaks of a water-spring where you could be cured of a bite from a rabid dog, which has been found. A famous plane tree once grew beside it, and I have a sneaking personal doubt whether Herodotos did not confuse it with the Falls of the Styx.

Kynaitha was wiped out by an invasion in the third century BC, and refounded perhaps under Hadrian as a Roman colony. It is a fine glen and the Romans who farmed there will have been contented. But Polybius gives the Kynaithians a very nasty reputation: he says their disgusting degree of aggression, their exiling and massacring and bloody-mindedness were due to their failure to be musical, their lack of training in music, which all the other Arcadians were famous for, and which they needed to offset their bleak environment. This is of course asinine, and used to be still quoted in my day to explain why Virgil set his *Eclogues* in Arcadia, and why all his shepherds sing. The only evidence Polybius can adduce against them is a massacre by which they offended the Spartans, from which all the other Arcadian cities dissociated themselves (4, 17–21). It seems that Polybius could say what he liked about them, and that his grievance was personal. Pausanias says very little about the place and less about the people, probably because in his day it was a Roman country town.

We sat down shocked, worn out and dazed in its main square, but no enquiry of the many we made brought us any closer to our waterfall: Chelmos to the people of Kalavryta was another world, as heaven is to earth. Then at last when Iannis was asking a taxi-man who had never heard of it, another taxi-man knew just what we wanted, and after some hunting found a tourist pamphlet that mentioned it. It was a drive of some ten miles back from Kalavryta up the mountain, and then by a by-road along the north face, as far as a car-park. From that point it was necessary to walk, but it was not seriously dangerous, nor was it excessively demanding. The five miles on foot would be too much for Giorgis all the same, and it was now late in the day. We all agreed about that and that having got so far we must give up the Falls of the Styx, and we should go home now. Iannis wanted to telephone home, and returned with the astonishing news that it was his brother's wedding day, he was supposed to be best man and we were to be witnesses, and if we left now we might just be in time. Whether his silence about this had been part of his exquisite courtesy to Giorgis and me, or due to his brother's talent for improvisation, I could not penetrate; I think it was both. We swiftly decided the inland road by Patras would be the best, though none of us knew it, and we were off.

This inner road turned out to be thrilling; it was not only extremely beautiful as the sun slid downwards, but had a number of antiquities that were all the more exciting to me because I knew that I would pass them only once, and when the sunlight melted as the snow was melting I would never see them again. There was no time to repine about that, or about Leake's waterfall in which by now I only half believed; the rush to the rescue of Iannis's brother and the charming Romanian bride preoccupied all three of us, though we kept pointing out of the car windows and exclaiming about the old houses, the magically perching villages, the valleys full of light and the sun-struck grazing grounds as we wound and whizzed our way towards the coast. That cannot have been a very long drive, but it was as memorable as certain dreams you long to dream again. The only thing that delayed us was the suburbs of Patras, which now extend many miles further into the country than even Giorgis had ever guessed. But some twisting and turning through garages brought us towards the sea and the old well-known National Road past the Cathedral. We eventually met the wedding party going in the opposite direction, in a lane outside Pyrgos. It turned out we would have been on time, but the ceremony had misfired because the village mayor, who was a friend and had agreed and had the power to perform the marriage, had misunderstood the date and wandered off to another town. It would all have to be fixed all over again, and next day her residence permit would expire. Still, these things are easier in Greece than under the Home Office, so they were not as worried as I would have been, or as I was.

Looking back at it now, after trying to write about it from the scratchiest notes, that seems a long and terribly hurried journey. It was one in which we missed a great deal, too. Had we paused at Lousoi and taken the side road to Lousiko, we would have seen the ruins of a temple of Artemis Lousiatis, the Washer-woman, some public buildings including one that interests me described as a meeting place built like a theatre but roofed. Not far away a cave goes deep into the mountainside; it must have been the cave of the Proitades and a lair of the magician Melampous, or Blackfoot: the Merlin of stalagmites, the Druid of stalactites. A tincture of the classics makes him somehow more credible that the Welsh wizard and more respectable, but there was no Arthur in north-western Arcadia, no Camelot on Chelmos, and no Tennyson, which is all a relief in this clear air. Yet when I woke the next morning that whole journey already seemed 'like the best kind of dream, I would like to repeat it slowly'.

That night we had supper at the Canada at Hagios Iannis to commemorate and honour Takis Sinopoulos the poet; one of his favourite expeditions was to that trout farm, to which he was the first to introduce Giorgis. It seemed then as if it was going to rain and rain hard. There was a south wind, the sort that comes loaded with sand from the Sahara and spatters things red. Mitsa had said ominously when we got home, 'Tonight it will rain red.' Perhaps it did during the night: when I woke at about half-past eight next morning the sun was just struggling up out of the mist, extremely hot; the sky was pure and cloudless and windless. The Greek connection with the Sahara is a very queer one. When their cousins in Arcadia were building at Alipheira with rocks six foot by three (and at Lepreon? who knows) the first Spartan colonists on the edge of the Libyan desert were living in tiny round huts like fishermen, where you could pick up stones with one hand, though the place, which is called Tocra, is a wonderful stone quarry. In Crete in certain weather conditions they see men robed in white walking and riding in the air. That is a mirage of a kind over the sea, the figures in white are Arabs. It is true of the Greeks perhaps as it is of those North Africans, that somewhere deep in them stretches a desert of sand.

Still, equally as the Egyptian sage remarks in Herodotos, the Greeks were always children. I do not know why so many albino blackbirds, trout singing like thrushes, and waterfalls that killed and others that cured, were crowded together in north-western Arcadia: maybe the fashion for wonders and peculiar animals, which flour-ished under the early empire and affected Pausanias among others, arose from scholars who had an access to the wildest mountains from Roman Kalavryta, or maybe it is just happy chance. Once when I was young I tried to learn German by reading through the massive *Encyclopaedia of Classical Studies* in twenty or thirty volumes that ruled our lives: but I did not get beyond the first page, because the first word was *Aal*, an eel. 'The Eel', it began sagely, 'is *ein heiliger flügendfisch*, a holy flying-fish for the Egyptians.' I was too entranced to want to read on, though I see that the modernised and compressed version of that encyclopaedia that I have used since 1979 just begins crossly, 'The eel in the *Iliad* is not a fish.' In the same way as the old encyclopaedia, these few pages of Pausanias on Arcadia are among my favourites from all his works. It is amusing to spot the books he is looking up, and to see for example how much material he shares with that other collector and scholar of natural wonders, Aelian: but it is even more amusing to go where he went and to halt, with one's own very different kind of curiosity and amazement, where he halted. All in all, if I had to start my life again, I would still start again at Pausanias: he is a satisfactory subject for study for second-rate minds like mine, and one that does not come to an end. I leave him now without regrets.

It was time to get ready to leave Greece. The hotel bill, which was under three hundred pounds for eleven nights, was not excessive: I think it was so modest only for Giorgis's sake. I met him at about eleven at his paper shop: the day was by then cloudy and windy just like England. Giorgis and I both had to face journeys that were beginning to colonise our minds. We had an ouzo with Iannis and sat on until a huge group had assembled, Barouxis who was better from his fever, a young and bearded radiographer, and for a moment even the old Maenad of the Doctor, with an equally unattractive teacher of English from Amaliada. They did not linger long, but the conversation seemed as if it would never stop. I liked the people more than ever but found the post-Communist intellectual flavour of the morning wearisome, and Giorgis was dazed by it too. Iannis did make a really funny joke about Derrida, but, alas, it was word-play and I do not remember it now. In fact I could only tell what they were on about by the recurring word *apodomosis*, which I deduced must mean deconstruction: they were running a literary magazine after all. Iannis produced a beautiful Bulgarian lady in trouble with Greek, and the Romanian lady appeared: it was all rather like Oxford forty years ago, where Eastern Europeans were a family speciality of the Cooper brothers.

But Iannis's mother knows the Pontic dialect of Greek very well, which is the one old Professor Dawkins, who had studied them all,

used to like best, because it was the closest to ancient Greek. It used
to be spoken in the three streets of Rizokastro which were a refugee
enclave of the Twenties under the Athenian akropolis, the way the
Persians climbed up when they conquered it. The Pontic families
had the most heavenly old-fashioned barrel organs covered in velvet
and stuck all over with pictures and bits of cheap jewellery, on
which in the Sixties they still played French 1920s dance music. You
saw them going about at night from tavern to tavern; I remember
them on my first evening in Athens, when there was a full moon and
one could go and see the Parthenon by pure moonlight, without
unnatural illuminations. I thought it magically beautiful, and in
those days you could wander all over it. Later that night I had dinner
with an American Jesuit at the Old University, once the most
dramatic of Greek taverns but now alas reclaimed by the State. Had
I known it, that was just on the edge of the Pontic-speaking enclave.
Now the dialect has dispersed, the barrel organs have fallen to pieces
or been bought by museums or millionaires, and the Old University,
the one where Makyriannis sat among the young men after the War
of Independence, and listened, I suppose, for the striking of Lord
Elgin's town clock, which Elgin had given the Athenians in return
for their marbles, has been turned into a set of civil service offices.

Yesterday the only person truly disappointed by the failure of the
wedding was Iannis's little son Dimitrakis, who was all washed and
dressed for it: but it was going to take place tonight, though without
us as witnesses alas. Iannis came home with us to lunch with Mitsa
and we said goodbye. In the late afternoon the sky cleared and the
swallows were swarming over all the roofs of Pyrgos. In the evening
we went to Giorgis's house again where we drank whisky, but Mitsa
was very ill with a throat infection, pausing only to laugh and to
groan, and to curse Giorgis about some pills not looking the same
as some other pills. Giorgis and I went out to dinner and ate fresh
fish at Barbadimis next door to the estate.

It is a curious fact that one of the few inscribed records of the
ancient dialect of the Eleians is the contract by which some land

was let at Salmone 'in perpetuity', perhaps a stone's throw away: 'between Theron and Aichmanor, *par tar gar tar en Salamonai*, eighteen measures . . .' The idea of most words ending in 'r' is jolly when you first encounter it, but it must have sounded extremely rustic, as if the Eleians chewed off the ends of words more or less at will. They used the digamma, too, when it was long out of fashion elsewhere. An agreement between Eleia and Heraia was inscribed in about 500 BC, *A Fratra toir Faleiois kai tois Er Fadiois* . . . 'F' being pronounced something like 'hw'. It is a great relief to me that we have not got any Eleian poetry: maybe Giorgis is the greatest Eleian poet there has ever been, or the last true Arcadian who has come down from the mountains.

Next day I was booked on to the new fast ferry from Patras. I was to be fetched by Christos's son and taken to the bus, and met by Dinos at Patras; at the offer of lunch he roared with laughter. It was as if I was deeply glued into the web of an extended family. All the same, Greek journeys have an inherent drama: they are never quite formless.

Epilogue:
Our Blood to This,
This to Our Blood Is Born

WHEN I got up at seven it was a pleasantly cool and cloudy day with much screaming of swallows. As for the people of the town, their faces in the street had never looked more Byzantine, so the least touch of peasant faces, common in Giorgis's and my generation, showed up at once: and, so I considered, did every quality of the Greeks ancient or modern, passing like cloud shadows over the Yorkshire moors. In the end I was taken to the bus station by not one car but two, Mr Kalamatianos's elder son, the one who could leap-frog higher than a horse, and Iannis who was even taller, with Giorgis to keep me company. The bus station was the same as ever with its grimy suffering crowd, the men in greasy flat caps and the women with queer parcels. A kilted highlander wandered through the crowd: from Edinburgh, Giorgis conjectured. I said he must be from a university, perhaps Glasgow, and when this turned out to be true my credit as a travelled man and connoisseur of nationalities soared.

The bus left at a quarter to ten; Giorgis prefers buses because on them as an old bus man he travels free and gets a good seat: this one was dustier than I remembered them but dreamlike also, and the journey enchanted, because it took the old road to Patras through all the intricate skein of the oldest villages. You did not feel you were whizzing across a plain between trees or farms, but fumbling

259

and rumbling along grassy, watery lanes from huge village to huge village. We passed Giorgis's grandfather's house and the church he built, both drowned in vegetation so prolific you could not tell what was wild, what was garden, and what was agriculture. There were some fine nut trees and fruit trees of his planting all the same. It is quite possible I had never been on this bus with Giorgis before. I had forgotten the windings, the heat, the suburban villages sprawling in the sun, and hoping to be taken for towns: something only Amaliada achieved, that queer place. The others hoped, but Amaliada pretended. We should have been in Patras before noon, but suddenly at half-past eleven we were lost and trapped in the most horrendous traffic jam.

The whole town was paralysed by the excavation of the main road, rendered worse by a fiendish one-way system, with screaming whistles, angry policemen, and bemused, anarchic drivers stopping to telephone, doing U-turns on the pavement, and so on. It was not just one hold-up; the jam went on as long as Patras, because the entire road was up for a mile or so, while one machine and two or three men laid down immense cement sections of piping. The others must have been away at lunch. Meanwhile the police barred traffic from all useful routes, and all short cuts had been skilfully blocked off. If you had entered Patras you must suffer. We were told this crisis had been going on for months. Fortunately we had allowed plenty of time, because I had thought of wandering off to see the bare Roman bones of Patras, which is an Augustan city after all and has a right to what is left of its Venetian colonnades, which are imitated from Zakynthos. There is a castle and a museum, neither of which I had seen for many years.

It was half an hour after noon when we got to the bus station and Dinos was nowhere to be seen. Searching did not produce him and small wonder: he was doubtless lost or imprisoned somewhere in the vast agglomerated traffic, tooting impotently. We therefore felt we must take a taxi back into the traffic and go in the wrong direction to the only point at which one could rejoin it. At last this cunning taxi-man got us to Pelikani, a region named after a pelican once befriended by a tavern-keeper, when the world was young that is, to the new flats opposite the brewery, but there we found Dinos was out and there was no public telephone. We were quite heavily encumbered, so no light manoeuvring was possible. We waited until we found a man going into the flats, and Giorgis cleverly got him to telephone for another taxi to rescue us. We tried to take the luggage to the harbour and dump it, and the driver said he knew just where we could eat, at a place 'opposite' our entrance, only it was not.

The information service of this part of the harbour could tell you about the weather, but not where to leave your baggage. It was apparently run by Wykhamists, highly agnostic on all subjects and bored and uninterested in mortal life. So we grabbed another taxi that was unloading, since the eating place was four hundred yards away and baggage 'should be left at the railway station', at the very far end of Patras beyond the traffic jam; the taxi we took, being asked to drive to Evangelatos where we would eat, set off in the wrong direction, but when Giorgis had cursed him for a bit he turned and we got there. This restaurant had moved a year or two ago from the old town where it had been one of the best in Greece, to be bigger and modern and downmarket, in an area of some new development near the Pelican. When we got in we found it occupied by about eighty working-class French people on holiday, who quarrelled over their bills. We were weary, but we ate and drank well enough; the only row was over a sealed bottle of water which I ordered, because Giorgis spotted that they brought an unsealed bottle they admitted to having filled from the tap. They claimed that the tapwater is rather good in Patras.

We took another taxi to the place where the new super-fast ferry docked, but no office in the long hall was open for it, so we doddered off to the Police and Passports, but in the course of doing so came across a policeman who showed me the right office, which had been open all the time, only it was blocked at one side because of a wind and opened only towards the road, for cars or lorries. Then I got on board and said goodbye to Giorgis, and felt it was all quite simple when you know how. My diary reads (about Pyrgos), 'The Alsatian on the roof had a tiny puppy friend today, a white-and-chestnut puppy which terrifies him and explains his fits of barking. I don't see well, though I saw half a dozen stars last night. It is blowing like fury from Italy. Yet as we left the harbour it calmed to the mildest roll, and we passed into a haze of sea and light, where the first Greek hills I ever saw loomed again enormous. The sea beaten and glittering. Shadow of Zakynthos like a woman lying naked on the sea, just out of the path of the sea. Levkas later like rocks to the right. It was as if the sun had sown the whole plain of the sea as far as Italy. At night we passed the low Italian coast south of Brindisi, lit up like a grand fleet; in the morning the sea was a rough silver on the surface of darkness, and as calm as a dark lake.'

The day was like May in England, like one of those days that are cloudy with a promise of rain and sun. For some reason, that reminded me yet again of 1947 and the river: 'I remember nothing about us then but the length of our legs, and the staidest boys frisking like colts in that variable sunshine.' Then we docked, but this new super-fast ferry did not dock at the normal ferry harbour where you might find a taxi or a bus or a porter or even a goods train; it docked in an industrial desert three miles away, where there were no taxis and no telephones, so when I had stumbled down the hellish moving stairs, helped with my unwieldy bag by some saint, I was faced with a grey, dusty walk of miles, across railway tracks and past repair shops and garages, to find the railway station. Before I got there I was arrested by three or four policemen for crossing one line too many. They looked dubiously at my passport and said, 'Ah, Irish.' No, I said, English. 'Yes,' they said, 'Irish.' Then with fatherly concern they let me go again, and at last I collapsed into the station self-service, where I got, to my surprise, a rather good lunch. I bought a ticket to Paris and off I went to Bologna. Reader, write upon your heart the maxim never to travel by rail in Italy on a Friday afternoon.

Off I went to Bologna, as I said, and there they offered a service from Bologna to Calais, so of course I took it, changing my ticket. The Bologna–Paris train was fully booked before leaving Venice, though I might have stayed a night and caught it, or gone to Venice and caught it, but I was becoming desperate. It had been impossible to book this train from Greece, as it nearly was from England. The train I was now after was advertised from a named platform, and I found that, but a strange silence made me suspicious, and some wily men watching a television screen somewhere underground confirmed that the only train went only to Milan and from another platform. This was the pleasantest part of the journey. At Milan I knew my old train left at nine, but it would be full so I took another for Paris leaving at eight. As for Calais, I doubt if any train ever goes there now, from Italy.

After long negotiations it turned out there was no room at all on this train, except in one carriage full of students, and in that there was standing room only. I decided to take it, because by now I was determined not to be beaten, and anyway I was too tired to walk one inch further. The sufferings of the night were great but I slept a bit. At about two in the morning police came because we were in France, and they removed a sweet-looking little Chinaman in a pink double-breasted suit who was resting on my suitcase like a cat, and a giant negro who looked sullen and carried a wooden statue of a pheasant, the tail of which he was clearly preparing to use as a knife. The Chinaman said he lived in Holland, so what right had the French of all people to arrest him for not having a passport? There was a sad, apprehensive-looking Arab they also took, who I was already convinced was a terrorist or a terrorist's cousin, but who really knows?

We were unfed and unwatered on that train but thank God I had consumed two quarter-bottles of a rather good wine called Fontana di Papa, and some mineral water, on the way to Milan. The journey, once it was light and I woke in France, was of great beauty through the forests and suburbs, only that about then a woman emerged from a compartment and began to be extremely sick. But the river and the trees had a delicacy like the beauty of some very old people, and I loved France more than ever, more even than the Lombard plain with castles melting in buttery yellow light, and the groves of poplars that used to be everywhere and seem to survive now only around Milan.

In Paris only a quarter of an hour late, which I put down to my pink-suited Chinese friend's expostulations, I staggered down a platform into the arms of a nice, efficient black taxi-man, who rushed me through the early emptiness to the Gare du Nord, where an almost nicer black ticket man popped me on to the Eurostar that left at eight, with minutes to spare (do not take it, reader, but it is better if you do so to go first class), and by ten in the morning I was in London. By half-past I was in Parliament Square, and before I fell asleep on the Gloucester train, I had just time to scribble down that England is like France south of Paris, only the country of the Eurostar route is dreary. Even Kent had that misty sweetness after rain that Giorgis noticed somewhere in Arcadia. Deirdre and Matthew met me and I was home for lunch and then I went to bed. It was the first of May; now it is half-way through July and I am going to have lunch and go to bed again.

Lament for Nikos Gatsos
died 12 May 1992

I

The seas have shrunk, what is lost what is past
is the one longed for unattainable coast:
in cafés that still live by poetry
the tongue shrivels, the poem is a ghost:

we came once to an enchanted grotto,
travelled to it all night by fishing-boat:
the sun had scarcely wiped his dewy eye
above the mountain when the sheep set out:

Avyerinos, dawn star, and the dawn's line
at break of day white as the surf of night
that never will flare up to noon again;
the sun on our mountain is out of sight.

II

Inside your café like a railway station
of marble in the cold and shaded air
you played for hours with a small coffee-cup,
the last free elephant in the Levant:
In the street the traffic hissed and squealed.
Where do American cars go when they die?

To Athens, where they join the taxi fleet,
heroes they race on Elysian asphalt.
Your corner table like a railway train
slowly clanking through years of afternoons,
sported in conversation, slowly moved
motionless like fresh water in a glass,
and your bare prose was secret poetry.
Summer night of dewfall, a breath of wind
found you high up where marble turns to cream
talking your mysteries in the starlight,
or under the plane tree, on the stone steps,
on the most rickety of wooden chairs.

The three streets of the Pontic barrel organ
with Paris tunes in crying Asian tones
haunted the long hours of our sleepless nights.
Day dawned for you where the last serving boys
came with their coffee in deserted squares.

III

Born to dry thunder in the stone mountains
and the thin blossom of the mountain pear,
the devastation of the Arcadian poor:
or village inn lost on a country road
going nowhere in the moon-visited hills:
to the undulating music of the reed,
forgotten songs and deep throbs of the drum:
to peace for ever, buried in peace for ever.
In all your life only the one poem
torn from you by the city and the times,
one moment Greece blazed up and lived in it,
there can be no poem like that again.
Those who died then starved to death in the street
to be carried off by cartloads at daybreak.
The living gambled shillings in the street,

and book by book you sold your library.
Now the dry lightning flashes in mid-air
and the pine trees are moaning in the ravine.

IV

The rotted moon hangs in the wind and sings:
O great loneliness, O dark loneliness,
hair full of shells and pebbles and shadows.
With his last music stinging in the air,
fresh consecrated in unhappy death,
the ghost of Lorca bowed to your poem,
your thin hand on the drowning broken strings
that plucked a hundred spirits from the wind,
and the air's ballad echoed in the mountains.
The dolphin hid her face in streaming waves
down to the fountainous sea-floors, and then
in naked sunlight showed her virgin face,
resurrection in sea-mist and sea-spray.
Virgil, the best Greek poet in Latin,
in his first flower still in your poem.
Now Virgil's book of love, 'with you alone
to wear away these ages of the world',
hangs open Nikos, wind-ruffled pages
as the mild wind opens the seeded grass
or as the dry scythe wheezing in the grass
wills shadows at the edges of the field,
where the pied watersnake swims in the cool
and still the sour fruit ripens in the heat.
Therefore, young men, with the wine in your mouth
with kisses and with green leaves in your mouth
go down, be naked in the water-streams
as the woodworker tracks the grain of wood,
and as the adder from the barley gardens
comes out with fury in her superb eyes,
and as the lightning threshes out our youth.

Do not laugh, do not weep, do not rejoice.
The poems crumbled into silence
of songs that were like songs from Edward Lear,
the boy Orestes as a nightingale
flying at twilight to the darker trees:
or as that other boy taken away,
bird on a branch, a swallow in a cage.
They whisper, and his brothers weep for him.
Words caught in wireless music, lost poems
still flickering in the ear of that sad God
that has compassion for what lives or grows.

V

Island in the smoke colours of the sea.
Noise of an apple dropping in the mist.
The unripe sun climbing the early sky
will not dry out your footsteps in the grass
the grass is printless, ghostly visitor:
and I am old now and a specialist
in words written to entertain the dead.
Here at the iron table I will set
fruits of the mist for you, the jug of wine
in the cold shade of coloured foliage
that smells of autumn in the increasing heat.
The bees have not abandoned the garden,
they maunder among ruins of bushes
and those late flowers that delight the dead.
We are undisturbed, we shall not fear sundown
or the cold rising of the mysterious moon
or the small goose-wail of the hunting horn.
Here by the cold river's estuary
I have set out these ragged offerings
in a small garden blazing with sealight:
hear the raw seagull crying on my roof
that travels with dead souls into the west.

We used to say that when you died old friend
they would find hoarded, unfinished poems
scribbled in drawers, torn papers in a chest,
imperfect, unrevised, fresh, unpublished,
to be the *arcanum* of our poetry,
like letters Makryiannis wrote to God.
But there is no more poetry to come,
only your ghost comes, friendly visitor
to pass an hour, to waste an autumn day:
and after the storm-winds the small rain comes.
Trees lounge away their life, shivering leaves
wanton in transmutations of daylight
groans of pigeons and whistles of small birds.

Tall ghost compact of massacred poems
knowing all things and altering all things
into the poem that you cannot speak,
be welcome to this island out of time,
and music straying like the twang of strings,
the conversations of eternity
being so old, so private and so mild.
In the hot afternoon you will not sleep,
coarse birds of winter squabble in the grove.
Our life now is the never written poem,
mountain music in the dead villages,
traditional sanctities of the silence.
The earth shakes and the vision is fading.
I kiss your white cheeks and your cold forehead.

VI

The falling sun whose yellow hair half seen
spangles the sea-water's unlighted green
dives to the west and limit of all things:
the murmurous air remurmurs with swan-wings,
midnight draws on the suffering spirit

to where world-wandering seas dumbly repeat
the infinite purgations of the waves
to the mind's ocean, where the ice-cap heaves
his mountainous white crest to the snow star,
and music and all voices come from far.
The friend of man is ice there, or owl-faced,
and the slow horn-beaked raven is the priest.
It is into that country we shall go,
and when we have been sprinkled with that snow,
and come to where pure suns swim in their west,
our soul shall settle on a place of rest.

from *The Rags of Time*,
Anvil Press, 1994

INDEX

Acheron, River, 223–4, 226–7
Actium, 26
Aelian, 234
Albania, 24–5
Alexander the Great, 231, 235–6
Alexiou, Dr, 133–4
Alipheira, 80, 255
Alpheios, 40–1
Alpheios (magazine), 171, 180, 182–3, 200, 217
Alpheiousa (*formerly* Polatsa), 173
Amalias, 43–4
Anaphonitria Abbey (Zakynthos), 153–4
Ancona, 10, 14–23, 185
Andrew, St: skull, 9
Andritsaina, 83
Antigonos One-Eye, 79
Antikythera (island), 10–11
Antipater, 235
Antoniou, D., 177
Apollo (god), 81, 83, 89, 91
Apostolatou, Vicky, 133
Apuleius, 233
Arcadia, 7, 78, 80, 89–94, 230–1, 246–8, 252, 255–6
Arekia (improvised couplets), 146, 151, 156
Aristophanes, 73

Aristotle, 232, 235
Arnold, Matthew: *Merope*, 237–9; 'The Scholar Gypsy', 239
Arrian, 234–5
Asea, 105, 113–18, 123, 180
Asquith, Raymond, 54, 61, 66
Auden, W. H., 164
Augustus Caesar, 26, 187

Barbasimis o Akourastos, 116
Barnes, William, 123, 160
Barouxis, Theodoros, 212, 256
Basho, 62
Bassai: Apollo temple, 81–5, 88–9, 91, 239
Baudelaire, Charles, 14, 164, 220–1; 'The Voyage', 221
Benton, S., 125
Berger, John, 121
Bertolucci, Attilio, 15–16
Biazis, Spyridon de, 141
Bios, Ioannis, 141
Bologna, 14–15
Bowra, Sir Maurice, 54–6, 63
Brandard, Edward Paxman, 97
Brindisi, 10–11, 14, 18
British Museum, 81
Brooke, Rupert, 55
Brooke-Papadopoulos, Mrs, 129